BLUEPRINTS

F O R   R E F O R M

BLUEPRINTS

FOR REFORM

PROJECT 2061

AMERICAN ASSOCIATION FOR THE ADVANCEMENT OF SCIENCE

OXFORD UNIVERSITY PRESS

NEW YORK   OXFORD

1998

OXFORD UNIVERSITY PRESS

OXFORD   NEW YORK

ATHENS   AUCKLAND   BANGKOK   BOGOTA   BOMBAY
BUENOS AIRES   CALCUTTA   CAPE TOWN   DAR ES SALAAM
DELHI   FLORENCE   HONG KONG   ISTANBUL
KARACHI   KUALA LUMPUR   MADRAS   MADRID
MELBOURNE   MEXICO CITY   NAIROBI   PARIS
SINGAPORE   TAIPEI   TOKYO   TORONTO

AND ASSOCIATED COMPANIES IN

BERLIN   IBADAN

First published in 1998 by Oxford University Press, Inc.
198 Madison Avenue, New York, New York 10016

Library of Congress Cataloging-in-Publication Data

Blueprints for reform/Project 2061,
American Association for the Advancement of Science
p.   cm.
Includes bibliographical references and index.
ISBN 0-19-512427-8

1. Science—Study and teaching (Elementary)—United States.
2. Science—Study and teaching (Secondary)—United States.
3. Mathematics—Study and teaching (Elementary)—United States.
4. Mathematics—Study and teaching (Secondary)—United States.
5. Technology—Study and teaching (Elementary)—United States.
6. Technology—Study and teaching (Secondary)—United States.
7. Educational change—United States. I. Project 2061 (American Association
for the Advancement of Science)

LB1585.3.B58   1998
507.1 ' 273—dc21
98-13962

CIP

Printed in the United States of America on acid-free paper

Table of Contents

Founded in 1848, the **American Association for the Advancement of Science** (AAAS) is the world's largest federation of scientific and engineering societies, with nearly 300 affiliate organizations. In addition, AAAS counts more than 140,000 scientists, engineers, science educators, policy makers, and interested citizens among its individual members, making it the largest general scientific organization in the world. The Association's goals are to further the work of scientists, facilitate cooperation among them, foster scientific freedom and responsibility, improve the effectiveness of science in the promotion of human welfare, advance education in science, and increase public understanding and appreciation of the importance and promise of the methods of science in human progress.

Project 2061 is a long-term initiative of AAAS to reform K-12 education in natural and social science, mathematics, and technology. Begun in 1985, Project 2061 is developing a comprehensive set of science education reform tools to help educators make science literacy a reality for all American students. With the publication in 1989 of *Science for All Americans*, Project 2061 defined science literacy in terms of the knowledge and skills that all high school graduates need. To provide more specific guidance on how students should progress toward science literacy, *Benchmarks for Science Literacy* (1993) describes what students should know and be able to do in science, mathematics, and technology by the end of grades 2, 5, 8, and 12. In 1997, the project published *Resources for Science Literacy: Professional Development*, a CD-ROM tool designed to provide educators with a better understanding of science literacy so they can help their students work toward it. Project 2061 continues to develop a variety of print and electronic tools and provides workshops and other professional development services to educators nationwide.

The AAAS wishes to express its gratitude to the following for their generous support of Project 2061:

Carnegie Corporation of New York
John D. and Catherine T. MacArthur Foundation
Andrew W. Mellon Foundation
Robert N. Noyce Foundation
The Pew Charitable Trusts
National Science Foundation
U.S. Department of Education

Preface

As *Science for All Americans* neared completion, questions of implementation came into view, and the need for Project 2061 to have a better understanding of the education system became more and more apparent. To that end, the project arbitrarily—but with lots of advice—identified a dozen key parts of the education system and then sought the help of experts in describing those parts and their interactions. The result of all of this was *Blueprints for Reform*.

Systemic reform in education can, it would seem, be approached as a line of action and a line of thought. Most of what has been happening has been on the action side—bringing the right organizations, institutions, and agencies together in common cause to solve urgent problems. A sensible and necessary step. But the thought side is also important, though it has received less attention. This is perfectly understandable. We know, after all, that reform will elude us unless we work in concert to find and carry out solutions, and we need to get on with it now; understanding seems less urgent.

There is a give-and-take between action and understanding. Through their actions, reformers have increased our understanding of what reform might entail. But to be effective in the long-run, our actions need to be informed by an understanding of education as a system. For that Project 2061 has found *Blueprints* useful and think it might be similarly useful for our colleagues who are engaged in and thinking about systemic reform in science, mathematics, and technology education.

This is at best, however, only a first step toward that understanding. *Blueprints* is on the Project 2061 Web site where it will serve as a focus of a national discussion on systemic issues in education. Hopefully, that will in time lead to deeper insights all around and hence contribute to enduring systemic reform.

F. JAMES RUTHERFORD
Director, Project 2061

COMET HALLEY, *Photographed from Las Campanas Observatory, Chile, March 1985*

Introduction

SYSTEM IS AN IDEA that helps us think about parts and wholes. It draws our attention to the interactions of the parts of something with one another and to the relation of the parts to the whole. The idea also emphasizes effects—what influences the behavior of something and what, in turn, that thing accomplishes. *Blueprints for Reform* was created on the premise that it is useful to think of education as a system. More particularly, it grew out of Project 2061's conviction that serious efforts to achieve the science literacy goals in *Science for All Americans* ought to be based on an understanding of education as a system.

Project 2061's approach to reform is national and systemic. We define the educational system to include more than students, teachers, and school administrators. The organizational structures where these people work and the laws and policies that affect them must also be included in systemic change. Further, business leaders, textbook and test publishers, academic and industrial scientists, and many others must be involved if change is to take place at the necessary scale and depth to make science literacy a reality.

THE IDEA FOR *BLUEPRINTS*

If a system is a collection of interrelated parts (objects, materials, phenomena, processes, ideas, principles, rules, organizations, people) that interact to form a distinguishable whole, what are the parts that make up a K-12 educational system? Because what constitutes a system is a matter of definition and varies according to purpose, the questions for Project 2061 became: What are the components of the education system that matter most in thinking about the attainment of science literacy by all K-12 graduates? What changes in them are desirable or possible? What are the system's boundaries? Do the constituent parts of the system interact in ways that need to be taken into account?

After extensive consultation with educators, scientists, policy makers, and funders, Project 2061 concluded that for its purposes it should examine these twelve aspects (listed alphabetically here) of the K-12 education system. To frame the issues for each of these components, we asked ourselves the following questions:

Assessment. Is the kind of learning recommended in *Science for All Americans* (*SFAA*) helped or hindered by current assessment practices— from in-class assessment during instruction, to program evaluation by schools, to monitoring education progress at state and national levels? Can new techniques really make a difference? If so, what will it take to change current approaches?

Business and Industry. In what ways do partnerships between business and education contribute to the attainment of science literacy? Can they be made more effective? Does the emphasis on workforce preparation by business and industry work for or against the goals of *SFAA*?

Curriculum Connections. Are there significant examples in today's schools of productive linkages among the natural sciences, mathematics, and technology? Between science, mathematics, and technology and the arts and humanities? Should there be more? How can such connections be fostered?

Equity. Which policies and practices impede the attainment of science literacy by all students and which foster it? What changes are desirable and possible? How should "all" be defined?

Family and Community. How are families and communities likely to respond to the recommendations in *SFAA*? What roles should family and community play in endorsing, supporting, or implementing the *Benchmarks* recommendations? Can family participation in science literacy be made more inclusive? Who speaks for a community?

Finance. What are the implications of Project 2061 reform recommendations for the allocation of money and other resources? Specifically, what are the costs of the equity-based idea of science literacy for all? What is the current financial base for education and the potential availability of resources for reform? Can schools be changed without incurring greater costs?

Higher Education. What changes in admissions standards, if any, will be necessary to respond to the reforms advocated by Project 2061? How should undergraduate education—from community colleges to research universities—build on the science literacy goals of *Science for All Americans*, especially for college students who might decide to become teachers? How can higher education faculty become more active partners in science education reform?

Materials and Technology. What new resources are needed for teachers to help students become science literate? How can existing resources be put to better use? What mechanisms are needed in assisting educators to identify, adapt, and improve materials so that they effectively target national science standards and the learning goals in *Benchmarks for Science Literacy*? How can this be done in a cost effective and timely way, avoiding "experimentation" on students?

Policy. Do current local, state, and federal education policies help or hinder the realization of Project 2061's science literacy goals? What changes in the laws and regulations that govern schools are needed and possible? How much would such changes cost, in dollars and politically?

Research. What kinds of research are likely to produce the knowledge needed to make science literacy a reality? What incentives would induce such research to be done? How can the findings of systematic research be reviewed, formulated, and disseminated to influence K-12 educational policies, teaching practices, materials development, and curriculum design more effectively than in the past?

School Organization. What will the realization of Project 2061's goals require of grade structure, teacher collaboration, control of curriculum materials and assessment, and how time and space in school are organized? What alternatives for school organization might better fit the reform directions set out in *Science for All Americans*?

Teacher Education. What promising innovations already are underway in the preparation of elementary and high school teachers of science, mathematics, and technology? What changes are needed in teacher preparation to produce teachers with the knowledge and skills necessary to implement curricula based on Project 2061 goals and principles? How much can be accomplished in preparation and how much must be part of career-long development? How can in-service education for teachers be made more coherent and effective?

Notice that there are some things missing from the above list that one might reasonably expect to find there. Learning goals have no blueprint because they are defined in *Science for All Americans* and *Benchmarks for Science Literacy*. They are ends for which the education system is the means. Similarly, although curriculum issues are embedded in several *Blueprints* chapters, curriculum has no separate blueprint because it is the central subject of Project 2061's forthcoming *Designs for Science Literacy*. Even though they are not a subject of a blueprint, students are the focus of all our work and their presence is felt in all of the components, especially assessment, equity, family and community, and research. And, finally, teaching has no separate treatment because the key issues concerning teaching cut across several components, including teacher education, higher education, school organization, materials and technology, assessment, and research.

HOW *BLUEPRINTS* WAS DEVELOPED

The development of both *Blueprints for Reform* and *Blueprints On-Line* has had input from many people.[1] Future efforts to improve and refine *Blueprints* will require similar work and help.

Teams of experts from around the country were commissioned to write reports for Project 2061 on each of the twelve topics described earlier. The authors were asked to keep in mind that the project's interest in this was more practical than scholarly, for it wanted to acquire whatever insights about the educational system as a system that would help it shape an effective reform strategy. In addition to *Science for All Americans*, drafts of *Benchmarks for Science Literacy* and other Project 2061 documents were furnished the authors.

The authors met as a group with the project staff (including representatives of the six Project 2061 School-District Centers that have worked with the project for the past several years) to learn more about Project 2061, share ideas with one another, and identify possible interactions among topics. After responding to external reviews of their drafts arranged by the project, the authors submitted their reports. Summaries

---

[1] See the acknowledgements section for the names of the persons who wrote reports, reviewed drafts, wrote summaries, and assisted Project 2061 staff in preparing the current chapters.

of the full reports were written by outside consultants so that the project staff could more readily study them as a set.

Guided by external reviews of the summaries and recommendations from three meetings of experts, the staff prepared the versions of the summaries that now appear on-line and in this print volume. These were written to serve the needs of state and school level reformers more than those of specialists, although experts in one field may find chapters outside their specialty enlightening. And to provide concrete examples of how some of the *Blueprints* recommendations are being carried out, Project 2061 has developed a database of bibliographies, exemplary projects, and science- and education-related organizations and agencies.

BLUEPRINTS ON-LINE

Even though the original reports and their summaries were prepared for internal use by Project 2061, several considerations led to the decision to make them available on-line. Colleagues have urged the project to share this work with them, and this seemed like a cost-effective way to do so. Another is that as the work progressed it became evident that the chapters, regardless of their depth or completeness, would stimulate productive discussions of systemic issues in science education reform. What better way to involve more educators in such discussions than by using the *Blueprints* chapters as the focus of on-line exchanges?

A third consideration is that the blueprint job is not over. Recall that the idea was to look at the pursuit of the goals expressed in *Science for All Americans* from the perspective of the education system as a system. That means taking interactions of the entire system's components into account, not being satisfied with twelve or any other number of individual aspects considered one at a time. It is one thing to identify issues in diverse parts of a complex system, another to describe relationships among them, and still another to develop directions and plans for action. The current state of *Blueprints* (although named for action planning) has, so far, provided a competent summary of some important issues and a few indications of prominent connections. The important activity of developing useful "blueprints" for taking action is still to be done, with the help of on-line contributors.

This is where *Blueprints On-Line* becomes a challenge. Is it possible that together we can somehow come up with a way of thinking about the education system that will break new ground, that is integrative, yet builds on a deep understanding of the individual components of the system? We believe that it can happen if enough of us can dig more deeply into the possibilities.

Twelve topics are far too many to consider simultaneously. Fewer topics and a context would help. To that end, the twelve chapters were divided into three groups. The chapters in each group have at least a surface relationship, although other groupings might also be valid. The groupings are:

The Foundation: Equity, Policy, Finance, and Research.

The School Context: School Organization, Curriculum Connections, Materials and Technology, and Assessment.

The Support Structure: Teacher Education, Higher Education, Family and Community, and Business and Industry.

The intent here is not to create a taxonomy but to focus the discussion fruitfully. In short, we invite you to work with us in an effort to develop a more coherent and integrated view of the education system as a system than now exists. Our joint purpose can be to create a blueprint for reform that will help all of us to be more effective in fostering science literacy. The reports and summaries submitted to Project 2061 and the resulting chapters presented both in print and on-line are a good starting place. As a next step, we would like you to help us move beyond them.

HOW YOU CAN PARTICIPATE

There are several ways interested educators, parents, community and business leaders, legislators, and others can respond to this challenge. These include the following:

1. Answer the monthly *Project 2061 Blueprints Survey* on our Web site (http://project2061.aaas.org/). This survey will focus on selected chapters or topics rather than on the whole collection of chapters. The results will be summarized and reported at the same on-line location.

2. Join on-line conferences and discussions about *Blueprints* topics. These will be announced well in advance to provide an opportunity for the kind of intense sharing of ideas that can benefit the participants as well as Project 2061.

3. Send email (blueprints@aaas.org) asking questions, expressing your reactions, and giving suggestions.

4. Help Project 2061 expand and update *Blueprints'* resources and bibliographies by sending information on relevant programs, projects, reports, and research studies.

Here are some questions that Project 2061 would like responses on, though you can react to any aspects of the material. The questions in the first list refer to each of the chapters, in the second list to the entire collection. With regard to each of the individual chapters:

1. Is the information up-to-date and accurate?
2. Are the issues addressed truly important?
3. Are significant issues missing?
4. Is there support in practice or research for the claims that are made?
5. Do the conclusions reached follow from the evidence given?
6. Are there important alternative points of view, arguments, or interpretations?
7. What additional key references to the literature, projects, and resources are needed?

With respect to the entire collection:

1. Are the twelve chapters sufficient for characterizing the education system as a system? What chapters, if any, should be added? Eliminated?
2. Is it helpful to sort the chapters into groups? Is there a better way to group them?
3. How might the chapters be modified to emphasize their interrelations?
4. Are there some themes that could be used to bring greater coherence to the collection?

CHARLES SHEELER, *The Open Door*, 1932.

PART I

The Foundation

THERE ARE MANY REASONS why making policy and financial decisions to foster equity in science education is difficult. The skill that diverse constituencies have in influencing federal, state, and local policy makers is one, and the lack of agreement on what constitutes equity is another. In the long run, making good policy decisions about equity is hard because the needed data and research on what works are limited. Despite these difficulties, Project 2061 remains committed to the idea of science literacy for all students and to setting standards and expectations to work toward this goal. Examples of successful programs provide plenty of reason to believe that the goal is possible, given the will and necessary resources.

It sometimes seems as though policy and finance are as inseparable as light and shadow. Policies usually have financial consequences, and financial resources generally influence, if not determine, policy. A school board policy decision, based on sound educational principles, to decrease the student/teacher ratio, lengthen the school year, or increase the number of after-school activities will add substantial costs to the annual budget. The same board, under the threat of a large budget deficit might, for sound financial reasons, increase the student/teacher ratio, shorten the school year, or decrease the number of after-school student activities.

To be sure, in practice the intertwining of policy and finance is not a simple matter. It is not always evident, for example, what the dollar cost of an educational policy decision will turn out to be nor what the educational cost of a budget decision will turn out to be. One thing we can be certain of, however, is that rarely will policy or financial decisions have the same impact on all students. Educational equity may be a great rallying cry in the United States, but it is far from having been achieved. Whether science for *all* Americans can become a reality any time soon depends on how thoughtfully policy and financial decisions are made in the years ahead—a daunting prospect in the face of the political pluralism and dispersed decision-making that characterizes our education system.

Systematic research in education of the right kind and quality is needed to inform education policies and practices. The case for thinking of research as a foundation for every aspect of education may rest more on optimistic hopes for the future than on incontrovertible evidence from the past. The current picture of research with its successes, failures, impediments and opportunities is notable for the absence of a clearly articulated research agenda built around the idea of science literacy. An important characteristic of such an agenda is that it should be interdisciplinary—not only in content but in research methodology. As a relatively new scholarly area, education research is only beginning to be productive in informing practitioners. The increasing use of qualitative methods may provide improved congruence between research and the classroom. Nevertheless, finding effective ways to bring researchers and teachers into closer and more active relationships remains a challenge for the future.

For the most part, the equity, policy, finance, and research chapters that follow do not explicitly address the interdependencies among them. Yet it is helpful to read them with an eye for implicit connections and for missed opportunities to put on the table. Some of the questions below bear on interconnections. The purpose of the questions is to prompt a conversation that will lead to a better understanding of the issues treated in the chapters, not to suggest either praise or criticism of them. Some of the questions appear to be answered directly in the chapters, and some not. In either case, we again urge you to raise your own questions as you peruse the chapters, then forward them for posting in the *Blueprints* News Room via blueprints@aaas.org.

EQUITY

1. Is it possible to reconcile a commitment to equity as equal opportunity with that of equity as equal outcomes? What measures of opportunity should be used? What measures of outcomes? What does research say about the relationship between opportunity and outcome?

2. What characteristics of the American educational system are the greatest barriers to equal opportunity or outcome? Which of these are most amenable to improvement?

3. Can science literacy for all be achieved given the current unequal distribution of financial resources? Would an equal distribution of resources be equitable? Are some kinds of resources more important than others in providing equal opportunity?

4. Which groups of students are most in need of help in science and mathematics? Are their needs the same? Will the same instructional, support, and organizational policies serve them equally well? The same proportional investment?

5. How can a common set of learning goals be achieved while honoring individual and cultural differences? Are new materials and teaching needed? How can we communicate and meet high expectations for all students?

POLICY

1. How do such entreaties as "set high standards of learning for all students," and "pay attention to individual, socioeconomic, and cultural differences," translate into policy decisions? Is there sound research to guide the making of those decisions?

2. Because policy decisions are made at federal, state, local, school, and classroom levels, what possibilities are there for ending up with coherent policies rather than conflicting ones?

3. If authority for making policy decisions is devolving from the federal government to state governments to school districts to individual schools, where does the responsibility rest for educational equity? What is the balance between the power of the purse and the power of the courts in shaping state and local policies that bear on educational equity?

4. Because state licensing authorities, teacher education institutions, and school district policies (hiring, salary, professional development opportunities, and tenure) all influence teacher quality, what can be done to improve it? What would it cost, and who would bear the burden? Are there state or federal policies that could improve the distribution of highly qualified teachers with regard to urban and remote school districts?

5. Are professional associations and unions effective in influencing education policy? If so, does that influence tend to foster or impede reform? In particular, are these organizations a force for educational equity?

FINANCE

1. What are the financial costs of adopting policies that place a top priority on having all students become science literate? What effect will such policies have on students who may be headed for careers in science and science-related fields? What research is needed to answer such questions?

2. If it matters more how money is spent for science and mathematics education (or any other disciplines) than how much is spent, what research-based principles are there to guide how best to spend whatever money is available? What basis is there for deciding what the threshold of investment is?

3. Is financing of reform an added cost or is it only a matter of reallocat-

ing existing funds? What knowledge is there to guide decisions on how to distribute reform costs among such things as retraining teachers, providing better materials for instruction, upgrading technologies, realigning organizational structures, and other components of the system?
4. In what ways do the funding policies of federal and state agencies and philanthropic foundations shape—or try to shape—educational reform? How could funding polices be changed to become more effective? Is coordination among funders of reform desirable? Possible?
5. Does it take financial incentives to get states and school districts to adopt voluntary standards? How costly would such incentives be and who would foot the bill? What other incentives are likely to prompt a response from states and schools?

RESEARCH

1. Given the total cost of the educational enterprise in the United States, what dollar investment should the nation make in research? What should be the balance of investment between research focusing on learning and research focusing on policy issues? Research to develop a knowledge base and research to help solve urgent problems? Research to inform instructional, policy, and financial decisions and research to determine the effects of those decisions?
2. What policies might lead to an educational research enterprise that meets scientific standards, is less fragmented than the current one, and can be sustained long enough to yield useful knowledge? Is a research agenda needed at all, or is the search for systematic knowledge in education better served by a support policy that funds the most creative researchers regardless of their focus?
3. How can research link standards-based reform efforts in a way that focuses on learning and policy questions about equity? Can such research produce knowledge that can be applied more generally?
4. How can knowledge, once created, be used to influence educational

policies and practices? What training would teachers, materials developers, administrators, and others who are part of the system of education need to be able to understand and apply research findings?

5. How can educational research be focused on long-term visions that could enlist and energize the entire research community? How can research be structured to reveal how learning progresses from childhood to adult literacy, and how understanding of important topics is developed? How can research be integrated so that knowledge about learning, teaching, instructional materials, and assessment are connected in ways that are useable by all educators?

1

Equity

A CENTRAL PROBLEM for reformers is to make science understandable, accessible, and perhaps even enjoyable to all K-12 students. All students are expected to achieve some degree of literacy in reading and mathematics. In contrast, science has been viewed as the province of a privileged few. Even today, there are opinions that most people can, at best, learn about science, rather than how to do science (Shamos, 1996).

This chapter explores the implications of science education for various groups of students who presently are underrepresented in science classes and science-related careers, do not achieve highly in science, have difficulty getting access to appropriate learning environments for science, or may not match current stereotypes of students who are interested in science. In addition, the chapter considers the needs of students from groups who have traditionally done well in the sciences in the United States and attempts to assess how science reform might affect them.

The chapter's purpose is threefold: to describe, discuss, and analyze equity in K-12 science education in American schools; to predict how reform might impact current barriers to equity and how, in turn, barriers to equity might affect efforts in science reform; and to make recommendations for both short- and long-term planning that will help science education reform achieve its aim, namely science literacy for all Americans.

THE CURRENT STATUS: DEMOGRAPHICS AND TRENDS IN SCIENCE EDUCATION

Although Americans are committed to the principles of fairness, equality of opportunity, and justice that are at the heart of democracy, that

---

The data in this chapter are from *Indicators of Science and Mathematics Education 1995* (National Science Foundation, 1996), 1995 *Digest of Educational Statistics* (National Center for Education Statistics, 1995), and *The Condition of Education 1996* (U.S. Department of Education, 1996).

commitment exists alongside clear evidence that some groups of Americans are more likely to participate and be successful in science than others. To put it bluntly, discrimination is alive and well in education, despite the best intentions. Although this chapter provides examples of problems (stereotyping, lack of resources, etc.) specific to one group or another, most of these examples represent more general issues that need to be addressed in order to achieve equity in science education. Groups do differ and, moreover, individuals within groups may not fit the group pattern. However, similar problems and possible solutions often apply to many different groups.

Gender. There is ample evidence that females are less likely than males to study and to enter occupations related to applied mathematics, physical science, and engineering. These gender differences become noticeable in high school and are clearly apparent during the college years. For example, although the percentages of bachelor's degrees awarded to women in engineering and physics have increased over the last decade, women are still significantly underrepresented in these fields. Social forces and personal beliefs play major roles in perpetuating these disparities.

Black Americans. Over the last ten years, Black American students, as well as Hispanic and American Indian students, have had greater increases in science and mathematics achievement scores than White and Asian students. However, the increases have been small, and a significant gap remains between the groups.

Hispanic Americans. The term "Hispanic" includes a variety of peoples of Spanish-speaking heritage, ranging from Mexican Americans who have lived in the United States for generations and may speak only English, to refugees recently arrived from countries such as El Salvador who may speak no English and may have had little exposure to formal schooling. Hispanics are the fastest growing group in the United States. In the last decade, although there has been some growth in the number

---

The chapter uses the terminology of the federal government in referring to the many ethnic groups. For example, the term "Black Americans" is the inclusive category rather than "African Americans" because many Caribbeans and Africans identify themselves according to their country of origin, and the term "Hispanics" includes the many different origin countries and cultures. Nevertheless, we recognize that it is important to refer to individuals and groups according to their own wishes, rather than imposing labels. The terms used here are for convenience, and not an attempt to lump groups together who have important individual characteristics.

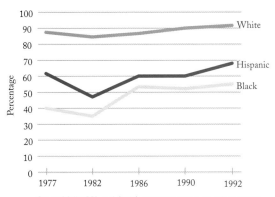

Seventeen-Year-Olds at or Above Basic Math Proficiency

Source: Mullis, I.V., et al. (1994). *NAEP 1992 trends in academic progress* (Report No. 23-TR01). Washington, D.C.: National Center for Education Statistics.

of undergraduate degrees awarded to Hispanics in science, mathematics, and engineering, their proportion relative to other groups has remained unchanged, and they continue to be seriously underrepresented in science-related fields.

American Indians/Alaskan Natives. Although American Indians and Alaskan Natives account for only 1% of the U.S. population, they include more than 500 tribes and 200 languages. The high school drop-out rate for American Indians/Alaskan Natives is higher than for any other group. Their rates of poverty and severe health problems (alcoholism, suicide, and accidents) are among the highest in the country. American Indians score significantly lower than Whites and Asian Americans but higher than Black Americans and Hispanics on most achievement measures of science and mathematics in grades K-12. Only a small percentage of American Indians and Alaskan Natives go on to receive undergraduate degrees in science fields.

Bachelor's Degrees Awarded in Science and Engineering in 1991

	Number	Percent
White	303,532	82.7
Black	23,170	6.3
Hispanic	17,021	4.6
Asian	21,628	5.9
Native American	1,594	0.4

Source: National Science Foundation (1996). *Indicators of science and mathematics education 1995.* Arlington, VA: Author.

Asian Americans. Asian Americans have been described as a "model minority" for their academic performance in general and have been stereotyped as "math or science whizzes" in particular. But as is the case with many groups, the use of an encompassing term, such as "Asian

Americans," masks the fact that the group includes substantially different subgroups, such as Filipino, Chinese, Korean, Japanese, Southeast Asian, Pacific Islander, South Asian and other Asian ethnic subgroups. There are significant differences among these groups in mathematics and science performance. The achievement of second and third generation Asian American students is much the same as Whites. The 1990 U.S. Census data indicate that Asian Americans account for about 3% of the overall U.S. labor force, but make up about 7% of natural scientists and engineers, and are as highly represented in these professions as their White counterparts.

Students with Disabilities. The term "disability" includes the following categories: learning disabilities; speech/language impairments; mental retardation; serious emotional disturbance; and hearing, visual, orthopedic, and other health impairments (including attention-deficit disorders, disabilities related to parental drug abuse, and disabilities acquired through trauma or illness). Currently, about 12% of American school children have an identified disability—which translates into nearly five million students. That number is growing as identification processes develop. Students with disabilities are frequently divided into two larger categories that can overlap. One group—about 1%—consists of individuals with physical impairments (for instance orthopedic, visual, or hearing disabilities). The remaining 99% of students with disabilities are those who manifest cognitive, social-personal, or intellectual difficulties that affect their ability to perform in regular classrooms.

Currently, about 12% of American school children have an identified disability—which translates into nearly five million students.

All students with disabilities do have potential in science. A major obstacle to their achievement is the tendency of educators and the public to believe that persons with disabilities lack intelligence. For example, persons with disabilities who do not express themselves well are assumed to be unable to understand and do science. Future technological advances and other accommodations are likely to improve the academic performance of children identified with disabilities. Currently, however, 50 to 60% of students with disabilities fail in one or more subjects, and their relative performance in science and mathematics is lower than in other subjects. These results are also reflected in lower SAT scores and other achievement measures. The gaps are not insurmountable, however, because about 8% of all undergraduates report having disabilities. While there are wide disparities in kind and extent of disability that may or may not affect academic achievement, it is clear that many students with disabilities are able to excel in school and go on to higher education.

English-Language Learners. A category that cuts across gender, ethnicity, and disabling conditions is "proficiency in English." The nearly six million children who are learning to speak English face challenges when they make the transition from the English as a Second Language (ESL) or bilingual classroom into the mainstream and cope with the demands of academic English. Nearly 75% of Hispanic and Asian children come from homes where a non-English language is spoken. For many Asian languages, few teachers are available for bilingual classes. And very few teachers can both speak the languages of American Indian/Alaskan Native children and teach science. Thus, bilingual students encounter particular difficulties in science courses.

The advantages of being bilingual in today's world are often overlooked when English-language learners are considered. Rather than repeating earlier mistakes of extinguishing first languages in favor of English, schools can provide opportunities for students to build on the advantage of speaking more than one language. The ability to speak English and a second language, combined with strong skills in mathematics and science, will provide unlimited opportunities—a fact that should be made more clear to English-language learners as they work to succeed in school.

Class/Socioeconomic Status. Ethnic groupings and operational definitions such as "students with disabilities" reflect only some aspects of what a student brings to the science classroom. Gender, socioeconomic status, geographic location, and proficiency in English language all interact with and have an impact on both the student's performance and the school's expectations of that student. Of these variables, socioeconomic status (SES) may be the single most powerful factor in determining who succeeds in American schools. Research suggests, for example, that only 12% of boys born in the bottom quarter of income rose as adults to the top quarter, while 69% remained in the lower half (Kahlenberg, 1995). This stubborn intransigence is echoed in other areas of achievement and progress, resulting in persistent gaps among various groups in mathematics and science education.

When considering group differences in science achievement, three points are central:

■ It is important to avoid confounding race with class. A disproportionate number of Black, Hispanic, and American Indian/Alaskan Native students are from low SES backgrounds.

■ A distinction must be made between the student's home background and the socioeconomic character of the school itself, because resources are not distributed equally across schools of different types.

■ Achievement levels of students are limited by the level and types of courses available—students cannot learn what is not taught.

For students with disabilities and students of color, many of these factors collide. Low SES schools place twice as many students in learning disability classes as high SES schools. They also have more Black American students in low math tracks, special education, and classes for students with mental retardation.

NEEDED CHANGES: IMPLEMENTING SCIENCE REFORM

SOCIAL FORCES AFFECTING SCHOOLING

There is a gap between the public's support for principles of equality and its support for policies designed to help bring equality about. Complicating this issue is the long-held American commitment to the notion of rugged individualism—the expectation that anyone, no matter how dire the circumstances, can bootstrap his or her way to success. Although group-level barriers are acknowledged, many Americans endorse the idea that such barriers can and should be overcome by individual efforts.

Consequently, if individuals do not seem to "take opportunities," their failure to achieve may be seen as their "fault." They may be viewed as not trying hard enough or as not having what it takes to succeed. This attitude plays itself out in science education. For instance, there is a well-documented tendency for Black, Hispanic, and American Indian students to take fewer courses in science and mathematics; Whites and Asian Americans take more (National Science Foundation [NSF],1996). Awareness of this problem has grown along with the commitment to the need for science for all and the recognition of the importance of gateway courses such as algebra and chemistry for future academic success.

Social attitudes, stereotyping, and discrimination are root causes of most inequities in science. It would seem difficult, if not impossible, to remedy underachievement and underrepresentation through reforms as long as such beliefs are at the core of what to do about "the equity issue." Instead, a very different way of thinking about and implementing reform may be needed.

For the moment, assume that the basic premises of the reform movement in the sciences are correct—that the curriculum, as currently constituted, is full of disconnected facts, organized in ways that interfere with how people learn and that it is focused on out-of-date knowledge that has little relevance to participatory democracy and everyday life, including spheres of work. Assume that instruction repeatedly covers the same low-level content and provides students with few (or no) opportunities to make sense of what they are encountering. Any reasonable person might disengage from the activities that are so offensive—not read the materials, not participate in class activities, ignore the teacher, talk to others, and undertake more meaningful activities. Not surprisingly, if tests were given, these individuals would perform badly. What is more, they might simply stop taking science courses.

Reform in science education needs to begin with those students who have resisted earlier school-based efforts to learn sciences.

If the above is a reasonable reaction to the inadequacies of school science, then the question is: Who, among students, is most likely to behave in this way? The answer is precisely those groups who are underachieving and underrepresented in science-related courses and careers—many low-income students; Hispanic, Black American, and American Indian/ Alaskan Native students; persons with disabilities; some females; and some students with exceptional ability (these categories are not, of course, exclusive). Instead of being stereotyped as not possessing scientific knowledge, being apathetic, or being deficient in some other way, maybe these students have been reacting in an understandable manner to what the reform movement has recently realized.

If the above analysis is even partly correct, it suggests at least three things. First, the discourse surrounding underachievement and underrepresentation needs to be expanded, if not changed entirely, because underachievement may be an early warning of the sad state of school science in general. Second, research needs to better address what features of a particular group might explain why these young people sense and react as they do. Third, reform in science education needs to begin with those students who have resisted earlier school-based efforts to learn science. These students are likely to be the best judges of whether the reform efforts have it right: Does the curriculum allow for sense making? Is the curriculum connected to the world in ways that are similar to the goals of scientific literacy? Does instruction really build on what students already know and understand? Is science a part of all students' lives?

If it is true that bias, stereotyping, and restriction of opportunity covertly or overtly influence who takes science courses, who succeeds in these courses, and who goes on to a career in a related area, then education designed to eliminate these negative forces ought to demonstrate very different results. Indeed, there is plenty of evidence that this is the case. For example, the extraordinary successes of women who graduate from all-female colleges and of Black Americans who graduate from historically Black colleges and universities are well-documented. The outstanding achievement of educators such as Jaime Escalante and Uri Treisman (1990) are proof that high expectations combined with strong content, mentoring, and attention to individual needs and cultures are effective. Casserly's work (1980) with high-achieving females in science identified approaches that can be effective for all students: recruiting promising students, negating bias in course placement, providing explicit encouragement in class by teachers, forming a critical mass of students, and forming nurturing social groups around academic science interests.

WORLD VIEW AND CULTURE

Students enter school and encounter school science with experiences, knowledge, and beliefs that are part of their cultural heritage. Differences in cultural and world views are not limited to students who have recently arrived in the United States. For example, while teachers might explain scientifically the causes for hurricanes and tornadoes, students may hold on to alternative explanations for these phenomena rooted in religious beliefs or fairy tales. There is thus a lack of "cultural continuity" between the science taught in the schools and the beliefs that guide the lives of people.

These observations on culture and world view have several implications. Children's cultures and backgrounds provide the starting point for learning science. For example, many students from other countries have an understanding of the metric system, and can offer ideas about scientific problems in other countries. Where scientific approaches to phenomena conflict with students' values, it is important that teachers better understand those conflicts and take steps to address them. Finally, it will be necessary for science education reformers to clarify their views on cultural pluralism and how it relates to the idea of science for all.

ALLOCATION OF EDUCATIONAL RESOURCES

There are vast differences in available resources across the country as one compares rural, urban, and suburban schools. School funding varies significantly across regions of the country and even within a state, affecting the resources (certified and qualified science teachers, professional development opportunities, curriculum materials, supplies and lab equipment, and technology) available to K-12 science students. These differences in conditions are exacerbated in science education because it is highly resource-dependent.

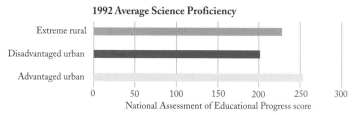

1992 Average Science Proficiency

National Assessment of Educational Progress score

Source: U.S. Department of Education, National Center for Education Statistics, National Assessment of Educational Progress. (1994, May). *NAEP 1992 trends in academic progress.* Prepared by the Educational Testing Service. Washington, D.C.: Author.

The costs of implementing science education reform will be substantial. To the extent to which science education reform is dependent upon resources, opportunities to learn science—especially for low-income schools and students—will be further stratified unless something dramatic is done. The situation is further compounded by the crisis in some urban schools, which are perceived as unsafe, unsound, and locked into permanent decline. Changing science education in some urban schools, even when money is available, may prove difficult to impossible because the structure of urban school systems allows them to swallow reforms and resources, simply incorporating them into the ineffective status quo. With a few exceptions such as the Coalition of Essential Schools, James Comer's schools, and the Accelerated Schools program, the restructuring of urban education has proven thus far almost totally resistant to remedy. These programs seem to produce positive changes on a school-by-school basis, rather than by system-wide change (see *Blueprints'* Resources for descriptions of these programs).

INSTRUCTIONAL MATERIALS AND TECHNOLOGY

It is fair to say that no one knows what it will cost to outfit a school to teach reformed science. The costs will vary dramatically depending upon the extant resources within a given school. The argument has been made that, in order to produce equitable outcomes in science across groups, it may be necessary to have unequal inputs for some students—more resources for underrepresented or low-income students. While this may be true, one would be pleased if, initially, all schools were simply provided the same resources as affluent schools currently have.

Money Matters If You Spend It Right

In 1989, as part of a court-ordered desegregation case in Austin, Texas, 16 elementary schools were given $300,000 per year for five years to improve achievement. At the end of the five years, two of the schools, Zavala and Ortega Elementary, were among the city's highest in attendance and achievement; the others showed no improvement. Both schools continued to draw students from the city's poorest neighborhoods, but somehow they achieved something extraordinary. The money made a major difference because of the way it was spent.

In 14 of the schools, the money was spent to reduce class size, but little was done to change what happened inside the classes. As one administrator put it, "…they had 10 students in class, but…two rows of five students, and the teacher would still be sitting up there in the front of the room, and still using ditto sheets…"

At Zavala and Ortega, class size was also reduced but as a part of a more comprehensive program. At the beginning of the year, the principal asked parents to read aloud the scores of the school's students on the statewide test. After their initial anger subsided, parents and teachers decided to adopt the reading and math curriculum that the district used only for gifted and talented children. Money was spent on professional development to help teachers learn the new curriculum and manage classes containing special-needs students. Health services were brought to the schools and parents became involved in the governance of the schools, including sitting on hiring and budget committees.

The answer these two schools discovered was to focus on one goal rather than trying to attack all fronts simultaneously. Once the goal of higher standards for achievement was set, the other components became manageable and supported that vision.

From Richard J. Murnane & Frank Levy, "Why Money Matters Sometimes," *Education Week*, September 11, 1996.

A sound understanding of the principles of technology is essential to science literacy, and widespread use of computers in science classrooms is important to learning. Yet many White and Hispanic girls have not had the same interest in computers as boys, and teachers have compounded the problem by viewing computers as a male technology with little meaning for the future careers of girls. In addition, the new CD-ROM technologies are marketed primarily for boys, and the preponderance of Internet users are male. There have been similar trends for Black Americans, whose use of home computers lags behind that of Whites and Asians.

Use of Computers at Home for School Work

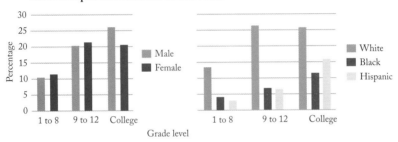

Source: National Center for Education Statistics. (1996). *1995 digest of educational statistics*. Washington, D.C.: Author.

SCHOOL ORGANIZATION

Current empirical research on the role of tracking in science education is in short supply. There is some older research, however, from which these general conclusions are relevant to the discussion of equity in science education reform: students in lower track classes are disproportionately more likely to be students of color (except Asian Americans), low-income students, and students with disabilities; they get fewer resources and experience science education very differently from students in higher track classes; and they achieve somewhat less well than their counterparts in heterogeneously grouped classes (Oakes, 1985). Variations in the selection of gateway science and mathematics courses (chemistry, geometry, etc.) for underrepresented groups result in these students being locked out of upper level courses, limiting their opportunities to pursue science, mathematics, and engineering careers.

Many of these problems may be solved simply by eliminating tracking; something that many schools are beginning to do. Students who are ready and motivated to go beyond the thresholds set by *Benchmarks for Science Literacy* (American Association for the Advancement of

Science, 1993) and *National Science Education Standards* (National Research Council, 1996) seem to have much to gain and little to lose in a de-tracked arrangement, especially if school organization patterns loosen lock-step grading practices. New technologies hold promise for opening many opportunities for students who are ready for more advanced work. Moreover, because the benchmarks are organized in grade bands (K-2, 3-5, 6-8, 9-12) that successively build knowledge and skills, a student who masters the concepts in a given band early can proceed to the next band. Dissolution of traditional, rigid age/grade science holds promise also for students other than the high achievers—some students with disabilities would be served well if they were allowed to progress more slowly.

Science Curriculum

The science curriculum differentiation in schools reflects both desired student outcomes and perceived limitations of teachers' and students' potential for understanding science (Oakes, Gamoran, & Page, 1992). The curriculum represents the science knowledge that scientists, teachers, community leaders, business leaders, legislators, and parents deem worthy and accessible for students in schools today. Science curriculum is thus embedded in the culture and cannot be separated from its myths, customs, taboos, and history. Curriculum developers face the difficult challenge of taking into account multiple frames of reference and different ways of viewing the world. *Benchmarks* and *Standards* provide the basis for addressing these issues, leaving open to the local school district how to teach the curriculum and creating the opportunity to design instruction that is relevant to community needs and concerns. At the same time, mastery of the benchmarks and standards can assure that the children of the community have the kind of sound and broad, nonidiosyncratic grounding in science that will allow further participation at the college and university level.

As new curriculum materials are developed, it is crucial that they not rely solely on print media that require expert reading ability. Children who are poor readers, English-language learners, and students with learning disabilities can learn science and demonstrate their understanding of concepts only if they have opportunities to do so with curricula that are not totally dependent on reading and writing. One can only wonder how many children with disabilities are lost in an educational system that insists that they communicate their science understanding only via the written word.

SCIENCE TEACHER PREPARATION
AND PROFESSIONAL DEVELOPMENT

Apart from selecting better and more diverse teacher candidates, what can be done to better prepare teachers to teach science to all? A handful of teacher education programs require that new teachers learn about teaching diverse students and specify a degree of familiarity with special education regulations. However, a survey of special education teachers revealed that (a) 42% received no training in science, (b) 38% of children in self-contained special education classes did not receive any instruction in science, and (c) among special educators who did teach science, nearly half devoted less than 60 minutes a week to science, and nearly 60% depended upon a textbook for science instruction (Patton, Polloway, & Cronin, 1986).

A survey revealed that 42% of special education teachers received no training in science.

Federal regulations mandate that all students be educated in regular classrooms unless it can be demonstrated that an alternative placement is necessary. School districts need professional development programs that provide teachers with the necessary support and training to help students with disabilities succeed in the regular classroom. Although there has been some progress in greater use of technology, little has been done to help general classroom teachers understand their responsibilities in meeting the needs of all students. Interventions such as creating and using adaptive materials, modifying lessons and strategies, modifying the laboratory environment to allow full participation, and adapting evaluation to students with disabilities are still perceived as responsibilities left for special educators.

A similar situation exists for science instruction for English-language learners. ESL and bilingual education teachers may be required to teach science to English-language learners, but often have little knowledge of science content or pedagogy. On the other hand, science teachers who have English-language learners in their classrooms usually have no training in second language instruction. Moreover, students are often released from ESL or bilingual education programs and mainstreamed as soon as they learn basic interpersonal communication skills. But cognitive/academic language proficiency takes from five to seven years to develop even when students have some basic literacy skills in their first language (Cummins, 1980). This means that most children will experience a gap between entering the mainstream and achieving well in traditional science. However, children taught context-rich, problem-based science in their first language can do excellent work as soon as they enter the mainstream (Fradd & Lee, 1995; Rosebery, Warren, & Conant, 1992). If teachers can connect science with students' home languages and cultures, they can teach science to these students. The challenge is to figure out how to adapt such successes for the monolingual English teacher whose students have many different language backgrounds and varying proficiencies in English. There are, of course, some basic strategies such as simplifying oral and written language, grouping students so that they can discuss science with one another (if not the teacher), translating materials into students' home languages, and coordinating instruction so that science and bilingual or ESL teachers are working together, rather than separately or at cross purposes. Additional research is needed to better understand these challenges and how to meet them.

SCIENCE TEACHING

Even in America's increasingly diverse science classrooms, students of color and females have difficulty finding role models that look like them. Schools need more teachers of color, more bilingual teachers, and teachers who can work with students with disabilities—and all of these teachers need to know science. But the issue is more than one of role models; it is a matter of finding teachers who understand the cultures and communities of their students (Banks, 1991). Successful teachers use knowledge and understanding of their students' home cultures and backgrounds to structure the norms for classroom behavior and discourse. For example, teachers should encourage students to communicate in the classroom following the rules that they learned at home for interacting with adults.

Most teachers are, to a certain degree, sensitive to the cultural values of their students in setting expectations, leading to differential treatment of students. The dilemma is that it is difficult to know whether differential treatment has positive or negative effects, because students may interpret the action as affirming or condescending. While it is possible to document patterns of differential treatment by gender and ethnicity, it is harder to know what to do about it. It is essential that schools hire and support teachers who not only are committed to science for all, but who are also willing to examine their teaching practice and to engage in professional development activities that support effective science teaching for students from all backgrounds.

The most effective strategies for teaching science to diverse learners support students in constructing their own understanding.

The most effective strategies for teaching science to diverse learners support students in constructing their own understanding in activities that are hands-on and relevant to their lives and cultures. Science educators should recognize that the success of hands-on, inquiry-based lessons is somewhat dependent upon the prior experiences of the child, his or her readiness to make inductive leaps, and opportunities for students to reflect on their hands-on experiences.

There is some, but not a great deal, of research on validated methods for teaching science to English-language learners. For preparing science teachers to teach English-language learners, Spurlin (1995) recommends the following activities:

■ Analyze written science materials for semantic, syntactic, and pragmatic problems.

■ Adapt and simplify written materials.

■ Teach demanding material in a hands-on context.

■ Help students construct their own meaning.

■ Observe English-language learners in schools, noting how they are treated and the kinds of instruction they receive.

■ Observe how language is used in instruction.

■ Identify how teachers can bring in the backgrounds and cultural experiences of diverse learners into the science classroom.

In addition, teachers can use promising methods to cut across all types of disabling conditions. These include hands-on instruction; discovery teaching; theme-based instruction; cooperative learning; and presenting science content in enriched and interesting settings.

EQUITABLE SCIENCE CLASSROOMS

Merely providing hands-on activities and group-work is insufficient for an equitable classroom environment. Rather, teachers must be vigilant and actively involved in creating classroom dynamics that allow all students to learn how to use equipment, operate computers, develop and test their ideas, and discuss observations and results. Girls participate more frequently and achieve better when teachers use noncompetitive teaching strategies, give extended examples of science in applied fields such as medicine, stress the creative components of mathematics and science, and provide extensive hands-on learning experiences.

Attention to equity issues should also be included during student teaching and in teacher evaluation systems within the school district. The kinds of changes in attitudes about gender and science that are necessary to achieve the goal of science literacy for all—for girls as well as boys, for students of all ethnic backgrounds, and for students with disabilities —require a major commitment of school district personnel. It seems somewhat incongruous to include a "soft" recommendation such as needing more "caring science teachers," but it is one that must be made. Science education needs more science teachers who care about their students and who define their jobs as teaching science to all students.

ASSESSMENT, EVALUATION, AND GRADING

Although assessments are potentially dangerous and damaging when they are misused, they also present opportunities to better understand and improve science education for those who have been bypassed by science education in the past. Documents like the National Council of Teachers of Mathematics' *Assessment Standards* (1993) and the National Research Council's *National Science Education Standards* (1996) are to be lauded for their attention to the instructional uses of assessment, their emphasis on what students know and can do, and their explicit attention to equity. Yet educators should not fool themselves. Assessment has been used primarily to classify and to track students; to diagnose what is wrong with their knowledge; and in general, to grant legitimacy to practices that constrain opportunity to learn. Educators need to be aware of the fine line between the traditional uses of assessment and the new uses envisioned by reformers. Schools are conservative and will be tempted to retrofit current practices to new assessments. For instance, there will be pressure to track students along the new lines of ability that are revealed through more authentic forms of assessment. Safeguards to prevent these sorts of actions have simply not been developed.

There is a great deal of hope that changing assessment to more "authentic" forms will reduce the stubborn ethnic and gender gaps in mathematics and science achievement measures—that new assessments may be less dependent upon background knowledge, experiences, and reading skills and, therefore, less biased. Each of these assumptions requires more empirical exploration. The expectation that alternative assessments can be used to leverage improved curriculum and teaching is counteracted by fears that initial increases in student disparities will be used to legitimize draconian consequences for students of color. For

The development, administration, and scoring of open-ended assessment tasks are ripe for bias.

example, some fear that open-ended tasks will be so culturally biased as to stack the deck against some children, or that programs to enhance educational opportunity will be improperly monitored or discontinued.

The development, administration, and scoring of open-ended assessment tasks are ripe for bias. For example, an early version of the California mathematics assessment contained an item on which a student from High School X believed that she was sure to be accepted to college because College A and College B each accept half of that school's graduating class. The task was to explain what was wrong with this reasoning. Although the task called on mathematical reasoning, it also was biased: half or more of the students who take the California assessments will not go on to college and as a result are unlikely to really care about this question.

Written items may also contain subtle bias. For example, students who speak languages other than English may be able to do the tasks, but have difficulty writing their results in English. These students may need more time to fully develop and edit their responses than is available for standardized tests. Many scoring rubrics purposefully confound written expression with science performance. This is partly because it is very difficult—some think it is impossible—to separate the two; some people cite substantive reasons for not separating them (Fradd & Larringa-McGee, 1994). The typical test-development strategy is to discard items that seem biased or fail to predict overall student performance. One alternative might be to develop multiple tasks that require similar kinds of competence but are set in different contexts. Students would be expected to select one or more items from a menu. Another strategy is to diversify the persons who write and develop assessments.

Assessment results can and should be used to hold both students and schools accountable for learning and teaching science. As states have begun to publish school-level assessment results, schools have been able (and in some cases, encouraged) to exclude students. To affect their average test scores, schools may only administer the tests to those who will score adequately. Students with disabilities, English-language learners, and Black Americans from educationally needy environments may be asked not to attend school during testing days (Darling-Hammond, 1991; Lacelle-Peterson & Rivera, 1993). This is often done under the guise of not wishing to embarrass a student. But because these students are frequently taught science by the least qualified teachers (special education and ESL/bilingual education teachers with little background in science, or the weakest science teachers), one wonders who is being saved from embarrassment. If the teacher doesn't assess student progress in some meaningful way, how is he or she to know what the student is actually learning? In turn, how would one know if the curriculum is effective or suitable? States publish each school's performance relative to other schools that are similar in terms of student social class and other background variables. The reason for these practices is to hold schools accountable only for those things that they are believed to be able to affect. A student's entering language proficiency, special needs, and social class are among those things over which schools are assumed to have little control. Yet, practices that exclude low-performing student populations can result in inflation of a school's apparent performance.

Assessments such as advanced placement exams and the SAT open doors to students.

Many students with disabilities are unable to demonstrate their true level of understanding and competency in science under traditional testing conditions. Using the same measures for students with disabilities as the non-disabled students with no adjustment in the conditions of testing or the reporting mechanisms could result in discouraging scores, rather than a valid assessment of what actually has been accomplished.

Ironically, although some students have had opportunities to learn denied them due to assessments that assigned them to lower tracks and inferior instruction, it is also true that assessments such as advanced placement exams and the SAT open doors to students. Increasing numbers of females and students of color are taking these tests, using them to gain access to further education.

Number of Students Taking Advanced Placement Exams

	1987	1996	Percent Increase
White	175,556	345,189	96.6
Black	8,141	22,373	174.8
Hispanic	9,632	45,021	367.4
Asian	21,101	58,778	176.6
Native American	643	2,491	287.4

Source: Published on the College Board's World Wide Web site at http://www.collegeboard.org/

Assessment can, in the long run, have other positive effects. Assessment reports might emphasize changes in test scores from baseline data, rather than reporting heterogeneous group means, or disaggregate data for students who are learning English, have learning disabilities, or are receiving Title I funds (low-income children). These reports could assuage the community's worries about whether all segments of the student population are progressing and learning. Reports could also help target areas that need special attention. If school reform is spurred by assessment results, then it would be desirable to chart the science progress of students with disabilities, for instance, rather than ignoring these students in science assessment.

STUDENTS, FAMILIES, AND COMMUNITIES: ATTRIBUTION THEORY

Equity issues begin with the individual student, but each student is, in turn, the developing product of his or her entire community. In discussing a student's progress toward science literacy, as well as the unique skills, abilities, attitudes, and beliefs each child brings to the science classroom, we must equally consider the society, culture, community, and family that help to form that child's constellation of individual characteristics.

Among equity issues, gender and science education has recieved the greatest research attention in the past. Gender issues affect all ethnic groups and every socioeconomic stratum, albeit differentially. Lately, we have begun to see how generalizations about gender and science education that may be true for a White middle class population may operate differently for other ethnic groups or in various socioeconomic strata.

Jacque Eccles and her colleagues at the University of Michigan have built and tested a model that explains how social forces act on young women's decisions to study science. They have researched psychological and social factors influencing long- and short-range achievement goals and behaviors, such as career aspirations, vocational and avocational choices, course selections, persistence on difficult tasks, and allocation of effort across various achievement-related activities (Eccles, 1992).

Drawing upon the theoretical and empirical work associated with decision-making, achievement theory, and attribution theory, Eccles and her colleagues have elaborated a model of achievement-related choices. This model links educational, vocational, and other achievement-related choices to two sets of beliefs: the individual's expectations for success and the importance the individual attaches to the various options perceived to be available. The individual's beliefs are formed by cultural norms, experiences, and aptitudes. The psychological processes underlying individual choice are socialized processes that grow out of years of experiences at home, in one's community, and at school. Consequently, society is just as responsible for disparities in these processes as it is responsible for inequities in the experiences provided at school.

Young people of all abilities, ethnicities, and backgrounds will be less likely to participate in math and science if they express low confidence in their abilities to master mathematics and science and to succeed in careers requiring these skills; if they value success and participation in these fields less than they value success and participation in other fields; if they do not enjoy mathematics and science; and if they experience a nonsupportive environment for learning mathematics and science, either in school or at home. Therefore, it is particularly important to remedy these conditions for groups that are already underrepresented in mathematics and science.

RECOMMENDATIONS

Equity issues are among society's most challenging. They simultaneously demand acknowledgment and response and foster resistance because no one is defined solely in terms of group membership, but rather as an individual who is complexly situated in terms of gender, ethnicity, social class, ability or disability, language and other attributes.

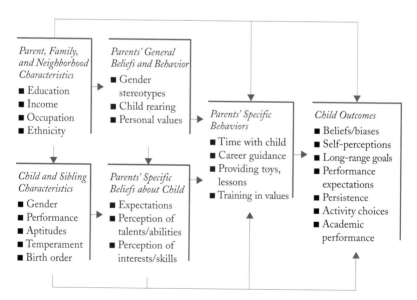

Adapted from Eccles, J. S. (1992). School and family effects on the ontogeny of children's interests, self-perceptions, and activity choice. In J. Jacobs (Ed.), *Nebraska symposium on motivation, 1992*. Lincoln, NE: University of Nebraska Press.

Science education reform can be characterized by the title work of Project 2061: *Science for All Americans.* The danger, of course, is that this credo can be diluted and weakened to the extent that it becomes just another slogan that people see as political rhetoric, virtually impossible to realize. Consequently, a first recommendation is that science education raise its profile regarding equity issues.

■ To begin, science educators and their professional organizations may wish to expand their contacts with and listen to educational agencies and organizations particularly concerned with equity issues. These include the Office of Bilingual Education and Minority Language Affairs, National Urban Coalition, Council for Exceptional Children, Quality Education for Minorities, Council of Great City Schools, Equity 2000 (The College Board), American Indian Science and Engineering Society, and American Association of University Women. Science education reform philosophy and goals should be disseminated with and through these organizations, as well as through the professional science education groups that have been targeted in the past.

■ Second, science education organizations should begin to develop public relations materials that can be used by parent groups, PTAs, civic organizations, churches, businesses, and industry. Given the current political climate—cutbacks in educational budgets and existing funds being handled more and more at the state level—it will be important for science education reformers to leverage their guidance into state and civic efforts. In the face of federal budget cutbacks, it may be more important than ever for Project 2061, the National Research Council, the National Council of Teachers of Mathematics, and the National Science Teachers Association to show solidarity and congruence with regard to equity issues.

■ The third recommendation is to expand research about diverse groups. Although a growing body of literature is emerging, the knowledge base about issues of diversity and equity is very limited at present. Project 2061's approach to science education and its accompanying benchmarks hold a great deal of promise for educating those who have been bypassed by science in the past. Researchers are right to look for "landmarks" by which to navigate explorations around equity issues. Research that focuses on how all students can achieve benchmarks and standards in an equitable and fair way should be the central goal for science educators.

■ Science educators should carefully consider the unfortunate prospect of further stratification of opportunity that reform may engender. There is some evidence that more affluent schools and districts are already well out in front of low-income schools and districts in implementing reform. Consequently, it will be important to target first those areas of greatest need. Inequity seems to begin at the level of state funding patterns. We recommend that science education organizations such as Project 2061 and the National Research Council explore the creation of a science education equity instrument that might be used on the state, local school district, school, or classroom level to examine equity issues.

■ Finally, science educators should honestly examine the current reward system in science education and ask if it could be replaced or adjusted to include equity goals. Teachers who have discovered successful methods for teaching science to all, schools that involve teams of educators working together to create innovative and effective science classrooms, and communities that promote and sponsor extracurricular science activities for students who otherwise would not have had the opportunity should be recognized and rewarded. Currently, the reward system seems geared to the accomplishments of the "academically talented." This recommendation to restructure rewards is not merely an exercise in building self-esteem, but an attempt to define science literacy in human terms.

Science educators, including Project 2061, have set into motion a reform effort that promises to deliver something far greater than slogans. The steps toward implementing the standards and benchmarks that have been developed should more specifically address the equity goals that are so crucial to the vision of science for all. In the world of today, scientific literacy is not only for the privileged few. There is no longer an option of not providing equitable resources necessary for all students to meet ambitious standards. The survival of democracy depends on opportunity for all, avoiding a drift toward "haves" and "have-nots," which is the consequence if science for all is not achieved. Literacy in science is necessary for survival not only in the job market and in daily life, but as a way to join the mainstream society and enjoy the benefits and culture of the information age.

REFERENCES

American Association for the Advancement of Science. (1993). *Benchmarks for science literacy.* New York: Oxford University Press.

Banks, J. A. (1991). Teaching multicultural literacy to teachers. *Teaching Education, 41*(1), 135–144.

Casserly, P. L. (1980). Factors affecting female participation in advanced placement programs in mathematics, chemistry and physics. In L. Fox, L. Brody, & D. Tobin (Eds.), *Women and the mathematical mystique.* Baltimore, MD: The Johns Hopkins University Press.

Cummins, J. (1980). The cross-lingual dimensions of language proficiency: Implications for bilingual education and the optimal age issue. *TESOL Quarterly, 14*(2), 175–187.

Darling-Hammond, L. (1991). The implications of testing policy on quality and quantity. *Phi Delta Kappan, 73*(3), 220–225.

Department of Education. (1996). *The condition of education 1996.* Washington, D.C.: Author.

Eccles, J.S. (1992). School and family effects on the ontogeny of children's interests, self-perceptions, and activity choice. In J. Jacobs (ed.), *Nebraska symposium on motivation, 1992.* Lincoln, NE: University of Nebraska Press.

Fradd, S. H., & Larringa-McGee, P. (1994). *Instructional assessment: An integrative approach to evaluating student performance.* Reading, MA: Addison-Wesley.

Fradd, S. H., & Lee, O. (1995). *Promoting science literacy for all Americans including culturally and linguistically diverse students: Keeping the promise.* (NSF Grant No. REC-9552556). Coral Gables, FL: University of Miami.

Kahlenberg, R. (1995). Class, not race. *The New Republic, 21,* 24–27

Lacelle-Peterson, M., & Rivera, C. (1993). *Will the national goals improve the progress of English language learners?* (ERIC Document Reproduction Service No. ED 362073).

National Center for Education Statistics. (1996). *1995 Digest of educational statistics.* Washington, D.C.: Author.

National Council of Teachers of Mathematics. (1995). *Assessment standards for school mathematics.* Reston, VA: Author.

National Research Council. (1996). *National science education standards.* Washington, D.C.: National Academy of Sciences.

National Science Foundation. (1996). *Indicators of science and mathematics education 1995.* Arlington, VA: Author.

Oakes, J. (1985). *Keeping track.* New Haven, CT: Yale University Press.

Oakes, J., Gamoran, A., & Page, R. N. (1992). Curriculum differentiation: Opportunities, outcomes, and meanings. In P. W. Jackson (Ed.), *Handbook of research on curriculum.* New York: MacMillan Publishing.

Patton, J., Polloway, E., & Cronin, M. (1986). *Science education for students with mild disabilities: A status report.* ED370329.

Rosebery, A. S., Warren, B., & Conant, F. R. (1992). Appropriating scientific discourse: Findings from language minority classrooms. *The Journal of the Learning Sciences, 2,* 61–94.

Shamos, M. (1996). *The myth of scientific literacy.* New Brunswick, NJ: Rutgers University Press.

Spurlin, Q. (1995). Making science compatible for language minority students. *Science Teacher Education, 6*(2), 71–78.

Treisman, E. U. (1990). *Academic peristroika: Teaching, learning, and the faculty's role in turbulent times.* Fund for the Improvement of Postsecondary Education lecture. California State University, San Bernadino.

BIBLIOGRAPHY

Allen, B. A., & Boykin, A. W. (1992). African American children and the educational process: Alleviating cultural discontinuity through prescriptive pedagogy. *School Psychology Review, 21*, 586-596.

Allen, N. J. (1995). *Voices from the bridge. Kickapoo Indian students and science education: A world view comparison.* Paper presented at the annual meeting of the National Association for Research in Science Teaching, San Francisco, CA.

Alsalam, N., Fischer, G. E., Ogle, L. T., & Smith, T. M. (1993). *The condition of education 1993.* Washington, D.C.: U.S. Government Printing Office.

American Association for the Advancement of Science. (1993). *Benchmarks for science literacy.* New York: Oxford University Press.

American Association for the Advancement of Science. (1989). *Science for all Americans.* New York: Oxford University Press.

American Association of University Women. (1992). *How schools shortchange girls.* Washington, D.C.: Author.

American Indian Science and Engineering Society. (1995). *Educating American Indian/Alaska Native elementary and secondary students.* Arlington, VA: The National Science Foundation.

Atkinson, J. W. (1964). *An introduction to motivation.* Princeton, NJ: Van Nostrand.

Bach, R. L. (1984). *Labor for participation and employment of Southeast Asian refugees in the United States.* Washington, D.C.: Department of Health and Human Services.

Bandura, A. (1977). Self-efficacy: Toward a unifying theory of behavior change. *Psychological Review, 84*, 191-215.

Banks, J. A. (1991). Teaching multicultural literacy to teachers. *Teaching Education, 41*(1), 135-144.

Barringer, H. (1990). Education, occupational prestige, and income of Asian Americans. *Sociology of Education, 63*(1), 27-43.

Barth, P. (1994). *Curriculum Connections Blueprint.* Paper prepared for the American Association for the Advancement of Science, Project 2061, Washington, D.C.

Bay, M., Staver, J. R., Bryan, T., & Hale, J. B. (1992). Science instruction for the mildly handicapped: Direct instruction versus discovery teaching. *Journal of Research in Science Teaching, 29*(6), 555-570.

Becker, J. R. (1981). Differential treatment of females and males in mathematics classes. *Journal of Research in Mathematics Education, 72*, 119-132.

Benjamin, D. (1986). *The Japanese school: Lessons for industrial America.* New York: Praeger Publishers.

Betz, N. E., & Hackett, G. (1981). The relationship of career-related self-efficacy expectations to perceived career options in college women and men. *Journal of Counseling Psychology, 28*, 399-410.

Bobo, L. (1988). Group conflict, prejudice, and the paradox of contemporary racial attitudes. In P. Katz and D. Taylor (Eds.), *Eliminating racism: Profiles in controversy.* New York: Plenum Press.

Booth, W. (1995, July 21). University of California ends racial preferences. *The Washington Post*, pp. A1, A13.

Boswell, S. (1979). *Nice girls don't study mathematics: The perspective from elementary school.* Paper presented at the annual meeting of the American Educational Research Association, San Francisco, CA.

Bourdieu, P. (1977). Cultural reproduction and social reproduction. In J. Karabel and A. H. Halsey (Eds.), *Power and ideology in education.* New York: Oxford University Press.

Boykin, A. W. (1977). Experimental psychology from a black perspective: Issues and examples. *Journal of Black Psychology, 2*, 29-49.

Brody, L., & Fox, L. H. (1980). An accelerated intervention program for mathematically gifted girls. In L.H. Fox, L. Brody, & D. Tobin (Eds.), *Women and the mathematical mystique.* Baltimore, MD: The Johns Hopkins University Press.

Brophy, J. E., & Good, T. (1974). *Teacher-student relationships: Causes and consequences.* New York: Holt, Reinhart, and Winston.

Brush, L. (1980). *Encouraging girls in mathematics: The problem and the solution.* Boston, MA: ABT Books.

Callahan, C.M. (1979). The gifted and talented woman. In A.H. Passow (Ed.), *The gifted and talented: Their education and development. The Seventy-Eighth Yearbook of the National Society for the Study of Education.* Chicago, IL: The University of Chicago Press.

Campbell, J. R. (1991). The roots of gender equity in technical areas. *Journal of Research in Science Teaching, 28*(3), 251-264.

Campbell, J. R., & Connolly, C. (1987). Deciphering the effects of socialization. *Journal of Educational Equity and Leadership, 7*(3), 208-222.

Caplan, N., Choy, M. H., & Whitmore, J. K. (1992). Indochinese refugee families and academic achievement. *Scientific American, 266*(2), 36-42.

Casserly, P. (1975). *An assessment of factors affecting female participation in advanced placement programs in mathematics, chemistry, and physics.* Report to the National Science Foundation. Reprinted in L. H. Fox, L. Brody, and D. Tobin (Eds.), (1980), *Women and the mathematical mystique.* Baltimore, MD: The Johns Hopkins University Press.

Casserly, P. L. (1980). Factors affecting female participation in advanced placement programs in mathematics, chemistry and physics. In L. Fox, L. Brody, & D. Tobin (Eds.), *Women and the mathematical mystique.* Baltimore, MD: The Johns Hopkins University Press.

Cawley, J. F., Kahn, H., & Tedesco, A. (1989). Vocational education and students with learning disabilities. *Journal of Learning Disabilities, 22*, 630-634.

Cawley, J. F., Miller, J., Sentman, R., & Bennett, S. (In progress). *Science for all children (SAC).* Unpublished science curriculum. Buffalo, NY: State University of New York at Buffalo.

Ceci, S. J. (1991). How much does schooling influence general intelligence and its cognitive components? A reassessment of the evidence. *Developmental Psychology, 27*, 703-722.

Chan, S., & Wang, L. (1990). Racism and the model minority: Asian Americans in higher education. In M. T. Nettles (Ed.), *The effect of assessment on minority student participation* (New Directions for Institutional Research, No. 65) (pp. 43-67). San Francisco, CA: Jossey-Bass.

Chipman, S., & Thomas, V. G. (1987). The participation of women and minorities in mathematical, scientific, and technical fields. In E. Z. Rothkopf (Ed.), *Review of Research in Education, 14*, 387-430. Washington, D.C.: American Educational Research Association.

Cleminson, A. (1990). Establishing an epistemological base for science teaching in light of contemporary notions of the nature of science and how children learn science. *Journal of Research in Science Teaching, 27*(5), 429-445.

Clewell, B. C., & Ficklen, M. S. (1986). *Improving minority retention in higher education: A search for effective practices* (Report No. RR-86-17). Princeton, NJ: Educational Testing Service.

Clewell, B. C., Thorpe, M. E., & Anderson, B. T. (1987). *Intervention programs in math, science, and computer science for minority and female students in grades four through eight.* Princeton, NJ: Educational Testing Service.

Crandall, V. C. (1969). Sex differences in expectancy of intellectual and academic reinforcement. In C.P. Smith (Ed.), *Achievement-related behaviors in children* (pp. 11-45). New York: Russell Sage Foundation.

Cummins, J. (1980). The cross-lingual dimensions of language proficiency: Implications for bilingual education and the optimal age issue. *TESOL Quarterly, 14*(2), 175-187.

Darling-Hammond, L. (1991). The implications of testing policy on quality and quantity. *Phi Delta Kappan, 73*(3), 220-225.

Delpit, L. (1988). The silenced dialogue: Power and pedagogy in educating other people's children. *Harvard Educational Review, 58*, 280-898.

Donahoe, K., & Zigmond, N. (1988). *High school grades of urban LD students and low-achieving peers.* Paper presented at the annual meeting of the American Educational Research Association, San Francisco, CA.

Donmoyer, R. & Kos, R. (1993). *At-risk students: Portraits, policies programs and practices.* Albany, NY: State University of New York Press.

Doran, R. L., Cawley, J. F., Parmar, R. S., & Sentman, R. (1995). *Science for the handicapped.* Final report to the National Science Association. Buffalo, NY: State University of New York at Buffalo.

Dresselhaus, M. S., Franz, J. R., & Clark, B. C. (1994, March 11). Interventions to increase the participation of women in physics. *Science, 263*, 1392-93.

Dunteman, G. H., Wisenbaker, J., and Taylor, M. E. (1978). *Race and sex differences in college science program participation.* Report to the National Science Foundation. Research Triangle Park, NC: Research Triangle Institute.

Dweck, C. S., & Elliott. (1983). Achievement motivation. In E. M. Hetherington (Ed.), *Socialization, personality, and social development: Vol. 4* (pp. 643-691). New York, NY: Wiley.

Dweck, C. S., & Licht, B. G. (1980). Learned helplessness and intellectual achievement. In J. Garber and M.E.P. Seligman (Eds.), *Human helplessness: Theory and applications.* New York: Academic Press.

Eccles, J. S. (1984). Sex differences in mathematics participation. In M. Steinkamp and M. Maehr (Eds.), *Women in science.* Greenwich, CT: JAI Press, Inc.

Eccles, J. S. (1989). Bringing young women to math and science. In M. Crawford and M. Gentry (Eds.), *Gender and thought.* New York: Springer Verlag.

Eccles, J. S. (1992). School and family effects on the ontogeny of children's interests, self-perceptions, and activity choice. In J. Jacobs (Ed.), *Nebraska symposium on motivation, 1992.* Lincoln, NE: University of Nebraska Press.

Eccles, J. S., & Blumenfeld. (1985). Classroom experiences and student gender: Are there differences and do they matter? In L.C. Wilkinson and C. Marrett (Ed.), *Gender influences in classroom interaction* (pp. 79-114). Hillsdale, NJ: Lawrence Erlbaum Associates.

Eccles, J. S., & Harold, R. D. (1990). Gender differences in educational and occupational patterns among the gifted. In N. Colangelo, S.G. Assouline, & D.L. Amronson (Eds.), *Talent development: Proceedings from the 1991 Henry B. and Jocelyn Wallace National Research Symposium on Talent Development.* Unionville, NY: Trillium Press.

Eccles, J. S., & Harold, R. D. (1992). Gender differences in educational and occupational patterns among the gifted. In N. Colangelo, S. G. Assouline, & D. L. Amronson (Eds.), *Talent development: Proceedings from the 1991 Henry B. and Jocelyn Wallace National Research Symposium on Talent Development* (pp.3-29). Unionville, NY: Trillium Press.

Eccles (Parsons), J. S., Adler, T. F., & Meece, J. L. (1984). Sex differences in achievement: A test of alternate theories. *Journal of Personality and Social Psychology, 46,* 26-43.

Eccles, J.S., Jacobs, J.E., & Harold, R.D. (1990). Gender-role stereotypes, expectancy effects, and parents' role in socialization of gender differences in self-perceptions and skill acquisition. *Journal of Social Issues, 46,* 182-201.

Encyclopedia Britannica. (1992). *Full option science system.* Chicago, IL: Encyclopedia Brittanica, Co.

Endo, J. J. (1990). Assessing the educational performance of minority students: The case of Asian and Pacific Americans. In M. T. Nettles (Ed.), *The effect of assessment on minority student participation* (New Directions for Institutional Research, No. 65) (pp. 37-52). San Francisco, CA: Jossey-Bass.

Entwisle, D. R., & Alexander, K. L. (1992, February). Summer setback: Race, poverty, school composition, and mathematics achievement in the first two years of school. *American Sociological Review, 57,* 72-84.

Fallows, J. (1987). Grandgrind's heirs. *Atlantic Monthly,* 16-24.

Farrell, Edwin (1994). *Self and school success: Voices and lore of inner-city students.* Albany, NY: State University of New York Press.

First, J. M. (1988). Immigrant students in U.S. public schools: Challenges with solutions. *Phi Delta Kappan, 70*(3), 205-210.

Fox, L. H. (1976). Sex differences in mathematical precocity: Bridging the gap. In D. P. Keating (Ed.), *Intellectual talent: research and development.* Baltimore, MD: The Johns Hopkins University Press.

Fox, L. H. & Denham, S. A. (1974). Values and career interests of mathematically and scientifically precocious youth. In J. C. Stanley, D. P. Keating, & L. H. Fox (Eds.), *Mathematical "talent": Discovery, description and development.* Baltimore, MD: The Johns Hopkins University Press.

Fox, L. H., Benbow, C. P., & Perkins, S. (1983). An accelerated mathematics program for girls: A longitudinal evaluation. In C. P. Benbow and J. Stanley (eds.), *Academic precocity: Aspects of its development.* Baltimore, MD: The Johns Hopkins University Press.

Fradd, S. H., & Larrinaga-McGee, P. (1994). *Instructional assessment: An integrative approach to evaluating student performance.* Reading, MA: Addison-Wesley.

Fradd, S. H., & Lee, O. (1995a). Science for all: A promise or a pipe dream for bilingual students? *The Bilingual Research Journal, 19,* 261-278.

Fradd, S. H., & Lee, O. (1995b). *Promoting science literacy for all Americans including culturally and linguistically diverse students: Keeping the promise* (NSF Grant No. REC-9552556). Coral Gables, FL: University of Miami.

Gamoran, A. (1992). Access to excellence: Assignment to honors English classes in the transition from middle to high school. *Educational Evaluation and Policy Analysis, 14,* 185-204.

Gamoran, A., & Berends, M. (1987). The effects of stratification in secondary schools: Synthesis of survey and ethnographic research. *Review of Educational Research, 57,* 415-435.

Gamoran, A. & Mare, R. D. (1989). Secondary school tracking and educational inequality: Compensation, reinforcement or neutrality? *American Journal of Sociology, 94,* 1146-1183.

Garcia, E. (1995). Educating Mexican-American students: Past treatment and recent developments in theory, research, policy and practice. In J. A. Banks and C. M. Banks (Eds.), *Handbook of research on multicultural education* (pp. 372-387). New York: MacMillan.

Gibbons, A. (1992). Minority programs that get high marks. *Science, 258,* 1190-1196.

Gordon, B. J. & Addison, L. (1985). Gifted girls and women in education. In S. Klein (Ed.), *Sex equity through education.* Baltimore, MD: The Johns Hopkins University Press.

Greene, M. S. (1995, June 25). Daily struggles, distant dreams. *The Washington Post,* pp. A1 & A16-A18.

Gregory, J., Shanahan, T., & Walberg, H. (1985). Learning disabled 10th graders in main streamed settings: A descriptive analysis. *Remedial and Special Education, 6*(4), 25-33.

Grossen, B. (1995, July). *What works in middle school: Teaching big ideas in science.* Paper presented at the National Science Foundation/American Association for the Advancement of Science conference on science and learning disabilities, Washington, D.C.

Grossen, B., Romance, N. R., & Vitale, M. R. (1994). Science: Educational tools for diverse learners. *School Psychology Review, 23,* 442-463.

Haberman, M. (1995, June). Selecting "star" teachers for children and youth in urban poverty. *Phi Delta Kappan,* 777-781.

Hamilton, V. L., Blumenfeld, P. C., Akoh, H., & Miura, K. (1989). Citizenship and scholarship in Japanese and American fifth grades. *American Educational Research Journal, 26*(1), 44-72.

Harnisch, D., and Wilkinson, I. (1989). *Cognitive return of schooling for the handicapped: Preliminary findings from high school and beyond.* Paper presented at the annual meeting of the American Educational Research Association, San Francisco, CA.

Hartka, E. (1994). A study of students excluded from the 1992 National Assessment of Educational Progress trial state assessment. In R. Glaser & R. Linn (Eds.), *The trial state assessment: Prospects and realities: Background studies* (pp. 69-114). Stanford, CA: National Academy of Education.

Heath, S. B. & McLaughlin, M. W. (1993). *Identity and inner-city youth: Beyond ethnicity and gender.* New York: Teachers College Press.

Hess, R. D., & Azuma, H. (1991). Cultural support for schooling: Contrasts between Japan and the United States. *Educational Researcher, 20*(9), 2-8.

Hess, R. D., Chih-Mei, C., & McDevitt, T. M. (1987). Cultural variations in family beliefs about children's performance in mathematics: Comparisons among People's Republic of China, Chinese-American, and Caucasian-American families. *Journal of Educational Psychology, 79*(2), 179-188.

Hilton, T. L., Hsia, J., Solorzano, D. G., & Benton, N. L. (1988). *Persistence in science of high ability minority students.* Princeton, NJ: Educational Testing Service.

Hirayama, Y. (1989, January). Where Japan is second-best. *World Press Review, 55.*

Hirschman, C. & Wong, M. G. (1984). Socioeconomic gains of Asian Americans, Blacks, and Hispanics: 1960-1976. *American Journal of Sociology, 90*(3), 584-607.

Hodgkinson, H. (1990). *The demographics of American Indians: One percent of the people: Fifty percent of the diversity.* Washington, D.C.: Institute for Educational Leadership Publications.

Hoffer, T. (1992). Middle school ability grouping and student achievement in science and mathematics. *Educational Evaluation and Policy Analysis, 14,* 205-227.

Hofmeister, A., Carnine, D., & Clark, R. (1994). *A Blueprint for action: Technology, media and materials.* Paper prepared for the American Association for the Advancement of Science, Project 2061, Washington, D.C.

Holahan, G. & DeLuca, C. (1993). *Classroom science interventions via a thematic approach.* Unpublished research paper, Buffalo, NY.

Hsia, J. (1988). Asian Americans fight the myth of the super student. *Educational Record, 68*(4), 94-97.

Huston, A. C. (1983). Sex-typing. In P. Mussen & E. M. Hetherington (Eds.), *Handbook of Child Psychology, Vol. 4.* New York: John Wiley.

International Association for the Evaluation of Educational Achievement. (1988). *Science achievement in seventeen countries: A preliminary report.* New York: Pergamon.

Kahle, J. (1984). *Girl friendly science.* Paper presented at the annual meeting of the American Association for the Advancement of Science, New York, NY.

Kahlenberg, R. (1995, April 3). Class, not race. *The New Republic, 21,* 24-27.

Kahlenberg, R. (1995, July 17 & 24). Equal opportunity critics. *The New Republic, 20, 22,* 24-25.

Kellogg, J. B. (1988). Forces of change. *Phi Delta Kappan, 70*(3), 199-204.

Klopfer, L. E., & Champagne, A. B. (1990). Ghosts of crises past. *Science Education,* *74,* 133-154.

Kluegel, J. & Smith, E. (1986). *Beliefs about inequality: Americans' views about what ought to be.* New York: Aldine de Gruyter.

Kohr, R. L., Masters, J. R., Coldiron, J. R., Blust, R. S., & Skiffington, E. (1991). The relationship of race, class, and gender with mathematics achievement for fifth-, eighth,-, and eleventh-grade students in Pennsylvania schools. *Peabody Journal of Education, 66,* 147-171.

Kozol, J. (1991). *Savage inequalities.* New York: Crown Publishers.

Kulik, C. L. C., & Kulik, J. A. (1982). Effects of ability grouping on secondary school students: A meta-analysis of the findings. *American Educational Research Journal, 19,* 415-428.

Lacelle-Peterson, M. & Rivera, C. (1993). *Will the national educational goals improve the progress of English language learners?* (ERIC Document Reproduction Service No. ED 362 073).

Ladson-Billings, G. (1994). *The dream keepers.* San Francisco, CA: Jossey Bass.

Lane, M. (1990). *Women and minorities in science and engineering.* Washington, D.C.: National Science Foundation.

Lapointe, A. E., Askew, J. M., & Mead, N. A. (1992). *Learning science.* Princeton, NJ: Educational Testing Service.

Lee, E. S., & Rong, X. (1988). The educational and economic achievement of Asian-Americans. *The Elementary School Journal, 88*(5), 545-560.

Lee, O. (1995). *Children's science conceptions and world views in social and cultural contexts: Making sense after a natural disaster.* Paper presented at the annual meeting of the American Educational Research Association, San Francisco, CA.

Lee, O. & Fradd, S. H. (in press). *Literacy skills in science performance among culturally and linguistically diverse students.*

Lee, O., & Fradd, S.H. (1995). *Science literacy with diverse students.* Coral Gables, FL: University of Miami.

Lee, O., Fradd, S. H., and Sutman, F. X. (1995). Science knowledge and cognitive strategy use among culturally and linguistically diverse students. *Journal of Research in Science Teaching, 32,* 797-816.

Lee, S., Ichikawa, V., & Stevenson, H. W. (1987). Beliefs and achievement in mathematics and reading: A cross-cultural study of Chinese, Japanese, and American children and their mothers. In M. L. Maehr & D. A. Kleiber (Eds.), *Advances in motivation and achievement: Enhancing motivation* (pp. 149-179). Orlando, FL: JAI Press.

Lewin, K. (1938). *The conceptual representation and the measurement of psychological forces.* Durham, NC: Duke University Press.

Lipton, E. (1995, June 25). In Fairfax high tech equals power. *The Washington Post,* pp. A1 & A11.

Luchins, E. H., & Luchins, A. S. (1980). Female mathematics: A contemporary appraisal. In L. H. Fox, L. Brody, & D. Tobin (Eds.), *Women and the mathematical mystique* (pp. 7-22). Baltimore, MD: The Johns Hopkins University Press.

Lynch, S. (1990). Fast-paced science for the academically talented: Issues of age and competence. *Science Education, 74*(6), 585-596.

Lynch, S. (1994). Ability grouping and science education reform: Policy and research base. *Journal of Research in Science Teaching, 31*(2), 105-128.

Lynch, S. (1995, April). *The missing link: The pre-implemented curriculum in Project 2061.* Paper presented at the annual meeting of the National Association for Research in Science Teaching, San Francisco, CA.

Lynch, S., & Mills, C. J. (1990). The skills reinforcement project: An academic program for high potential minority youth. *Journal for the Education of the Gifted, 13,* 364-379.

Lynch, S., & Mills, C. A. (1993). Identifying and preparing disadvantaged and minority youth for high-level academic achievement. *Contemporary Educational Psychology, 18,* 66-76.

Lynch, S., & Thomas, G. (1995). Hands-On Universe at Robinson Secondary School. In S. Rockman (Ed.), *Evaluation of the Hands-On Universe Project for the 1994-1995 academic year.* San Francisco, CA: Lawrence Berkeley Laboratory.

Mastropieri, M. A., & Scruggs, T. E. (1992). *Guidelines for effective mainstreaming in science.* West Lafayette, IN: Purdue Research Foundation.

Mathematical Sciences Education Board/National Research Council. (1990). *Reshaping school mathematics: A philosophy and framework for curriculum.* Washington, D.C.: National Academy Press.

Matyas, M. L. (1991). Fostering diversity at higher education institutions. In M. L. Matyas & S. M. Malcom (Eds.), *Investing in human potential: Science and engineering at the crossroads.* Washington, D.C.: American Association for the Advancement of Science.

Matyas, M. L., & Malcom, S. M. (1991). *Investing in human potential: Science and engineering at the crossroads.* Washington, D.C.: American Association for the Advancement of Science.

Mau, R. Y. (1990). Barriers to higher education for Asian/Pacific-American females. *Urban Review, 22*(3), 83-97.

Melnick, S. L. & Raudenbush, S. W. (1986). *Influence of pupils' gender, race, ability, and behavior on prospective and experienced teachers' judgements about appropriate feedback, research series no. 175* (Report No. Sp 028 405). East Lansing, MI: Michigan State University, Institute for Research on Teaching. (ERIC Reproduction Document Service No. ED 028 405).

Mordkowitz, E. R., & Ginsberg, H. P. (1987). Early academic socialization of successful Asian-American college students. *The Quarterly Newsletter of the Laboratory of Comparative Human Cognition, 9*(2), 85-91.

Morrison, J. W. (1990). *Compensatory preschool teachers' interaction patterns with the classroom minority.* (Report No. PS 018 650). Syracuse, NY: Syracuse University. (ERIC Document Reproduction Service No. ED 317 271).

National Center for Education Statistics. (1992). *Language characteristics and academic achievement: A look at Asian and Hispanic eighth graders in NELS: 1988.* Washington, D.C.: U.S. Department of Education.

National Center for Science Teaching and Learning. (1994). *School organization blueprint.* Paper prepared for the American Association for the Advancement of Science, Project 2061, Washington, D.C.

National Center on Research for Teacher Learning. (1994). *A blueprint for the education of Project 2061 science teachers.* East Lansing, MI: Michigan State University.

National Council of Teachers of Mathematics. (1995). *Assessment standards for school mathematics.* Reston, VA: Author.

National Council of Teachers of Mathematics. (1991). *Professional standards for teaching mathematics.* Reston, VA: Author.

National Council of Teachers of Mathematics. (1989). *Curriculum and evaluation standards for school mathematics.* Reston, VA: Author.

National Education Goals Panel. (1994). *Data Volume for the National Education Goals Report: Vol. 1.* Washington, D.C.: Author.

National Research Council. (1996). *National science education standards.* Washington, D.C.: National Academy Press.

National Research Council. (1989). *Everybody counts.* Washington, D.C.: National Academy Press.

National Science Foundation. (1994). *Women, minorities, and persons with disabilities in science and engineering* (1994 ed.). Arlington, VA: Author.

Nicholls, J.G. (1975). Causal attributions and other achievement-related cognitions: Effects of task outcomes, attainment value and sex. *Journal of Personality and Social Psychology, 31,* 379-380.

Oakes, J. (1985). *Keeping track.* New Haven, CT: Yale University Press.

Oakes, J., Gamoran, A., & Page, R. N. (1992). Curriculum differentiation: Opportunities, outcomes, and meanings. In P. W. Jackson (Ed.), *Handbook of research on curriculum* (pp. 570-608). New York: MacMillan Publishing.

Ogbu, J. (1992, November). Understanding cultural diversity. *Educational Researcher,* 5-14.

Olsen, L. (1988). Crossing the schoolhouse border: Immigrant children in California. *Phi Delta Kappan, 70*(3), 211-218.

Parmar, R., & Cawley, J. (1993). Analysis of science textbook recommendations to meet the needs of students with disabilities. *Exceptional Children, 59,* 518-531.

Parsons, J. E. Adler, P. A., & Kaczala, C. (1982). Socialization of achievement attitudes and beliefs: Parental influences. *Child Development, 53,* 310-321.

Parsons, J. E., Kaczala, C., & Meece, J. L. (1982). Socialization of achievement attitudes and beliefs: Classroom influences. *Child Development, 53,* 322-339.

Parsons, J. E., Ruble, D. N., Hodges, K. L., & Small, A.W. (1976). Cognitive-developmental factors in emerging sex differences in achievement-related expectancies. *Journal of Social Issues, 32,* 47-61.

Raizen, S. (1988). *Increasing educational productivity through improving the science curriculum.* Washington, D.C.: The National Center for Improving Science Education.

Raspberry, W. (1995, September 25). Hugh Price's children's crusade. *The Washington Post,* p. A21.

Rawls, J. (1971). *A theory of justice.* Cambridge, MA: Belknap Press.

Redden, M.R. (1978). What is the state of the art? In H. Hofman (Ed.), *Science education for handicapped students.* Washington, D.C.: National Science Teachers Association.

Reyes, L. H., Stanic, G. M. A. (1988). Race, sex, socio-economic status and mathematics. *Journal for research in mathematics education, 19,* 26-43.

Rockman, S. (1995). In school or out: Technology, equity, and the future of our kids. *Communications of the ACM, 38,* 25-29.

Rodney, C. A., Perry, R. P., Parsonson, K. & Hrynuik, S. (1986). Effects of ethnicity and sex on teachers' expectations of junior high school students. *Sociology of Education, 59,* 58-67.

Rohlen, T. P. (1983). *Japan's high school.* Berkeley, CA: University of California Press.

Rosebery, A. S., Waren, B., & Conant, F. R. (1992). Appropriating scientific discourse: Findings from language minority classrooms. *The Journal of the Learning Sciences, 2,* 61-94.

Rotberg, I. C. (1990). Resources and reality: The participation of minorities in science and engineering education. *Phi Delta Kappan, 71*(9), 672-679.

Sanders, Jo (1994). *Lifting the Barriers.* Port Washington, NY: Jo Sanders Publications.

Scantleberry, K. & Kahle, J. B. (1993). The implementation of equitable teaching strategies by high school biology student teachers. *Journal of Research in Science Teaching, 30,* 537-546.

Secada, W. G. (1989). Educational equity versus equality of education: An alternative conception. In W. G. Secada (Ed.), *Equity in education.* Philadelphia, PA: Falmer Press.

Secada, W. G. (1991/1992). Agenda setting, enlightened self-interest, and equity in mathematics education. *Peabody Journal of Education, 66*(2), 22-56.

Secada, W. G. (1994). Equity and the teaching of mathematics. In M. Atwater (Ed.), *Proceedings of a seminar on multi-cultural education in mathematics education.* Athens, GA: Department of Science, University of Georgia. (Obtained from the author with permission to use).

Shavelson, R. (1992). Performance assessments: Political rhetoric and measurement reality. *Educational Researcher, 21,* 22-27.

Simpson, R. D. and Oliver, J. S. (1990). A summary of major influences on attitude toward achievement in science among adolescent students. *Science Education, 74,* 1-18.

Slavin, R. E. (1990). Achievement effects of ability grouping in secondary schools: A best-evidence synthesis. *Review of Educational Research, 60,* 471-499.

Sleeter, C. E. and Grant, C. A. (1991). Mapping terrains of power: Student cultural knowledge versus classroom knowledge. In C.E. Sleeter (Ed.), *Empowerment through multi-cultural education* (pp. 49-68). Albany, NY: State University of New York Press.

Smith-Hefner, N. J. (1990). Language and identity in the education of Boston-Area Khmer. *Anthropology and Education Quarterly, 21*(3), 250-268.

Snow, R. E., & Yallow, E. (1982). Education and intelligence. In R. J. Sternberg (Ed.), *Handbook of human intelligence* (pp. 493-585). London: Cambridge University Press.

Snyder, T. (1993). *Digest of educational statistics.* Washington, D.C.: Government Documents.

Spencer, B. D. (1994). A study of eligibility exclusion and sampling: 1992 trial state assessment. In *Trial state assessment: Prospects and realities: Vol. 2. Background studies* (pp. 1-68). Palo Alto, CA: National Academy of Education.

Spurlin, Q. (1995). Making science comprehensible for language minority students. *Science Teacher Education, 6*(2), 71-78.

Terman, L. M. (1926). *Genetic studies of genius: Vol. 1.* Palo Alto, CA: Stanford University Press.

Tidball, M., & Kistiakowsky, B. (1976). Baccalaureate origins of American scientists and scholars. *Science, 193,* 747-52.

Tikunuff. (1985). *Applying significant bilingual instructional features in the classroom.* Washington, D.C.: National Clearinghouse for Bilingual Education.

Tobin, D., & Fox, L. H. (1980). Career interests and career education: A way to change. In L. H. Fox, L. Brody, and D. Tobin (Eds.), *Women and the mathematical mystique.* Baltimore, MD: The Johns Hopkins University Press.

Tomlinson-Keasey, C., & Smith-Winberry, C. (1983). Educational strategies and personality outcomes of gifted and non-gifted college students. *Gifted Child Quarterly, 27,* 35-41.

Traub, J. (1995, July 17). It's elementary. *The New Yorker,* 74-79.

Treisman, E. U. (1990, March). *Academic peristroika: Teaching, learning and the faculty's role in turbulent times.* Fund for the Improvement of Postsecondary Education lecture at California State University, San Bernadino.

United States Commission on Civil Rights. (1992). *Civil rights issues facing Asian Americans in the 1990s.* Washington, D.C.: U.S. Government Printing Office.

Webster's encyclopedic unabridged dictionary of the English language. (1989). New York: Gramercy Books.

Weiner, B. (1974). *Achievement motivation and attribution theory.* Morristown, NJ: General Learning Press.

Welch, W. W. (1994). *Blueprint for reform: Assessment.* Paper prepared for the American Association for the Advancement of Science, Project 2061, Washington, D.C.

Weldon, S. (1995, July 12). Magnet schools saved, but at what cost to system? *The Silver Spring Gazette,* p. A13.

White, M. (1987). *The Japanese educational challenge: A commitment to children.* New York: The Free Press.

Wilkinson, L. C., & Marrett, C. (1985). *Gender influences in classroom interaction.* Hillsdale, NJ: Lawrence Erlbaum Associates.

Wright, P., & Santa-Cruz, R. (1983). Ethnic composition of special education programs in California. *Learning Disability Quarterly, 6*(4), 387-394.

Yao, E. L. (1988). Working effectively with Asian immigrant parents. *Phi Delta Kappan, 70*(5), 223-225.

Ysseldyke, J., Thurlow, M., Christenson, S., & Weiss, J. (1987). Time allocated to instruction of mentally retarded, learning disabled, emotionally disturbed and non-handicapped elementary students. *The Journal of Special Education, 21,* 23-42.

2

Policy

SCIENCE EDUCATION REFORMERS have identified three barriers to change in American classrooms: the state of science curricula, the state of teachers' knowledge, and public awareness of the need for educational reform in science. Most current science curricula are designed to have students memorize a vast number of unrelated facts rather than having them explore in depth an integrated series of concepts and principles that cut across traditional disciplines and prepare them for a lifetime of learning. Most teachers have been trained in the former style of curriculum and therefore are often unprepared to implement the latter. The public is generally unaware of these issues and is less interested in science education than in reading and mathematics, for example.

Like many curriculum reform efforts today, Project 2061 aims to solve these problems by creating a more student-centered, hands-on, and experiential way of learning science. In addition, Project 2061 strongly suggests that educators move away from the standardized science curriculum offered by widely used textbooks toward developing science education that is dynamic, flexible, and locally meaningful. *Benchmarks for Science Literacy* (*Benchmarks*) (American Association for the Advancement of Science [AAAS], 1993) creates a framework around which teachers, schools, and districts can design class work that will suit the unique needs of their individual students.

CURRENT STATUS OF REFORM

While the goals of current science and mathematics education reform are commendable, many of its essential aspects are not dissimilar to large-scale curriculum reform efforts undertaken between the 1950s and 1970s. These projects also saw curriculum and teacher training as key problems and searched for a more hands-on, student-centered approach to science instruction, all the while understanding that major change was a gradual process that would require many years to implement. Despite these laudable efforts and despite the investment of resources, expertise, and federal money (at least $117 million between 1954 and 1975), little of the substance of these changes remained by the mid-1970s. Student learning once again focused primarily on the acquisition of computational skills, and students rarely engaged in activities that allowed for creativity and reflection. The key question for today's science and mathematics education reformers clearly becomes, "Why did these efforts fail?"

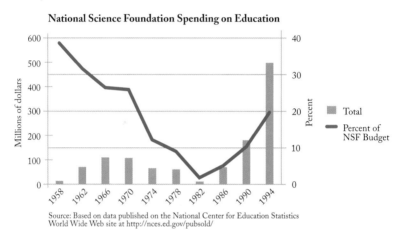

National Science Foundation Spending on Education

Source: Based on data published on the National Center for Education Statistics World Wide Web site at http://nces.ed.gov/pubsold/

The answers are surely multilayered, but reformers who wish to avoid the disappointing results of the earlier efforts must recognize two key points. First, the link between the school curriculum and the science practiced in laboratories and universities must be as close as possible so that research scientists, engineers, and other professionals in science-related disciplines can work together with K-12 teachers. Scientists cannot be expected to know all that one should know about teaching and instruction. Likewise, K-12 science teachers and curriculum developers cannot know all that one should know about the nature of research-based science. But the tighter this link, the better school and university science curriculum and instruction will be.

Second, many teachers are unprepared to implement science education as envisioned by *Benchmarks* and the National Research Council's 1996 *National Science Education Standards* (*Standards*). Any reform effort will fail if teachers are poorly prepared to teach science. Most teachers have grown up learning science as a series of unrelated facts to be memorized and recalled, and they continued to learn science

Elementary and secondary school teachers have little or no access to the kinds of professional networks common in the community of academic scientists.

that way in the science courses that were required in teacher-education programs. In addition, elementary and secondary school teachers have little or no access to the kinds of professional networks common in the community of academic scientists and thus do not have regular access to conversation about what "real" science is. Some of the projects in the 1970s recognized this deficiency and acknowledged the paramount importance of engaging teachers with scientists in the development of new curricula. Recent teacher enhancement projects, such as those sponsored by the National Science Foundation and the U.S. Department of Education, have also worked to develop professional networks, aided by the increasing availability of electronic communications in schools. However, when these projects end, schools and universities often find it difficult to support continued funding for the activities. Teachers lose contact with the academic scientists they have worked with and are again left without a professional network to support their reform efforts.

While it is important that reformers recognize these problems as they prepare to proceed with development and implementation, they must also recognize that change will occur incrementally. Therefore, short-term goals must be designed that focus on the following questions:

■ What role can government policy play at the federal, state, and local levels to support science reform?

■ How can local school district policy be encouraged to support science reform at the school and the classroom level?

■ What role should the construction of curriculum play in professional development? To what extent should curricula be ready to implement in the classroom?

■ How can public support of science education reform be developed at both national and grass-roots levels?

The short-term goals that emerge from the answers to these and perhaps other questions should be considered in the context of top-down and bottom-up reform strategies, and strategies that combine ingredients of both. This chapter is divided into four sections that focus on these questions and offer options for reform strategies that address them.

TOP-DOWN REFORM:
NEEDED CHANGES IN GOVERNMENT POLICY

Government policy—federal, state, and local—has the power to effect fundamental change in classroom practice. Although federal funding has some influence on K-12 school programs, local school boards continue to have direct control over American schools. And in the last 25 years, the role of states in U.S. education—even at the local level—has grown considerably (Goertz, 1993). The increased focus on course requirements and state comparisons during the 1980s helped move even more power to the state level. Although this movement increased the number of students from all backgrounds taking academic courses (Porter, Kirst, Osthoff, & Schneider, 1993), little attention was paid to what was being taught in those courses. Now states around the country are beginning to use policy instruments, such as curriculum frameworks, assessments, and teacher certification requirements, to directly impact both content and instruction in schools. Many are doing so under the rubric of a policy and governance strategy called "systemic reform." This strategy calls for states to develop a common set of standards or principles around which their schools should operate, then use these standards to develop goals for curriculum, instruction, and assessment. This reform also requires states to organize and distribute resources more effectively to meet standards-based goals.

States around the country are using policy instruments, such as curriculum frameworks, assessments, and teacher certification requirements, to directly impact both content and instruction in schools.

States give their districts and schools varying degrees of flexibility to design their own strategies for meeting state-imposed standards. For example, state-mandated textbooks and assessments narrow the options that individual districts and schools have for designing their own programs. If science and mathematics educators hope to see reforms implemented on a wide scale, they must work to influence state-level policies that support more flexibility. Reforms should include comprehensive attention to curriculum frameworks, assessment, teachers, and curriculum materials. If state policy impacting these four areas runs antithetical to the goals of science education reform, it will surely kill reform efforts. But policies that at least open the space for innovation—and at best actively support science and mathematics education—can be a key ingredient to the success of reform.

CURRICULUM FRAMEWORKS

In the past, state guidelines for instruction in various disciplines received little attention from educators. However, these guidelines—commonly called curriculum frameworks—are beginning to play a greater role in guiding statewide instruction. Frameworks are now often developed in a public forum, and many states use them as catalysts for school reform. When this chapter was written, many states were publishing new or revised statewide curriculum frameworks—37 in science and 33 in mathematics—and most were already in the process of implementing them (Blank & Pechman, 1995). More and more of these frameworks are beginning to mirror the goals of science and mathematics reform by using standards that emphasize the conceptual ideas of a field rather than its highly specialized details. These standards include *Benchmarks* (AAAS, 1993), *National Science Education Standards* (National Research Council, 1996), and *Curriculum and Evaluation Standards for School Mathematics* (National Council of Teachers of Mathematics, 1989).

Nonetheless, frameworks take very different forms from state to state. For instance, California and South Carolina provide a relatively high level of detail, discussing the larger conceptual ideas of science, its pedagogy, the sequencing of instruction, and assessment. Texas and Mississippi limit their frameworks to statements of the science content goals and objectives, offering only optional suggestions for instruction. Finally, states such as Pennsylvania have developed nondisciplinary frameworks that do not discuss sequencing or pedagogy. Content-only and nondisciplinary approaches may be used more often in states with a history of strong local control because they provide more flexibility to school districts. Some of the states that proposed detailed content and pedagogy have been forced to rewrite their frameworks by powerful groups who oppose values and attitudes statements that are often expressed or implied in more detailed frameworks. Some coalitions strongly oppose goals such as problem-solving, higher-order thinking, and heterogeneous grouping because they feel it detracts from student learning of specific subjects. These groups have forced several states to switch from the development of frameworks that make suggestions for teaching and learning science processes to more discipline-based frameworks.

State frameworks that do not contain at least some degree of specificity or instructional guidance will have little practical value to teachers and school administrators.

Although the "bare-bones," discipline-based frameworks do not always align perfectly with *Benchmarks*—mainly because they are often grade-level or course specific rather than interdisciplinary across grade ranges— they are much more viable politically. In addition, they make it possible to provide a great deal of guidance and flexibility to teachers. On the other hand, state frameworks that do not contain at least some degree of specificity or instructional guidance will have little practical value to teachers and school administrators who must figure out how to translate the broad concepts of the frameworks into classroom units and lesson plans. To solve this problem, local school districts can use *Benchmarks*, which provides both a high degree of specificity and a great deal of flexibility. Project 2061's proponents will have a powerful tool to advance reforms if they extend their influence on the development of state science curriculum frameworks to include the work that local districts do to implement those frameworks.

ASSESSMENT

Like state influence in general, the influence of statewide (and even nationwide) testing has grown dramatically in the last 20 years. As discussed at length in *Blueprints'* Chapter 8: Assessment, these tests often are the most important influence on what gets taught in the classroom. Recognizing this, many science and mathematics educators have become increasingly concerned about the limitations of multiple-choice, standardized tests, and have begun to focus increasing attention on developing so-called "authentic assessments." These authentic assessments often include portfolios of student work, performance-based exams, and open-ended response items that are designed to test students' ability to think reflectively rather than reflexively. Many hope, and science education reformers must also hope, that the use of these assessments will continue to increase. They have great potential to promote more experiential learning and critical thinking skills, two key goals of science and mathematics education reform.

Costs and public acceptance are barriers to the development and use of authentic assessments. Larger states are able to pay for the

State Assessment Accountability

State Assessment is:	Number of States*
Used for school accountability	30
Used to make decisions on consequences	27
About school funding	13
About school probation	11
Used for student accountability	26
High school exit requirement	17
Aligned with state curriculum standards	23**

*45 states have statewide assessment systems
**21 states in the process of analyzing alignment
Source: National Goals Panel. (1996). *Profile of 1994-95 state assessment systems and reported results.* Washington, DC: Author.

development of science assessments that are aligned with their own frameworks and that include open-ended and performance items. States with fewer resources must use "off-the-shelf" commercial tests that are mainly multiple-choice format and often are poorly aligned with the state framework. School districts face similar difficulties in aligning frameworks and assessments. Although many states have begun to use enhanced multiple-choice exams (e.g., exams that include graphs, measuring tools, and so on) and open-ended items in statewide assessments, a variety of technical issues still plague authentic assessments and make them problematic for policymakers concerned about public accountability. Likewise, several groups resist authentic assessments because of their inability to clearly quantify a student's performance. California and Kentucky, for example, had to shelve their authentic assessments in the face of public criticism that they were not sufficiently objective and reliable.

Whether a state or school district uses authentic assessments or relies heavily on standardized, multiple-choice testing, assessments exert a powerful influence on curriculum and instruction. And the higher the stakes associated with performance on the exam, the more it will influence the curriculum. Though some of the indirect results of high-stakes exams—such as teaching to the test, focusing on skills and vocabulary, and taking time away from instruction—are inconsistent with many of the aims of reform, educators must recognize the power that assessments exert on practice and must therefore be prepared to attempt to influence the design of state and national exams, following the suggestions in Chapter 8.

TEACHERS
Reforms have little chance of producing more than isolated impact without fundamentally affecting teachers. A recent study indicated that there are major problems in the teaching force, including many out-of-subject and non-certified teachers, and high rates of turnover and

leaving the field (National Commission on Teaching & America's Future, 1996). The report identified ten indicators of teacher quality:

- percent of unqualified hires,
- percent of out-of-field teachers,
- teachers as a percent of total staff,
- professional accreditation,
- required time in student teaching,
- student teaching experience with diverse learners,
- new teacher induction,
- professional standards,
- nationally certified teachers, and
- incentives for national board certification.

Of these ten indicators, one state currently meets seven, three states meet none, and the majority of states meet fewer than four.

States use a wide variety of policies to influence the quality of the teaching force, including salaries, incentive pay, certification and license renewal, evaluation, and staff development. The surest way for science and mathematics education reformers to make fundamental change is to place strong emphasis on the certification, evaluation, and staff development of teachers, administrators, and policymakers.

Certification. Just as assessment influences classroom practice, a state's certification process for teachers affects the practices of teacher-training institutions. Though it is difficult to change the content of higher education curricula, institutions have changed their teacher-training programs when high numbers of students have not passed certification exams. In an attempt to change the nature of its teaching force, Oklahoma is now tying its certification requirements to standards devised by the National Board for Professional Teaching Standards (NBPTS) for high-performing, experienced teachers. Teacher educators would be well-advised to work with NBPTS or similar organizations in determining the content of their programs.

Evaluation. In the 1980s, many states attempted to strengthen their teacher evaluation processes. However, these efforts were not very successful in influencing education. First, teacher shortages in some states and localities precluded districts from eliminating teachers, no matter how they performed on the evaluations. In addition, teaching evaluations have tended to focus on generic teaching competencies. For instance, Minnesota's Educational Effectiveness Program, created in 1983, used

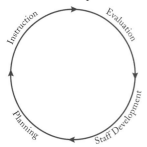

Cycle of Standards-Based
Instructional Improvement

15 general "effective schools" criteria as a basis for evaluation and assistance. It is important to recognize that the context of a teaching situation, the content of what is being taught, and the particular instructional goal all must be considered in defining and evaluating effective teaching (Sclan & Darling-Hammond, 1992). Reformers should develop and refine models of teaching science that align with the goals of *Benchmarks* and *Standards*, use them as the basis for evaluations systems, and tie staff development to evaluation to produce a system that builds science teaching competency toward standards-based goals.

Staff Development. Largely because supporters of staff development efforts lack political power, many states do not provide any funding at all for staff development, leaving it to individual districts. Even when states do provide funds for staff development, they rarely support the type of long-term, flexible, and developmental science learning process that Project 2061 envisions for teachers and students. Fiscal crises nationwide and broad popular support for belt tightening in state bureaucracies ensure that this political reality will remain unchanged for the foreseeable future.

Science and mathematics education reformers should work closely with states that do provide funding for staff development in order to help them create targeted, substantive programs for districts and schools. In states that provide minimal or no financial support for staff development, professional associations can try to influence teacher-training institutions and state certification processes. In these states, any efforts to influence staff development activities should be focused at the district level. A long-term goal can be to design workshops to introduce teachers to *Benchmarks* and *Standards*. A truly effective system would also include statewide networks of teachers, district offices, and "coaches" who have been similarly trained and who provide ongoing training and support to schools implementing these goals.

INSTRUCTIONAL MATERIALS

Although about half the states approve textbooks and other instructional materials for schools, mandantory adoption of those materials varies widely from state to state. Some policy makers have talked of moving away from textbook use, with frequent claims that textbooks are a mile wide and an inch deep, that they are written by publishers whose aim is not to offend, that they therefore address only the most watered down content, and that they limit teacher options and tend to stifle teacher creativity (Schmidt, McKnight, & Raizen, 1996). States have begun to respond to these criticisms. Not only have many states pushed the publishers of their textbooks to adopt higher standards of quality, they have also worked to diversify the materials that are eligible for adoption. For example, several states now encourage science teachers to use science kits, videodisks, or computer software programs in their classrooms. Science and mathematics educators would do well to take advantage of this climate of flexibility and reform. Providing students with more relevant, hands-on learning experiences is now the aim of science and mathematics educators and a growing number of policymakers.

Hands-on Work in Science Class

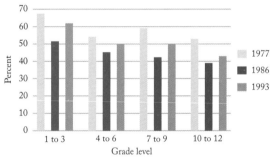

Source: National Science Foundation. (1996). *Indicators of mathematics and science education, 1995.* Arlington, VA: Author.

ADDING FLEXIBILITY

Many states are actively working to increase the flexibility of their policies, recognizing the limits of past efforts aimed strictly at top-down reform. Numerous states see standard-setting policies that are modeled after *Benchmarks* and *Standards* as a promising method for combining state-level accountability needs with local needs for control of instruction and curriculum design. Science and mathematics educators would be well advised to use these new mechanisms and their counterparts— deregulation, charter schools legislation, local needs assessment processes, and the like—to allow for local experimentation along lines consonant with reform ideals. The current climate of reform at the state level is one in which lasting, meaningful change can flourish.

BOTTOM-UP REFORM:
NEEDED CHANGES IN SCHOOL POLICY

By the mid-1980s, the substantial limits of top-down reform had begun to reveal themselves, and policy makers increasingly focused attention on "restructuring." Most restructuring policies held that teacher and parent empowerment was the key to effective education. Although the reasoning was logical and the intention admirable, most restructuring policies ignored curriculum content. Without such focus, it was difficult to effect changes in student learning (Porter, 1993).

DISTRICT-BASED REFORM

Theoretically, systemic reform attempts to address this issue by bringing subject-matter content into local empowerment strategies. Many of today's systemic reform initiatives, however, tend to decentralize control from the state to the school, bypassing the district. Policymakers should be careful not to get carried away with the romantic idea of delegating all decision-making to individual school sites. Spillane's 1994 study of a Michigan school district illustrates how powerful districts are in mediating between state policy and classroom practice. Despite a strong set of incentives and sanctions designed to make districts comply with new state reading standards, the district was instead able to focus professional development, curricular materials, and student assessments on more traditional forms of reading.

Districts play a major role in mobilizing and influencing local political support for reform initiatives, and their opposition can kill those efforts with ease.

The power of local districts should not be overlooked in any sweeping reform strategy. They are close enough to school sites to understand the subtleties of local context, but powerful enough to influence practice at a group of schools, eliminating the difficult task of making change on a school-by-school basis. Policymakers must consider that district administrators interpret policy changes in the light of their own organizational, social, and political context.

To bypass district administrators and focus on school personnel will not diminish the importance of the district in the change process. Districts play a major role in mobilizing and influencing local political support for reform initiatives, and their opposition can kill those efforts with ease.

As increased state-level control influences educational goals in the coming years, science and mathematics education reformers would do well to use districts as the unit of dissemination and development. Under current Goals 2000 plans, 90% of states' allocations of federal grants for goal setting will go to local districts. Science leaders might consider ways to provide (or ask states, foundations, or others to provide) incentive grants to local districts interested in implementing *Benchmarks* and *Standards*.

School-based Reform

As an overall change strategy, focusing on the school or district level as the unit of development holds promise. Building networks of schools or districts that aim toward science reform would allow them to learn from each other, cooperate to obtain technical assistance, and break down the isolation that so often plagues educators. Grants for start-up costs and implementation also may be more easily obtained by a coalition of schools with common goals.

There are several trade-offs involved in a school-centered strategy of bottom-up change. Certainly, school by school change is more expensive, and its reach is more limited. It also may miss the very schools that need help the most. Voluntary, bottom-up approaches do not provide the political leverage that is sometimes needed for change, and may only attract schools at the high end of the socioeconomic scale. School by school change increases the complexity of district administrators' jobs, which is to assure the public that programs are effective and students are achieving. These reasons argue that, although individual schools can and do manage to develop impressive changes, an overall strategy for reform in science education should not depend solely on school-level approaches.

Lessons from Project 2061 Sites

For any school or district wishing to put the goals of *Science for All Americans* (AAAS, 1989) into practice, the School-District Centers involved with Project 2061's reform efforts provide valuable lessons. Several factors have influenced the outcomes at the six sites: bottom-up design; external support and funding from AAAS; multilevel, multidisciplinary teams; encouragement to "dream big" and develop a vision unhampered by current school organization, design, or district politics; and a lengthy planning and development period (Massel & Hetrick, 1993).

Just as the sites provide lessons on how to ensure the success of science education reform, they also illustrate examples of the many pitfalls that await a district or school attempting such broad change. For instance, the open-ended nature of the project was in conflict with some important local realities, such as constraints on teachers' time, politicians' needs for accountability, and parental understanding. The long-term strategy of the project also made it difficult for some, especially those outside the core team, to stay actively involved. If reform is to engage teachers on an ongoing basis—and surely it should—these difficult realities will have to be addressed.

RECOMMENDATIONS FOR A PROFESSIONAL LEARNING STRATEGY

To address the difficult issue of teacher capacity, science and mathematics education reformers can consider focusing on a strategy of professional learning, with strong ties to curriculum development. This strategy would combine elements of both top-down and bottom-up approaches.

PROFESSIONAL CHALLENGES

The models of learning embraced by reformers—based on the idea that learners construct their own knowledge—force teachers to become more active decision makers in the classroom and to use materials and lessons that meet the unique needs of their students. In short, this approach may ask some teachers to teach in a way they have never been taught, which sometimes goes against the grain of today's classroom organization. In addition, it requires teachers to have much greater facility with subject matter than they currently do. They must be prepared to contend with a degree of complexity and uncertainty that was probably not a part of their training, and to not know the answer to many student questions. Overcoming these challenges is no small task. Research on the reforms of the mid-1970s, which were heavily supported and widely implemented, showed that most teachers who experimented with experience-based learning and new curriculum materials quickly returned to more comfortable, traditional methods (Stake, Easely, & Anastasiou, 1978).

STAFF DEVELOPMENT TODAY

Much staff development today is ineffective because it is fragmented in conception, episodic in delivery, and inconsistently distributed among teachers. It is often designed by experts distant from the classroom, with schools rarely taking responsibility for it. Teachers in most staff development exercises are consumers of knowledge produced elsewhere, a reali-

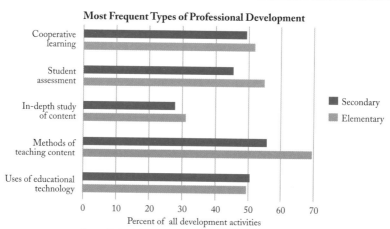

Most Frequent Types of Professional Development

Cooperative learning

Student assessment

In-depth study of content

Methods of teaching content

Uses of educational technology

■ Secondary
■ Elementary

0 10 20 30 40 50 60 70

Percent of all development activities

Source: National Center of Educational Statistics. (1996). *The condition of education, 1996.* (NCES 96-304). Washington, D.C.: Author.

ty that is wholly inconsistent with the goals and philosophy of reform (Little, 1993).

In addition, many teachers are poorly situated professionally to engage in the kind of networking that takes place among academic scientists at frequent conferences. Teachers can hardly be expected to provide hands-on activities and help children construct knowledge in science if they are not given the resources to construct their own ideas about science content and teaching. Likewise, it is not surprising that teachers might have difficulty implementing many science curricula. These materials are often developed by professional scientists, and teachers and professional scientists are almost completely isolated from each other.

Some successful efforts to confront these challenges have been made, such as the Urban Mathematics Collaborative (Webb, Heck, & Tate; 1996) and a smaller network of Math A teachers in San Francisco described by Adams (1992). Both of these efforts recognized that building long-term teacher development rests heavily on three factors: subject-matter expertise, knowledge of education policy, and a strong connection to a broader professional community. The Urban Mathematics Collaborative reaped the benefits of connecting teachers to influential people in their discipline and to state and national policy makers, while helping teachers to recognize expertise and incorporate it in their teaching.

Project 2061 school sites have in some ways functioned much like these two collaborative networks. In fact, several teachers who were trained at these sites and interviewed for this chapter said it was the best professional development they had received in their lives. Other studies

Building long-term teacher development rests heavily on three factors: subject-matter expertise, knowledge of educa-tion policy, and a strong connection to a broader professional community.

have shown that teachers tend to consider staff development most effective when it offers sub-stantive depth and focus, adequate time to grapple with ideas and materials, opportunity to consult with colleagues and experts, and a sense of doing real work rather than being "talked at" by experts. Project 2061's staff development includes several of these charac-teristics. Similar professional learning models, centered around curriculum analysis, are strate-gies that can be more widely implemented.

Nonetheless, there are serious barriers to implementing improved models of professional learning. First, the cost of all staff development is high. Second, it is difficult to engage already busy teachers in lengthy staff development exer-cises. It might be even more difficult to engage college and university faculty. Third, while reform emphasizes open-ended processes that promote ongoing learning and growth, politicians and the public often demand closure on the development process, and account-ability measures that match a certain timeline. In a similar vein, teachers demand closure on curriculum development. Not surprisingly, many teachers have expressed frustration in the past when curriculum reforms have been designed to serve the broad needs of an entire state or nation, and therefore have left teachers with the overwhelming responsibility of designing or adapting course units and activities. Science and mathemat-ics leaders must be aware of these realities and work to balance their objectives with the needs of teachers, administrators, and policy makers.

RECOMMENDATIONS FOR BUILDING SUPPORT

If reform leaders intend to reach the ambitious goal of changing the way science is taught in schools nationwide—in fact, if they hope to have any impact at all—one of their greatest challenges is to build widespread public support. Gaining public consensus and support is made more dif-ficult by the diversity in our educational and political systems, which respond to many interest groups with a variety of agendas. It is useful to think of the need to build public support in two areas: policymakers' sup-port for initial approval of reforms, and grass-roots support from teach-ers and parents for long-range classroom implementation. While advocates of reform must recognize the importance of building support among *both* of these constituencies, they must also recognize that the construction of such support will probably be done site by site or issue by issue rather than with a single, broad-based campaign. Finally, support for reform ideas will be most forthcoming if the public gains a sense of ownership through early and continued participation.

COALITIONS ON THE TOP

In order to develop the most effective effort to influence coalitions at higher levels of power, leaders must endeavor to understand the political contexts of different regions, states, and localities. For instance, while the state legislature may take the lead in influencing reform in one state, the state department of education may be the critical contact in another. Reform leaders should rank those who influence policy in terms of their positions, power, and salience across the following categories:

■ *insiders*, such as professional subject-matter associations, state science and mathematics systemic reform projects, curriculum policy makers, and textbook publishers;

■ the *near circle*, such as state boards of education, teacher unions, parent associations, and ideology groups;

■ the *far circle*, such as administrative organizations and business groups; and

■ *sometimes players*, such as school accrediting agencies.

Science education leaders might consider a variety of other tactics to spread their word to policy makers and the public. For example, to gain public and professional input on its Common Core of Learning (Vermont's curriculum framework), the Department of Education sponsored "focus forums"—meetings to discuss what students should know and be able to do. Such forums are an effective way to help parents and the public play a role in the development of new schooling programs and to give them a better understanding of the aims and philosophy of science education reform. Focused dialogues such as these serve to ease public resistance to change.

As science education reformers begin to develop public awareness, they must recognize other policy concerns as well. Interviews with 20 people from a range of constituencies (teachers, department heads, policy makers) highlighted some possible policy problems for reforms such as those proposed by Project 2061 (Kirst, Anhalt, & Marine, 1993). First, the interdisciplinary focus runs counter to many powerful institutional structures, such as professional associations, current textbooks, and advanced placement (AP) examinations. Second, current and past efforts at mixed-group instruction have often met fierce opposition from parents of gifted children, a group that tends to form a powerful lobby. Finally, while many interviewees were positive about the benchmarks, the flexibility they allow raises important questions for state policy makers, such as how to evaluate the diverse instructional programs that could arise under such an interdisciplinary approach.

GRASS-ROOTS COALITIONS

The task of mobilizing grass-roots support is distinct from influencing policy at higher levels. Direct contact with individual teachers is expensive, so reformers should work through organizations, beginning with subject-matter professional groups, teacher unions, and reform networks. But support from teachers will only be forthcoming if they understand the vision of reform and believe it will help solve the problems of the classroom, and if they have the external support to prepare for and implement reform ideas. Teacher support may grow if professional learning and curriculum development continue to be integral parts of reform strategies.

The policy scenarios and recommendations in this chapter are much easier said than done. But change is always a challenge, and recognizing complexity is the first step. The policy environment is ripe for science and mathematics education reform. Many stakeholders agree on the basic premises of systemic reform. The task will be to keep pushing on these fronts, to make some wise (and lucky) strategic choices, and to build on the philosophy and content of *Benchmarks* and *Standards*.

REFERENCES

Adams, J. (1992). *Policy implementation through teacher professional networks: The case of Math A in California.* Unpublished doctoral dissertation. Stanford, CA: Stanford University.

American Association for the Advancement of Science. (1993). *Benchmarks for science literacy.* New York: Oxford University Press.

American Association for the Advancement of Science. (1989). *Science for all Americans.* New York: Oxford University Press.

Blank, R., & Pechman, E. (1995). *State curriculum frameworks in mathematics and science: How are they changing across the states?* Washington, D.C.: Council of Chief State School Officers.

Goertz, M. (1993). *The role of state policy in mathematics and science reform.* Background paper prepared for the American Association for the Advancement of Science, Project 2061, Washington, D.C.

Kirst, M., Anhalt, B, & Marine, R. (1993). *Science for all Americans: A political blueprint.* Paper prepared for the American Association for the Advancement of Science, Project 2061, Washington, D.C.

Little, J. W. (1993). Teacher professional development in a climate of educational reform. *Educational Evaluation and Policy Analysis, 15*(2), 129.

Massell, D., & Hetrick, B. (1993). *Design and implementation in Project 2061: Lessons from the field.* Background paper prepared for the American Association for the Advancement of Science, Project 2061, Washington, D.C.

National Commission on Teaching & America's Future. (1996). *What matters most: Teaching for America's future.* New York: Author.

National Council of Teachers of Mathematics. (1989). *Curriculum and evaluation standards for school mathematics.* Reston, VA: Author.

National Research Council. (1996). *National science education standards.* Washington, D.C.: National Academy Press.

Porter, A. (1993). *State and district leadership for the implementation of Project 2061.* Background paper prepared for the American Association for the Advancement of Science, Project 2061, Washington, D.C.

Porter, A., Kirst, M., Osthoff, J., & Schneider, S. (1993). *Reform up close: A classroom analysis.* (Final report to the National Science Foundation, Grant No. SPA-8953446.) Washington, D.C.: National Science Foundation.

Schmidt, W., McKnight, C, & Raizen, S. (1996). *A splintered vision: An investigation of U. S. science and mathematics education.* Boston, MA: The NETWORK, Inc.

Sclan, E. & Darling-Hammond, L. (1992, March). *Beginning teacher performance evaluation: An overview of state policies.* Washington, D.C.: ERIC Clearinghouse on Teacher Education, American Association of Colleges of Teacher Education.

Spillane, J. P. (1994, April). *Districts matter: The local school district and state instructional policy.* Paper presented at the annual meeting of the American Educational Research Association, New Orleans, LA.

Stake, R. E., Easely, J. A., & Anastasiou, C. (1978). *Case studies in science education, Vols. I and II.* Champagne-Urbana, IL: University of Illinois, Center for Instructional Research and Curriculum Evaluation.

Webb, N., Heck, D., & Tate, W. (1996). The Urban Mathematics Collaborative Project: A study of teacher, community, and reform. In S. A. Raizen & E. D. Britton (Eds.), *Bold ventures, Volume 3, Case studies of U. S. innovations in mathematics education.* (pp. 245-360.) Dordrecht, The Netherlands: Kluwer Academic Publishers.

BIBLIOGRAPHY

Adams, J. (1992). *Policy implementation through teacher professional networks: The case of Math A in California.* Unpublished doctoral dissertation, Stanford University.

American Association for the Advancement of Science. (1989). *Science for all Americans.* New York, NY: Oxford University Press.

Blank, R. K. & Dalkalic, M. (1992). *State policies on science and mathematics education, 1992.* Washington, D.C.: Council of Chief State School Officers, State Education Assessment Center.

Choy, S. P. et al. (1993). *America's teachers: Profile of a profession.* (NCES 93-025). Washington, D.C.: U.S. Department of Education, National Center for Education Statistics.

Coley, R.J., & Goertz, M.E. (1990). *Educational standards in the 50 states: 1990.* Princeton, NJ: Educational Testing Service.

Curry, B., & Temple, T. (1992). *Using curriculum frameworks for systemic reform.* Alexandria, VA: Association for Supervision and Curriculum Development.

Elmore, R.F. (1993). *The development and implementation of large-scale curriculum reforms.* Background paper prepared for the American Association for the Advancement of Science, Project 2061, Washington, D.C.

Feistritzer, E. (1993). National overview of alternative teacher certification. *Education and Urban Society, 26*(1), 18.

Firestone, W. A. (1991). *Schools to facilitate professionals: Implications of the organizational and cognitive research on teaching.* New Brunswick, NJ: Consortium for Policy Research in Education.

Fuhrman, S. & Elmore, R. (Eds.) (1994). *The governance of curriculum, 1994 ASCD Yearbook.* Alexandria, VA: Association for Supervision and Curriculum Development.

Fuhrman, S. & Massell, D. (1992). *Issues and strategies in systemic reform.* New Brunswick, NJ: Consortium for Policy Research in Education

Fullan, Michael G. (1993). *Change forces: Probing the depths of educational reform.* Bristol, PA: The Falmer Press.

Goertz, M. (1993). *The role of state policy in mathematics and science reform.* Background paper prepared for the American Association for the Advancement of Science, Project 2061, Washington, D.C.

Green, J. (1987). *The next wave: A synopsis of recent education reform reports.* Denver, CO: Education Commission of the States.

Jackson, P. (1983, Spring). The reform of science education: A cautionary tale. *Daedalus, 112*(2), 143-166.

Kirst, M., Anhalt, B. & Marine, R. (1993). *Science for all Americans: A political blueprint.* Background paper prepared for the American Association for the Advancement of Science, Project 2061, Washington, D.C..

Koretz, D.M., Madaus, G., Haertel, E., & Beaton, A. (1992). *National educational standards and testing: A response to the recommendations of the National Council on Educational Standards and Testing.* Santa Monica, CA: RAND.

Langland, C. (1992, July 26). A bold new goal for schools. *The Philadelphia Inquirer,* F1-F4.

Lichtenstein, G., McLaughlin, M. & Knudsen, J. (1991). *Teacher empowerment and professional knowledge.* New Brunswick, NJ: Consortium for Policy Research in Education.

Little, J.W. (1993). Teachers' professional development in a climate of educational reform. *Educational Evaluation and Policy Analysis, 15*(2), 129.

Little, J.W. (1989). District policy choices and teachers' professional development opportunities. *Educational Evaluation and Policy Analysis, 11*(2), 165-179.

Marsh, P. (1964). *The Physical Science Study Committee: A case history of nationwide curriculum development, 1956-1961.* Unpublished doctoral dissertation, Harvard University.

Massell, D., with Hetrick, B.(1993). *Design and implementation in Project 2061: Lessons from the field.* Background paper. Washington, D.C.: American Association for the Advancement of Science.

Massell, D. & Fuhrman, S. (1993). *Ten years of reform: Update with four case studies* New Brunswick, NJ: Consortium for Policy Research in Education.

Massell, D. (1994). Achieving consensus: Setting the agenda for state curriculum reform. In S. Fuhrman & R. Elmore (Eds.), *The governance of curriculum.* Alexandria, VA: Association for Supervision and Curriculum Development.

Massell, D. (1994, February). Setting standards in mathematics and social studies. *Education and Urban Society.*

McCarthy, M. & Langdon, C. (1993, June). *Challenges to the curriculum in Indiana's public schools.* (PB-B20). Bloomington, IN: Indiana Education Policy Center.

McLaughlin, M.W. (1991). The RAND change agent study: Ten years later. In A. R. Odden (Ed.), *Education policy implementation* (pp.143-155). Albany, NY: State University of New York Press.

Millsap, M.A., Moss, M., & Gamse, B. (1992). *The Chapter 1 implementation study: Chapter 1 in public schools.* Draft final report to the U.S. Department of Education. Cambridge, MA: ABT Associates, Inc.

Moore, D. & Hyde, A. (1981). *Making sense of staff development: An analysis of staff development programs and their costs in three urban school districts.* Chicago, IL: Designs for Change.

Murphy, J. (1990). The educational reform movement of the 1980s: A comprehensive analysis. In J. Murphy (Ed.) *The educational reform movement of the 1980s: Perspectives and cases.* Berkeley, CA: McCutchan Publishing Corp.

Pechman, E. & Laguarda, K. (1993). *Status of new curriculum frameworks, standards, assessments, and monitoring systems.* Washington, D.C.: Policy Studies Associates, Inc.

Porter, A., M., Kirst, E., Osthoff, & Smithson, J. (1993). *Reform up close: A classroom analysis.* Report to the National Science Foundation, Grant No. SPA-8953446.

Porter, A. (1993). *State and district leadership for the implementation of Project 2061.* Background paper prepared for the American Association for the Advancement of Science, Project 2061, Washington, D.C.

Scannell, M.M. (1988). *Factors influencing state policies restricting entry to teaching.* Unpublished doctoral dissertation, George Washington University.

Smith, M. & O'Day, J. (1991). Systemic school reform. *Politics of Education Association yearbook 1990* (pp.233-267). New York: Taylor and Francis Ltd.

Stake, R., Easely, J. et al. (1978). *Case studies in science education, Volume I and II.* Urbana, IL: Center for Instructional Research and Curriculum Evaluation, University of Illinois.

Walker, D. (1990). *Fundamentals of curriculum.* Saddle Brook, NJ: Harcourt Brace Jovanovich.

Weiss, I.R. (1987). *Report of the 1985-86 national survey of science and mathematics education.* Research Triangle Park, NC: Research Triangle Institute.

Wohlstedter, P. (1993). Georgia case study. In D. Massell & S. Fuhrman (Eds.), *Ten years of reform: Update with four case studies.* New Brunswick, NJ: Consortium for Policy Research in Education.

Yee, G. & Kirst, M. (1994, February). Lessons from the new science curriculum of the 1950s and 1960s. *Education and Urban Society.*

3

Finance

WHAT FISCAL ISSUES might arise from implementing reforms in science education? How might we deal with the related problems? This chapter answers these questions by assessing the existing resource base for education; reporting what we know about how these resources are being spent currently; reviewing the contemporary debate over whether and how dollars make a difference in the improvement of pupil performance; and assessing the costs of implementing an ambitious reform initiative with goals such as Project 2061's. The chapter argues that there is more to understanding the fiscal implications of science education reform than developing projections of expected dollar costs and speculating about how easy or hard it will be to raise the necessary money. It concludes with recommendations for enhancing the prospects of the successful implementation of the Project 2061 vision of reform at several levels of the educational system.

THE RESOURCE BASE FOR EDUCATION

The United States raised more than $260 billion of revenue for its public elementary and secondary schools in 1993–94. Almost all of these resources were generated by taxes imposed by various levels of government, but state and local units of government contributed the largest shares (93%) with the federal government contributing the balance.[1] This distribution of governmental responsibility for generating public education revenues has been changing. For many years, the share contributed by local governments declined in favor of increased shares for other levels of government. The federal share peaked in 1980 and has been steady in recent years. In the 1990s, the state share began to decline, placing greater responsibility on local governments. The tax on

---

[1]These data all come from the National Center for Education Statistics (1996).

real property is the primary means by which local governments raise tax revenues; rising tax burdens at the local level have sparked taxpayer protests that are frequently focused on the property tax.

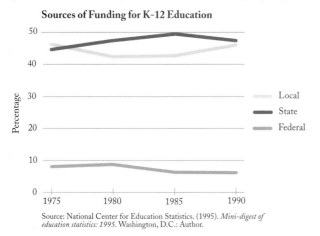

Sources of Funding for K-12 Education

Source: National Center for Education Statistics. (1995). *Mini-digest of education statistics: 1995.* Washington, D.C.: Author.

Changes have also been occurring in the absolute magnitude of the resource base for education in the United States. Evidence suggests that the level of investment has been increasing in real terms, although the precise magnitude of the increase is a matter of some dispute (cf. Rothstein, 1995; Odden, Monk, Nakib, & Picus, 1995). Odden estimates the increase at 200% in real terms per pupil over 30 years; according to Rothstein, estimates such as Odden's overstate the real growth by a factor of 40%. Much of the dispute over the precise magnitude centers around questions of changes in the needs of students and resulting changes in the nature of educational opportunities. If the public schools are delivering a significantly different product today than 20 years ago, it is clear that simple comparisons between what was spent then and now may be very misleading.

The basic conclusions that can be drawn are these:

■ A substantial investment in public education has been taking place.

■ The level of this investment has been rising in real terms.

■ The rate of increase is diminishing and is likely to continue to do so in the near term.

Education reformers need to be mindful of these trends, particularly if their reforms call for the infusion of new resources. Recent reductions in the share of support coming from state sources may be an opportunity for reformers to argue that states need to return to providing their historic share of support for the schools. Although there may be resistance to spending more state dollars to maintain the status quo, there may also be greater willingness to invest in well-designed reforms. The challenge will be to justify investments in education in relation to the pressing needs in most states for investments in health and other social services.

The rise of taxpayer frustration with the burden they carry to support schools is also prompting exploration of nontraditional revenue sources. In particular, interest is growing in user fees; proceeds of fund raising; and grants from private groups such as businesses, foundations, and booster clubs. In most places these revenues are playing only marginal roles, but some public schools are beginning to raise significant sums of money in these unorthodox ways. This success suggests that resources are available and that an important challenge for reformers is to identify new mechanisms for citizens to support their public schools.

SPENDING ON PUBLIC EDUCATION

There are a number of important questions to ask and answer about how the billions of dollars that are raised for public schools are being spent. For example, one might reasonably wonder about how much is spent on a typical pupil in the public schools. The answer for 1993–94 was $5,325 according to the National Center for Education Statistics (1996). But, this answer can be misleading because it does not reveal the tremendous amount of variation that occurs across individually organized schooling units. Some of this variation exists at the state level. For example, the highest spending state in 1993–94 was Alaska at $9,075, and the lowest spending state was Utah at $3,206 (a difference of more than 2.8 to 1).

Significant variation can also exist within the individual states. For example, in New York during the 1993–94 school year, the district in the 90th percentile of the spending distribution spent close to twice as much as the district in the 10th percentile. Considerably larger spending

Revenues for Public Education as a Percentage of All Revenues

State*	State Funds	Federal Funds
Hawaii	47.2	6.2
Nebraska	89.9	7.8
New Hampshire	31.0	5.9
New Mexico	72.7	12.2
Oregon	25.4	6.1
Washington	72.1	5.7
U.S. Average	47.3	5.7

*These are states with the highest and lowest percentages of state and federal funds, as a percentage of all sources.

Source: National Center for Education Statistics. (1996). *Current elementary and secondary expenditures—1990s and beyond.* Washington, D.C.: Author.

States . . . vary substantially in terms of the level of resources being invested in education.

discrepancies occur between districts at the extreme ends of the New York spending distribution curve.

The clear lesson to learn from these figures is that states, as well as individual schooling units, vary substantially in terms of the level of resources being invested in education. Some of the variation is due to factors such as differences in the cost of living, and some is due to fundamental, geographically based differences in fiscal capacity.

SPENDING BY FUNCTION

Schooling systems provide a vast array of services, including some that are only tangentially related to education (e.g., food and transportation services). Overall, we now know that 60% of the education dollar (nationwide) is spent on instructional services. The 60% figure is remarkably consistent across school districts of different size, wealth, spending level, region, incidence of minority populations, and incidence of children living in poverty (Odden et al., 1995). Thus, it appears that while districts have significantly different levels of resources to spend, they apportion their resources in much the same way. It also appears that the 60% level has remained steady over the past 35 years.

The remaining 40% of the education dollar is divided across other budget categories as shown in the table below. There has been a contentious debate in recent years over the level of spending on administrative services. Critics of the public schools have been known to talk about an "administrative blob" that is drawing resources away from the instructional core of the schools, particularly in large city schools. Research is showing little evidence of "blob-like" drains from the instructional budgets of the schools, even those located in the large cities (Odden et al., 1995). Indeed, some research is showing that, while never large, the percentage being spent on central administration has been dropping in recent years (Roellke, 1996).

Non-Instructional Spending

Percent	Category
8-10	Instructional support (curriculum development, professional development, student services, etc.)
9-11	Operation and maintenance of the physical plant
4-6	Transportation and food services
9-11	Administrative services

Source: Odden, A., Monk, D., Nakib, Y., and Picus, L. (1995, October). The story of the education dollar: No academy awards and no fiscal smoking guns. *Phi Delta Kappan,* 161-168.

SPENDING EARMARKED FOR SCIENCE EDUCATION
Various estimates have been made about the level of investment in science education. For example, the Federal Coordinating Council for Science, Engineering, and Technology (FCCSET) (1993) estimated that the federal government spent at least $2.2 billion on education programs specifically targeting science, mathematics, engineering, and technology (SMET). Total federal spending on education, including programs not focused specifically on SMET education, was estimated to be $24 billion in 1993 (FCCSET, 1993).

Recent research has looked at the allocation of instructional resources across different areas of the secondary school curriculum. For example, in 1992–93, New York State school districts on average provided 4.23 secondary science teachers per 1,000 district pupils. This allocation represented 12.2% of the teaching resource provided at the secondary level. The allocation of resources to secondary mathematics was larger, amounting to 4.65 teachers per 1,000 district pupils or 13.4% of the total teaching resource. (Monk, Roellke, & Brent, 1996).

The New York research also included analyses of how school district characteristics such as incidence of poverty were related to the allocation of resources to science and mathematics. Remarkably, wealth and per-pupil spending levels are largely unrelated to the allocation of teacher resources to science and mathematics. Indeed, it is only among the wealthiest and highest spending districts in the state that there is any evidence at all of an increase in the numbers of teachers in these key disciplines. The research shows that science and mathematics are not unique in this regard; the number of teachers in all academic curriculum subjects is relatively unaffected by differences in districts' wealth and overall spending levels.

Significantly different resource allocation practices have been found between remedial, regular, and advanced courses in mathematics and science. Specifically, a greater degree of course differentiation of this kind was found in New York for mathematics compared to science. In mathematics, 70% of teacher assignments were categorized as regular; in science, the comparable figure was 91%. Moreover, the differentiation that occurred in science took the form of more advanced (rather than remedial) offerings. In science, the proportion of remedial courses was 1%, while the comparable figure for mathematics was 21%.

According to the New York data, allocations of teachers to science and mathematics have been increasing. Between the 1982–83 and 1991–92 school years, the teacher supply per pupil grew by 6.02% in

Mathematics Teacher Allocations in New York
(Teachers per 1,000 students)

Level	1982-83	1991-92	Percent change
Advanced courses	1.21	1.55	+28.1
Remedial courses	1.64	1.96	+19.5
Regular courses	17.29	17.60	+1.8

Source: Monk, D.H., Roellke, C.F., and Brent, B.O. (1996). *What education dollars buy: An examination of resource allocation patterns in New York state public school systems.* Final report to the Consortium for Policy Research in Education. Ithaca, NY: Cornell University, Department of Education.

science and 4.31% in mathematics.

The longitudinal results regarding curricular differentiation are also of interest. Across all academic subjects there was growth in both advanced and remedial offerings that significantly outpaced growth in teachers allocated to the "regular" area of the curriculum. It is clear that most of the new staff going into the academic curriculum during this period of reform was directed away from the so-called regular offerings.

SPENDING ON A KEY INPUT: TEACHERS

Research has also been conducted on the level and nature of teacher compensation. There is a longstanding debate over what teachers should earn as they practice their craft. On the one hand, advocates of higher salaries argue that teaching is an undervalued profession. Proponents of this view typically cite as evidence the higher salaries that are received by accountants, architects, physicians, and lawyers. Evidence suggesting that teachers are poorly paid relative to certain civil servants is also often cited in this context. Those who question the wisdom of higher teacher salaries draw attention to the ten-month

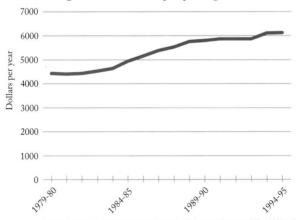

Average Nationwide Per-Pupil Spending (Constant 1995 Dollars)

Source: Published on the National Center for Education Statistics World Wide Web Site at http://www.ed.gov/NCES

nature of most teaching contracts, the relatively small number of hours spent in direct contact with students, and the high degree of job security and guarantees of due process that frequently accompany employment as a public school teacher.

The effects of new reform dollars coming into the educational system on teacher salaries are of special interest to science education reformers. A common worry is that new dollars could simply lead to higher salaries with little concomitant change in the nature of teachers' instructional efforts. Taxpayers would then find themselves paying more for the same product and thereby inadvertently contributing to a decline in the productivity of the schools.

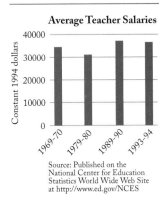

Average Teacher Salaries

Source: Published on the National Center for Education Statistics World Wide Web Site at http://www.ed.gov/NCES

High-spending districts could be compared with lower-spending districts to see how much of the extra resources are devoted to teacher salaries. Recent research of this type (e.g., Barro, 1992, and Picus, 1993) suggests that only a very small percentage of the additional dollars being spent in high expenditure districts can be traced to teacher salaries per se. The dominant uses of the higher spending levels are for more teachers (i.e., smaller average class sizes), more services for students with special educational needs, and noninstructional services.

There is a renewed interest in designing teacher compensation systems that establish stronger ties between compensation and performance. The history of these efforts (see Murnane & Cohen, 1986) is not encouraging. However, some new ideas have been advanced in recent years that involve reliance on group rewards and "gain-share" strategies that use compensation to stimulate performance (Odden, 1994). As Murnane and Cohen (1986) observed, the idea that compensation is tied to performance can foster a willingness among taxpayers to invest in education. Progress on the reform of teacher compensation practice needs to be a high priority for any reform-minded group in education.

Research on how resources are spent on teachers consistently finds that typically less than 1% of the budget is earmarked explicitly for teachers' continuing professional development (Darling-Hammond, 1994; National Commission on Teaching and America's Future, 1996). There seems to be a growing awareness that teachers need strengthened professional development programs, and there may well be greater willingness to spend new dollars on professional development rather than upgraded salaries and benefits for teachers.

THE DOLLARS DO/DON'T MATTER DEBATE

Before real progress can be made toward understanding the implications of differences in spending levels on education, insight is needed into the productivity of the existing educational system. Many critics find serious productivity problems (e.g., Hanushek with others, 1994). The underlying research literature on the topic is vast and largely inconclusive, with researchers sometimes drawing conflicting conclusions from the same studies (cf. Hanushek, 1989, and Hedges, Laine, & Greenwald, 1994). The chief lessons to learn are these:

1. It matters how dollars are spent. Not even the harshest critic of the productivity of schooling systems will claim that dollars "can't" make a difference. The debate is generally focused on whether good value is being realized for the dollars that are currently being expended. A corollary argument is that if current dollars are not being spent wisely, it would be folly to devote additional resources to the system.

2. There are examples of remarkably effective schools.[2] It is therefore clear that improvements are possible. The challenge lies in finding ways to move the system toward the level of performance that some experiences suggest is possible.

3. Incentives can be adjusted in ways that promote school effectiveness. Incentive analysis and manipulation is a promising and largely unexplored tool for making improvements in performance. Economists have argued that a major problem with public education is that the existing incentives block meaningful progress toward improvements in efficiency (Hanushek with others, 1994). For example, teacher compensation practices have been criticized on the grounds that all teachers earn virtually the same salaries as long as they have comparable levels of training and experience. Recent efforts at fostering systemic reform can be viewed as attempts to "get the incentives right" within the system, and a number of interesting and promising experiments have gone for-

---

[2]See the collection of papers edited by Robert Berne and Lawrence Picus (1994).

ward in states like South Carolina and city school systems like Dallas (Clotfelter & Ladd, 1996).

4. Innovations have promise but can impede growth in productivity. As computing and related technologies become increasingly prevalent in schools, care needs to be exercised so that innovations do not inadvertently erode productivity in education. Costs could outweigh benefits if these technologies serve only as add-ons to existing classroom activities.

ASSESSING THE COSTS OF REFORM

It is useful for policymakers to have cost estimates of proposed reforms before they make decisions about implementing them. This is particularly true for the ongoing efforts to implement site-based decision-making, redesign curricula, raise academic standards, reform pupil assessment practices, and further "professionalize" the field of teaching.

Certainly, it would be desirable to have estimates of the costs associated with implementing science education reform. However, there are at least three reasons why it is difficult to obtain even first approximations of the real costs associated with such reform, and these need to be understood by those who are seeking to implement the reform.

First, significant reforms entail significant departures from current practice. It is relatively easy to estimate costs of current practice because there is a track record that can be studied. But where policymakers are debating whether to pursue a significantly new set of practices, the track record is less available. Sometimes pilot efforts can be considered, but cost analysts still rely heavily on assumptions about what would happen if the pilot were fully operational.

Significant reforms are difficult to "cost out" because they entail significant departures from current practice.

Second, there is the "supplement versus supplant" problem. The very reason that a reform is being contemplated suggests problems with existing practice. To the extent that reform measures can *substitute* for existing practice, some savings need to be factored into estimates of the marginal cost of reform. It follows that the cost of a reform should *not* be viewed as a simple add-on to existing practice. However, it is also the case that the analyst is not entitled to simply subtract the cost of all practices deemed deficient. The implementation of reform is often difficult and the reluctance to change fundamental practice needs to be taken into account in estimating costs.

Third, suppose enhanced scientific literacy significantly improves the quality of public discourse over land use, the disposal of nuclear waste, and a host of other technologically connected issues. Society could find itself avoiding the costs of future mistakes, and these savings are relevant to a full cost/benefit accounting of science education reform. Of course, it is difficult to do much more than recognize that these savings/benefits could be significant.

Although these difficulties are daunting, it is nevertheless important for policy makers to have a grasp of the resources that reform will require. There have been some cost estimates for efforts similar to this reform, but current science education reform is unique in terms of the breadth of its goals.

This being said, there are some estimates that can begin to inform the debate. For example, at least $117 million were spent between 1954 and 1975 on National Science Foundation reforms (Jackson, 1983). And Elmore (1993) reports that the Physical Sciences Study Committee spent between $1 and $1.5 million from 1956 to 1961 in direct development costs and probably three times that amount in indirect costs. He also notes that the Biological Sciences Curriculum Study has spent in the neighborhood of $10 million in direct expenditures and several times that amount in indirect expenditures.

Other efforts to estimate these costs include the work of Borg and Gall (1989), who argue that the cost of developing a single minicourse that provides 15 hours of instruction was more than $100,000 in the early 1970s. They estimate that a similar major curriculum project today costs several million dollars. They also note that the ratio of 1:10:100 is used in industry to estimate funding requirements for research and development: if $1 million are required to do the basic research for a new curriculum product, it would require $10 million more to develop the product through the operational field test and revision phase, and 10 times that amount ($100 million more) to manufacture and disseminate the product.

Efforts have also been made to estimate the costs of continuing teacher professional development, another central element of science education reform. Miller, Lord, and Dorney (1994) estimated that between 1.8 and 2.8% of the operating budgets in the districts they studied was devoted to professional development, amounting to

Cost analysis can provide insight into the barriers that make implementing reform difficult.

$1,755 to $3,529, per regular classroom teacher. It has long been noted that it is unusual for school districts to devote more than 1% of their budget allocations to professional development (Darling-Hammond, 1994). If states invested 1% of the $117 billion that they raised for public K-12 education in 1993–1994, the effort would require $1.2 billion dollars.

In addition to generating estimates of resource requirements for anticipated reforms, cost analysis can provide insight into the barriers that make implementing reform difficult, i.e., costly. Economists are interested in the role incentives play in explaining the behavior of the various parties within educational systems. A cost can be thought of as a disincentive or impediment that needs to be overcome; sometimes those costs take subtle forms. For example, consider the case of a staff development program that periodically requires teachers to leave their classrooms in the hands of a substitute teacher. At first glance, the cost of this program would include the cost of funding the substitute teachers to free the classroom teacher for participation. However, teachers may still be reluctant to leave their classrooms on the grounds that their departure is disruptive, has adverse effects on the performance of their students, and requires more work for the teachers on their return. In such a case, the true cost of the program has been underestimated, perhaps to a significant degree. The failure to identify and offset these subtle costs may go a long way toward explaining why reform has been so difficult to implement. There is perhaps no surer way to compromise the effectiveness of a reform than to underfund it.

RECOMMENDATIONS

The following are recommended as broad strategies:

■ Educate the public about the importance of a science literate population. Use public education as a strategy to prevent or at least limit erosion of the existing resource base for public education.

■ Leverage new resources for reform. Capitalize on the basic good will people have for schools by demonstrating that any new dollars will be invested wisely.

■ Stimulate changes in how existing—as well as new—resources are utilized. Changes need to be made in certain "iron" laws of resource allocation, especially in the area of teachers' continuing professional development.

■ Discard practices that have been discredited and draw attention to the fact that the resulting savings can help to finance new strategies.

■ Face the full costs of reform squarely and resist the temptation to ignore hidden costs.

■ Continue to articulate a bold vision for reform.

■ Avoid trying to pursue all aspects of reform simultaneously. Instead, pursue tactics designed to make incremental progress at selected sites in carefully chosen areas of reform.

It is crucial to create and keep current, accurate records of the successes and failures that surround efforts to reform science, mathematics, and technology education. Educators may well find that an accurate and frank record of the experiences of Project 2061 and other reform efforts becomes their most enduring legacy for the long-term improvement of the nation's ability to make fundamental and cost-effective reforms of its educational system.

REFERENCES

Barro, S. (1992). *What does the education dollar buy? Relationships of staffing, staff characteristics, and staff salaries to state per-pupil spending.* Madison, WI: University of Wisconsin, Consortium for Policy Research in Education.

Berne, R., & Picus, L. O. (Eds.) (1994). *Outcome equity in education.* Thousand Oaks, CA: Corwin Press.

Borg, W. R., & Gall, M. D. (1989). *Educational research: An introduction.* New York: Longman.

Clotfelter, C. T., & Ladd, H. F. (1996). Recognizing and rewarding success in public schools. In H. F. Ladd (Ed.) *Holding schools accountable* (pp. 23–64). Washington, D.C.: The Brookings Institution.

Darling-Hammond, L. (1994). *The current status of teaching and teacher development in the United States.* Background paper prepared for the National Commission on Teaching and America's Future, New York.

Elmore, R. F. (1993). *The development and implementation of large-scale curriculum reforms.* Background paper prepared for the American Association for the Advancement of Science, Project 2061, Washington, D.C.

Federal Coordinating Council for Science, Engineering, and Technology. (1993). *The federal investment in science, mathematics, engineering, and technology education: Where now? What next?.* Washington, D.C.: Author.

Hanushek, E. (with Benson, C. S., Freeman, R. B., Jamison, D. T., Levin, H. M., Maynard, R. A., Murnane, R. J., Rivkin, S. G., Sabot, R. H., Solmon, L. C., Summers Finis Welch, A. A., & Wolfe, B. L.). (1994). *Making schools work: Improving performance and controlling costs.* Washington, D.C.: The Brookings Institution.

Hanushek, E. A. (1989). The impact of differential expenditures on school performance. *Educational Researcher, 18*(4), 45–51.

Hedges, L. V., Laine, R. D., & Greenwald, R. (1994). Does money matter? A meta-analysis of studies of the effects of differential school inputs on student outcomes. *Educational Researcher, 23*(3), 5–14.

Jackson, P. (1983). The reform of science education: A cautionary tale. *Daedalus, 112*(2), 143–166.

Miller, B., Lord, B., & Dorney, J. (1994). *Staff development for teachers: a study of configurations and costs in four districts.* Newtonville, MA: Education Development Center.

Monk, D. H., Roellke, C. F., & Brent, B. O. (1996). *What education dollars buy: An examination of resource allocation patterns in New York state public school systems.* Final report to the Finance Center, Consortium for Policy Research in Education. Ithaca, NY: Cornell University, Department of Education.

Murnane, R. J., & Cohen, D. K. (1986). Merit pay and the evaluation problem: Why most merit pay plans fail and a few survive. *Harvard Educational Review, 56*(1), 1–17.

National Center for Education Statistics. (1996). *Statistics in brief: Revenues and expenditures for public elementary and secondary education: School year 1993–94.* (NCES 96-303). Washington, D.C.: Author.

National Commission on Teaching and America's Future. (1996). *What matters most: Teaching for America's future.* New York: Columbia University, Teachers College.

Odden, A. (1994). *The financial implications of Project 2061 for teacher professional development and compensation.* Background paper prepared for the American Association for the Advancement of Science, Project 2061, Washington, D.C.

Odden, A., Monk, D., Nakib, Y., & Picus, L. (1995, October). The story of the education dollar: No academy awards and no fiscal smoking guns. *Phi Delta Kappan,* 161–168.

Picus, L. O. (1993). *The allocation and use of educational resources: District-level analysis from the schools and staffing survey.* Madison, WI: University of Wisconsin, Consortium for Policy Research in Education.

Roellke, C. F. (1996). *The local response to state initiated education reform: Changes in the allocation of human resources in New York State schooling systems, 1983–1995.* Unpublished doctoral dissertation. Ithaca, NY: Cornell University.

Rothstein, R. (with Miles, K. H.). (1995). *Where's the money gone? Changes in the level and composition of education spending.* Washington, D.C.: Economic Policy Institute.

BIBLIOGRAPHY

American Association for the Advancement of Science. (1993). *Benchmarks for science literacy.* New York: Oxford University Press.

American Association for the Advancement of Science. (1990). *Science for all Americans.* New York: Oxford University Press.

Barnett, W.S. (1991). Benefits of compensatory preschool education. *Journal of Human Resources, 27*(2), 279-312.

Barnett, W.S. (1985). Benefit-cost analysis of the Perry preschool program and its policy implications. *Educational Evaluation and Policy Analysis, 7,* 333-342.

Barth, P. (1993). *Curriculum connections blueprint report.* Paper prepared for the American Association for the Advancement of Science, Project 2061, Washington, D.C.

Bishop, J.H. (1993). *Incentives to study and the organization of secondary instruction.* (Working Paper 93-08). Ithaca, NY: Cornell University, Center for Advanced Human Resources.

Boe, E. E., Boruch, R.F., Landau, R., & Richardson, J.A. (1993). *State policies fostering the entrepreneurial restructuring of public schools: Identification and classification based on a survey of the fifty states.* Philadelphia, PA: University of Pennsylvania, Graduate School of Education.

Borg, W.R. & Gall, M.D. (1989). *Educational research: An introduction.* New York: Longman.

Cameron, J. & Pierce, W.D. (1994). Reinforcement, reward, and intrinsic motivation: A meta-analysis, *Review of Educational Research, 64*(3), 363-423.

Carlsen, W.S., Cunningham, C.M., & Lowmaster, N.E. (1994). *But who will teach it?* Review of the book *Benchmarks for science literacy.* Prepared for the American Association for the Advancement of Science, Project 2061, Washington, D.C.

Chriss, B., Nash, G., & Stern, D. (1992). The rise and fall of school choice in Richmond, California. *Economics of Education Review, 11*(4), 395-406.

Clune, W.H. (1993). *2061 and educational equity.* Background paper prepared for the American Association for the Advancement of Science, Project 2061, Washington, D.C.

Cohn, E. & Teel, S.J. (1991). Participation in a teacher incentive program and student achievement in reading and math. *The 1991 Proceedings of the American Statistical Association.* Washington, D.C.: American Statistical Association.

Cooley, V. E. & Thompson, J.C. (1990). *Mandated staff development in the fifty states: A study of state activity 1983-1989: A presentation for the National Council of States on Inservice Education.* (ERIC Document Reproduction Service No. ED 327 495).

DiMasi, J.A., Hansen, R.W., Grabowski, H.G., & Lasagna, L.(1991). Cost of innovation in the pharmaceutical industry. *Journal of Health Economics, 10,* 107-142.

Donmoyer, R., et al. (1993). *School organization: Blueprint report.* Prepared for the American Association for the Advancement of Science, Project 2061, Washington, D.C.

Elmore, R.F. (1993). *The development and implementation of large-scale curriculum reforms*. Background paper prepared for the American Association for the Advancement of Science, Project 2061, Washington, D.C.

Federal Coordinating Council for Science, Engineering and Technology. (1993). *The federal investment in science, mathematics, engineering. and technology education: Where now? What next?* Washington, D.C.: Author.

Feistritzer, E. (1993). National overview of alternative teacher certification. *Education and Urban Society, 26*(1), 18-28.

Fullan, M.G. with Stiegelbauer, S. (1991). *The new meaning of educational change*. New York: Teachers College Press.

Gold, S.D., Smith, D.M., Lawton, S.B & Hyary, A.C. (1992). *Public school finance programs of the United States and Canada*. Albany, NY: American Education Finance Association and The Center for the Study of the States. (Available from The Center for the Study of the States, Albany, New York).

Hawley, W.D. (1987). The high costs and doubtful efficacy of extended teacher - preparation programs: An invitation to more basic reforms. *American Journal of Education, 45*(2), 275-298.

Hoenack, S.A. (1988). Incentives, outcome-based instruction, and school efficiency. In D.H. Monk and J. Underwood (Eds.), *Microlevel school finance* (pp. 113-142). Cambridge, MA: Ballinger.

Hofmeister, A., Carnine, D., & Clark, R. (1994). *A blueprint for action: Technology, media, and materials*. Prepared for the American Association for the Advancement of Science, Project 2061, Washington, D.C.

Hornbeck, D.W. &. Salamon, L.M. (Eds.). (1991). *Human capital and America's future*. Baltimore, MD: Johns Hopkins University Press.

Houston, R. W. & Freiberg, J.H.(1979). Perpetual motion, blindman's bluff, and inservice education. *Journal of Teacher Education, 30*(1), 7-9.

Jackson, P. (1983). The reform of science education: A cautionary tale. *Daedalus, 112*(2), 143-166.

King, J.A. (1994). Meeting the educational needs of at-risk students: A cost analysis of three models. *Educational Evaluation and Policy Analysis, 16*(1), 1-20.

Kirst, M., Anhalt, B. & Marine, R. (1993). *Science for all Americans: A political blueprint*. Background paper prepared for the American Association for the Advancement of Science, Project 2061, Washington, D.C.

Lepkowski, A. (1987, September 21). Precollege science, math education enhanced by volunteers. *Chemical & Engineering News, 65*, 38.

Levin, H.M. & Kelley, C. (1994). Can education do it alone? *Economics of Education Review, 13*(2), 97-108.

Little, J. W. (1993). Teachers' professional development in a climate of educational reform. *Education Evaluation and Policy Analysis, 15*(2), 129- 151.

Little, J.W. (1989, Summer). District policy choices and teachers' professional development opportunities. *Educational Evaluation and Policy Analysis, 11*, 165-179.

Massell, D. & Goertz, M. (1994). *2061 policy blueprint*. Prepared for the American Association for the Advancement of Science, Project 2061, Washington, D.C.

Massell, D. with Hetrick, B. (1993). *Design and implementation in Project 2061: Lessons from the field*. Background paper prepared for the American Association for the Advancement of Science, Project 2061, Washington, D.C.

McLaughlin, M.W. & Yee, S.M. (1988). School as a place to have a career. In A. Liberman (Ed.), *Building a professional culture in schools*. New York: Teachers College Press.

McLaughlin, M. (1990). The RAND change agent study revisited: Macro perspectives and micro realities. *Educational Researcher 19*(9), 11-16.

Millman, J & Sykes, G. (1992). *The assessment of teaching based on evidence of student learning: An analysis*. Research monograph prepared for the National Board for Professional Teaching Standards, Washington, D.C.

Monk, D.H. (1994a). Subject area preparation of secondary mathematics and science teachers and student achievement. *Economics of Education Review, 13*(2), 125-145.

Monk, D.H. (1994b). *The costs of Project 2061: Conceptual issues and background information*. Background paper prepared for the American Association for the Advancement of Science, Project 2061, Washington, D.C.

Monk, D.H.. (1994c). Incorporating outcome equity standards into extant systems of educational finance. In R. Berne & L. Picus (Eds.), *New conceptions of equity in educational finance*. Newbury Park, CA: Corwin Press.

Monk, D.H. & Kadamus, J.A. (1994). The reform of district organizational structure: New York's experimental use of a collaborative study process. In W.J. Fowler, B. Levin, & H. Walberg (Eds.), *Organizational influences on educational productivity*. Greenwich, CT: JAI Press.

Monk, D.H. & Roellke, C. (1994). *The origin, disposition, and utilization of resources within New York state public school systems: A progress report*. Paper presented at the annual meeting of the American Education Finance Association, Nashville, TN.

Monk, D.H. (1993). *The costs of systemic reform: Conceptual issues and preliminary estimates*. Final Report to the New Standards Project, Center for the Study of Education and the Economy, Rochester, NY.

Monk, D. H. & King, J. (1993). Cost analysis as a tool for education reform. In S.L. Jacobson and R. Berne (Eds.), *Reforming education: The emerging systemic approach*. Newbury Park, CA: Corwin Press.

Moore, D., & Hyde, A. (1978). *Rethinking staff development: A handbook for analyzing your program and its costs*. New York: Ford Foundation.

Murnane, R.J. & Cohen, D.K. (1986). Merit pay and the evaluation problem: Why most merit pay plans fail and a few survive. *Harvard Educational Review, 56*(1), 1-17.

Murnane, R.J., Singer, J.D., Willett, J.B., Kemple, J.J., & Olsen, R.J. (1991). *Who will teach? Policies that matter*. Cambridge, MA: Harvard University Press.

O'Day J.A. & Smith, M.S. (1993). Systemic reform and educational opportunity. In S.H. Fuhrman (Ed.) *Designing coherent education policy* (pp. 250-312). San Francisco, CA: Jossey Bass.

Odden, A.R. (1994). *Including school finance in systemic reform strategies: A commentary*. New Brunswick, NJ: State University of New Jersey.

Odden, A.R. (1994b). *The financial implications of Project 2061 for teacher professional development and compensation*. Background paper prepared for the American Association for the Advancement of Science, Project 2061, Washington, D.C.

Orlich, D. C. & Evans, A. (1990). *Regression analysis: A novel way to examine staff development cost factors.* (ERIC Reproduction Service Document No. ED 331 808).

Parent Teacher Association. (1993). *A blueprint for action: Parents and community.* Prepared for the American Association for the Advancement of Science, Project 2061, Washington, D.C.

Perry Associates, Inc. (1994). *Business and industry's role in Project 2061: A blueprint for the AAAS.* Prepared for the American Association for the Advancement of Science, Project 2061, Washington, D.C.

Picus, L.O. (1994). *The $300 billion question: How do public elementary and secondary schools spend their money?* Paper presented at the annual meeting of the American Educational Research Association, New Orleans, LA.

Porter, A.C. (1993). *State and district leadership for implementation of Project 2061.* Background paper prepared for the American Association for the Advancement of Science, Project 2061, Washington, D.C.

Porter, A.C. (1991). Creating a system of school process indicators. *Educational Evaluation and Policy Analysis, 13*(1), 13-30.

Ramsey, N. (1992). How business can help the schools? *Fortune,* Education/ Special Report, 147-174.

Reich, R.B. (1991). *The work of nations: Preparing ourselves for 21st century capitalism.* New York: Knopf.

Richards, C.E., Fishbein, D., & Melville, P. (1993). Cooperative performance incentives in education. In S.L. Jacobson & R. Berne (Eds.), *Reforming education: The emerging systemic approach* (pp. 28-42). Thousand Oaks, CA: Corwin Press.

Rosenholtz, S. (1989). *Teachers' workplace: The social organization of schools.* New York: Longman.

Rumberger, R.W. (1987). The potential impact of technology on the skill requirements of future jobs. In G. Burke & R.W. Rumberger (Eds.), *The future impact of technology on work and education.* Bristol, PA: Taylor & Francis.

Shepard, L. & Kreitzer, A. (1987). The Texas teacher test. *Educational Researcher, 16*(6).

Stern, D., Gerritz, W. & Little, J.W. (1989, Winter). Making the most of a school district's two (or five) cents: Accounting for investment in teacher's professional development. *Journal of Education Finance, 14,* 368-379.

Sommerfeld, M. (1994, September 28). Report notes 'consistently slow growth' in corporate giving. *Education Week,* 8.

Welch, W.W. (1991) *Blueprint for reform: Assessment.* Prepared for the American Association for the Advancement of Science, Project 2061, Washington, D.C.

4

Research

WHAT KNOWLEDGE IS NEEDED to allow the ideas in *Science for All Americans* (American Association for the Advancement of Science [AAAS], 1989) to become common practice? What kinds of research are needed to ensure informed decision making that will lead to the kind of science literacy for all envisioned by Project 2061 and other science reform efforts? These are critical questions for a research agenda.

The definition of science literacy in *Science for All Americans* and *Benchmarks for Science Literacy* (AAAS, 1993) is not limited to the natural sciences; mathematics, technology, and the social sciences are also included. Adding to the complexity of a broad definition of science literacy is the deeper understanding of curriculum that has developed during the last two decades. Correspondingly, educational research has also become far more complex. Together, these factors all contribute to the challenge of developing a blueprint for needed research.

Building on *Benchmarks'* Chapter 15: The Research Base, this chapter highlights three major areas for research focus: understanding what students and teachers know and how they learn about science; the possibilities and consequences of building stronger connections among the natural sciences, mathematics, technology, and social studies; and linking educational research with practice.

Since 1985 there have been at least six attempts to set research agendas in science, mathematics, and technology education[1]. Reports detailing these attempts can inform the research agenda. They all agree on the need to coordinate the efforts of researchers and other stakeholders who

---

[1] They include: *Mathematics, Science, and Technology Education: A Research Agenda* (Committee on Research in Mathematics, Science, and Technology Education, 1985); *Establishing a Research Base for Science Education: Challenges, Trends, and Recommendations* (Linn, 1987); *Setting a Research Agenda: Research Agenda for Mathematics Education* (Sowder, 1989); *Establishing a Research Agenda: Critical Issues of Science Curriculum Reform* (Shymansky & Kyle, 1992); *Toward a Research Base for Evolution Education: Report of a National Conference* (Good et al., 1993); *Blueprints Research Conference* (Science Education Research Agenda Coalition [SERAC], 1994).

try, usually separately, to improve science education. They also stress how important it is for teachers and curriculum developers to know how students' and scientists' conceptions of nature differ. A third theme is the need to recognize that learning is situated in a complex set of variables, including class, race, and gender.

THE RESEARCH BASE: WHAT'S MISSING

As noted in *Benchmarks for Science Literacy* the coordinated, long-term research needed to inform many decisions about reform is largely unavailable. *Benchmarks'* Chapter 15: The Research Base summarizes the research that supports statements about what students should know and be able to do at specific grade levels. The summary is organized by the chapters in *Benchmarks* and *Science for All Americans*, which present a comprehensive and interdisciplinary view of science literacy. Following are examples from this summary, by area of science literacy, of further research that is needed.

The Nature of Science. There are few studies at the elementary school level, and much of the research that is available is limited to multiple-choice questionnaires. How might the results of nature-of-science research change if students were provided with adequate instruction in this area?

The Nature of Mathematics. Researchers have not emphasized the relationships between mathematics and science or mathematics as a modeling process. We must learn more about how students develop connections between phenomena and symbols or expressions and about how they judge the fit of representations to real objects.

The Nature of Technology. Only a small body of research exists on students' understanding of technology and how it relates to science and society.

The Physical Setting. Although much more research has been done in the physical sciences, few studies exist on students' understanding of the processes that shape the earth, or on long-term teaching interventions in the physical and earth sciences. Is it possible for elementary school students to understand many commonly-taught ideas about moon phases, our solar system, galaxy, and universe? To what extent can students of various ages understand the atomic/molecular nature of matter and related microscopic (abstract) ideas? How are students' concepts of forces and motion influenced by instructional and noninstructional factors?

The Living Environment. Little has been published on students' understanding of cells, the flow of energy through the living environment or on effective instructional interventions. Evolution of life as the central organizing scheme in biology and how precursor concepts are learned (or mis-learned) is also understudied.

The Human Organism. Much research is needed on elementary student's conceptions about the human organism.

Human Society. Studies on student learning of cultural effects on behavior, social change and conflicts, and global interdependence are limited. To what extent can students of various ages understand political and economic systems?

The Designed World. There is a very small body of research on what students know and how they learn about the structures and functions of the designed world.

The Mathematical World. Mathematics has benefited from a great deal of research, especially on how children build the ideas of number and space. However, more studies are needed about how students learn graphic skills and the relationship between graph production and interpretation, especially with microcomputer-based laboratories. In algebra, how do students come to understand what a solution means and why it is important? How might students be helped to understand the concepts of argument and proof?

Historical Perspectives. Much more research is needed to assess how historical understanding develops and how students' concepts of time are interrelated.

Common Themes. Insight is needed into how students understand the use of models in science.

Habits of Mind. Although a great deal is known about mathematics computational skills, little is known about how estimation skills relate to other scientific habits of mind or how students can be helped to relate theory to evidence and judge inadequacies in arguments.

These examples represent a bare outline of the research agenda that is needed to focus on how students develop the knowledge to become science literate. In addition, each benchmark across the K-12 grades raises related questions about curriculum and instruction.

STUDENT AND TEACHER KNOWLEDGE

Research on students' understandings of particular concepts at certain grade levels was an important influence on where benchmarks were placed. Project 2061's committment to the use and promotion of educational research in its reform efforts is further underscored by *Benchmarks'* Chapter 15: The Research Base. Although that chapter identifies more than 300 studies, the research is unevenly distributed across the 12 areas of literacy described in *Benchmarks*. These studies also tell us little about the nature of conceptual change within grade levels. Understanding the knowledge that students bring and how they are able to change that knowledge in classrooms and through other learning opportunities is crucial.

Most of the research reviewed in Chapter 15 relates to students' understanding of particular benchmarks; however, studies that report on the development of students' ideas across the span of grades K-12 are rare. Studying the nature of conceptual change in students over long periods of time for all benchmarks is an important area of needed research. Such research would entail a comprehensive, long-term project involving many researchers, including teachers.

Understanding the knowledge that students bring and how they are able to change that knowledge in classrooms and through other learning opportunities is crucial.

In addition to understanding the cognitive aspects of student learning, it is important to know how interests and other noncognitive factors contribute to students' attainment of science literacy goals. These contextual factors (Cole & Griffin, 1987) are part of the overall picture of student understanding and should be part of the research agenda. The role of the teacher in helping students attain science literacy goals is also important. However, there is less agreement on what it means to be an effective teacher and only an emerging consensus on how teachers should be prepared as professionals. Agreement with the goals of *Science for All Americans* provides a basis for consensus on teacher effectiveness. Unfortunately, there is little research-based evidence about how we can educate teachers to use guidelines such as *Benchmarks* and the *National Science Education Standards* (National Research Council, 1996) creatively to promote science literacy.

Many of the same misconceptions that research has documented for K-12 students can be found in college students, including prospective science and mathematics teachers. However, much more research on teachers' misconceptions is needed. How do these conceptions manifest themselves in teachers' instructional strategies and what effects might they have on students' understanding of science? Many other contextual factors at the levels of classroom, school, community, and beyond contribute to the understanding of how teachers convey important science concepts.

INTERDISCIPLINARY CONNECTIONS: RESEARCH IMPLICATIONS

Developing connections and common themes across disciplines should encourage more collaboration of K-12 teachers with educational researchers. Perhaps more than any other this theme stresses the importance of rethinking the meaning of science literacy. An interdisciplinary, thematic approach to curriculum organization would require research to determine appropriate curriculum design and instructional strategies as well as studying how learning occurs across traditional disciplines.

SCIENCE AND MATHEMATICS
The connections between mathematics and science are so numerous and so fundamental that it seems almost irresponsible of educators to not highlight their interrelatedness. The literacy envisioned by Project 2061 requires nothing less than a serious research and development effort to make these connections far more explicit in curriculum and instruction.

Ideas about the nature of mathematics have a clear impact on a research agenda related to teaching and learning mathematics. When mathematics is viewed as fundamentally grounded in natural phenomena, the need to connect science and mathematics education seems more pressing. Guidance on the needed research can be gained from a number of sources including *Benchmarks* and the *Curriculum and Evaluation Standards for School Mathematics* (National Council of Teachers of Mathematics [NCTM], 1989), both of which emphasize the importance of connections between mathematics and science. For example, an especially relevant recommendation can be implied from *Benchmarks*:

> Little emphasis has been given to students' understanding of mathematics as the study of patterns and relationships, or to the relationship between mathematics, science, and technology, or to the nature of mathematical inquiry as a modeling process (AAAS, 1993, p. 333).

Statements in the NCTM standards emphasize the importance of connections of mathematics with science and other disciplines and underscore the need for research in this area. For example:

As students in grades 5–8 become aware of the world around them, probability and statistics become increasingly important connections between the real world and the mathematics classroom. Weather forecasting, scientific experiments, advertising claims, chance events, and economic trends are but a few of the areas in which students can investigate the role of mathematics in our society (NCTM, 1989, p. 86).

An important area for connections between mathematics and science is quantitative reasoning. Students reason about quantities as they construct abstract ideas in mathematics, try to understand phenomena, and represent their thinking. Another theme is reasoning that is grounded in imagery of objects and phenomena, which supports students' construction of the quantities themselves, and from which they develop ideas related to patterns, functional relationships, and geometric properties (Thompson, 1994).

An important area for connections between mathematics and science is quantitative reasoning.

The alliance between mathematics and science has a long history in which both disciplines try to discover general patterns and relationships and, therefore, are part of the same endeavor. An excellent source for examples of this mutually beneficial relationship and, by extension, the implications they have for research, is *On the Shoulders of Giants* (Steen, 1990). The book's essays on pattern, change, dimension, quantity, shape, and uncertainty provide rich and relevant ideas about mathematics and its connections with other disciplines.

SCIENCE AND SOCIAL STUDIES

A research agenda should build a more solid foundation for curriculum decisions about when and how students can understand the social science content described in *Benchmarks'* Chapter 7: Human Society. *The Handbook of Research on Social Studies Teaching and Learning* (Shaver, 1991), for example, addresses the interrelations between social studies and other curriculum areas, but shows that connections between science and social studies have not been a major research agenda item.

Much of the critical research in social studies education is directed at the question of equity. What practices in society, and education in particular, result in inequitable treatment for people? To achieve science literacy for all will require knowledge of how the current system might discriminate against some students while favoring others. Other areas of research include exploring how science/technology/society (STS) issues (such as population growth, water resources, world hunger, food resources, and extinction of plants and animals) might be connected to issues of interest to social studies researchers (Hickman, Patrick, & Bybee, 1987). Many natural connections seem to exist between STS and social studies. Research can help to identify these connections and explore ways to use them effectively in schools.

SCIENCE AND TECHNOLOGY

It can be useful to keep in mind the fundamental differences between science and technology when considering implications for curriculum and instruction as well as for research. Chapter 15 in *Benchmarks* concludes that the research base for technology education is small. This is not surprising, because technology is largely ignored in U.S. schools. We need to understand in a much more detailed way what students think about the purposes of experimentation, as well as how science teachers convey the differences between scientific and engineering approaches to problems and experimentation.

Models developed in engineering may be more closely tied to relevant, everyday problems and may be more beneficial for teaching science than models organized by abstract principles (Linn, 1994). It is important to include teaching about technology to help students understand both the differences and similarities between science and technology. Research on these issues is needed as curriculum and instruction based on *Benchmarks* are used to promote reform.

RESEARCH CONNECTIONS
AMONG *BLUEPRINTS* CHAPTERS

Most of the chapters in *Blueprints* identify research knowledge that will be necessary to allow the ideas they address to become common practice. In this section, the importance of a comprehensive research agenda for science education reform is underscored. Many of the observations and suggestions for research can be traced to the *Blueprints* chapters themselves, while others grow out of other sources.

EQUITY

Issues of equity are clearly on the minds of many educators involved in science education reform. In *Creating a Civic Culture in a Scientific World*, Ladson-Billings (1994) writes:

Unfortunately, one of the last issues given consideration in all of this talk of standards is that of equity. Thus, the essential question for me is: What will national standards mean for those students who traditionally have been ill-served by the public schools? (p. 2)
She goes on to say:

If teachers are not prepared to engage in rigorous debate about the intersections of social and scientific studies, creating standards that list them cannot make them happen. If opportunities for educational excellence are seriously compromised because students are poor, speak a language other than English, are members of non-white racial or cultural groups, or are female, the standards are likely to do nothing more than reproduce the same inequalities. (p. 11)

How can the tools of science education reform, such as *Benchmarks* and *Standards*, be used to target the ill-served in our society? Especially for the children of this nation's poor, how can the vision of *Science for All Americans* be translated into learning opportunities that allow an escape from poverty? A research program designed to focus our attention on possible answers to these questions is sorely needed.

SCHOOL ORGANIZATION

Is it necessary to alter traditional school organization to accomplish the science literacy goals of reform? How can research help in answering this question? Research on school organization should continue to be a part of systemic reform efforts as schools adopt various alternatives to the traditional discipline-based, grade-level option most commonly found in our schools. Decision making at the grassroots level empowers teachers, parents, and others to make necessary changes. A great deal of locally generated information on school organizational change will be needed to find what works in the many different schools in the country. Case studies of alternative school organizations will provide valuable information as schools use *Benchmarks*, *Standards*, and other reform tools to improve science literacy.

CURRICULUM CONNECTIONS

The case studies described in *Blueprints'* Chapter 6: Curriculum Connections illustrate attempts to weave connections among the traditional school subjects—mathematics, science, language arts, and social studies—through projects that involve student learning inside and outside of schools. Research is needed to determine the effectiveness of these kinds of interdisciplinary curricula in terms of agreed-upon measures of science literacy. As pointed out in *Blueprints'* Chapter 8: Assessment, multiple measures and alternative assessment strategies are needed to reflect student learning in these new curricula. Most teachers want to know if and how these kinds of interdisciplinary curricula work. Assessment research will therefore need to be tied closely to research on curriculum development.

MATERIALS AND TECHNOLOGY

Little research has been done on how teachers and students access and use resources in teaching and learning science. Likewise, few studies describe the effect of various materials on teachers and students. We need to answer questions like those raised by Berger, Lu, Belzer, and Voss (1994): What are the capabilities of hypermedia, microworlds, expert tutoring systems, and telecommunications that allow students to share, exchange, and even reconsider what they have learned? What are the capabilities of database systems that permit students to retrieve information and make flexible connections between related ideas? What are the effects of microcomputer simulation environments that give students the opportunity to make hypotheses, test them, observe results, and come to conclusions?

Little research has been done on how teachers and students access and use resources in teaching and learning science.

ASSESSMENT

The most important question facing science education reform efforts with regard to *Benchmarks* and *Standards* is this: How will student progress through benchmarks at each grade level be monitored, and how can science literacy at the end of K-12 be assessed? Consensus on this issue will not be easy to attain. Who will decide and how will it be decided? Moreover, how can we know what students might be able to achieve if schools could provide ideal learning conditions? Extensive research on conceptual change will be needed to inform the assessment component of science education reform.

As reported in *Blueprints'* Chapter 8: Assessment, research suggests that teachers often are unaware of good assessment techniques. How can they be helped to improve their assessment strategies? This important research question relates both to assessment and to teacher education chapters, as discussed in *Blueprints'* Chapters 8 and 9. The issue of fairness has implications for research related to assessment and to equity which are addressed in *Blueprints'* Chapters 8: Assesment and 1: Equity. How should fairness of assessment measures be judged? How well do teachers recognize the degree of fairness of a test?

TEACHER EDUCATION

Assuming that teachers teach as they were taught in college science courses and that more science knowledge is important for inquiry-based teaching, the vision of *Blueprints'* Chapter 9: Teacher Education is tied closely to undergraduate education in the sciences. However, it seems prudent to at least question the assumption that K-12 science teachers teach as they were taught in college science courses. Of the many factors that influence how school science is taught, how influential are college science teachers? Can we turn to research-based knowledge for guidance? Unfortunately, the answer is no.

A research program designed to sort out the influence of content knowledge and teaching models in university and college science courses would be very helpful. How and where do effective K-12 science teachers learn to teach? How much of their effectiveness can be attributed to the influence of college science teachers? How much and what aspects of their effectiveness can be explained by their knowledge and understanding of science? A teacher education program informed by research must be able to answer these and related questions.

HIGHER EDUCATION

Blueprints' Chapter 10: Higher Education assumes that as science education reform goals are reached in K-12 schools, colleges and universities can build upon these achievements. During their preparation as undergraduates, many prospective science teachers take more science courses than education courses. *Blueprints'* Chapter 9: Teacher Education argues that these college-level science courses should be changed to provide prospective teachers with good models of science teaching. These assumptions raise interesting research questions probed earlier: What are the effects of college science teaching on prospective teachers' ideas about science teaching? How do these ideas get translated into actual teaching strategies? Careful study of the effects of college science teaching on the teaching ideas and habits of future school teachers should be undertaken to establish more clearly the "sensible" conclusion that we teach as we were taught in college.

FAMILY AND COMMUNITY

Research on family involvement in schooling should be carried out at the early stages of reform to allow for better informed decision making throughout reform. Just as teacher-education research shows that it is important to involve teachers in decision making, research on parent involvement shows that learning improves when parents have meaningful roles in their children's education (see *Blueprints'* Chapter 11: Family and Community). Given the wide variety of home environments of today's children, what kind of family involvement is reasonable to expect? A research program that can provide answers to this question will be helpful to science education reform.

BUSINESS AND INDUSTRY

Blueprints' Chapter 12: Business and Industry states that evidence of the effectiveness of business involvement in education is mainly anecdotal. The chapter also assumes that this involvement is desirable, focusing mainly on how to make the partnership more effective. A research agenda in this area would include questions designed to probe the nature and consequences of various kinds of involvement of business and industry in education.

CONNECTING RESEARCH WITH PRACTICE

Research and practice in education are multifaceted and can influence each other in many ways. This section considers some of the common views of education research and practice, and the relationships between them. Suggestions are offered on ways to connect these often separate enterprises within the reform framework.

RESEARCH IN CONTEXT

How can research on schooling be improved? How can research be tied more closely to practice? The journey that education research has taken from the 1960s to the 1990s can be thought of as a transition toward placing research in more meaningful context. Qualitative research methods are often better able to capture the rich detail of teaching and learning in complex classroom and school settings than are the quantitative, experimental methods that dominated pre-1970s education research. Having more research methods to use in trying to answer questions of interest to researchers and teachers ensures more realistic and meaningful results and conclusions. It seems obvious, but it is crucial to

Teachers must come to see the value of conduct-ing informal research in their classrooms.

know that both the discipline/subject content and the pedagogy used in teaching that content will influence the results of research on teaching or learning. Research that ignores one or the other lacks that context necessary to provide teachers with meaningful information.

The next step toward achieving a necessary richness of context in education research is developing the teacher-as-researcher or research-partner concept. The teacher-as-researcher is seen by many to be an important component in making the research-practice connection. Teachers must come to see the value of conducting informal research in their classrooms. At the same time, university researchers must come to understand the value of having teachers become members of the formal education research community. A continual exchange of ideas is critical to both initial and long-term change in instructional practice.

Multiple Meanings of Educational Research

Trying to connect research with practice requires a careful definition of research so we can know better where some useful connections can be made. Research is now defined in many different ways, in contrast to the earlier notion of quantitative methods. Among the terms used to refer to these approaches are qualitative, descriptive, interpretive, naturalistic, ethnographic, and phenomenological. The purpose here is not to sort out the nuances of modern forms of research but to emphasize the complex nature of the research picture.

Romberg (1992) noted the importance of understanding the various "conceptual lenses" used by researchers. These lenses often affect researchers' initial assumptions about the world to be investigated. For example, in studying schooling, these perspectives reflect researchers' assumptions about what knowledge is to be taught, how learning occurs, the role of teachers and other professionals, and the classroom environment.

Teacher as Researcher

A primary reason for including teachers is to provide a rich context for research efforts. Few people in the educational research community have as much knowledge of what goes on in schools as teachers, yet teaching is mainly studied by outside researchers. There are probably many reasons for this situation, but one that should be considered is the lack of value placed on teachers' knowledge of their own classroom and school environments. Researchers generally see a narrow range of the depth and complexity experienced by teachers every day, year after year. There are a few signs that this situation is beginning to change (for examples, see Cochran-Smith & Lytle, 1993; Schon, 1990; Whyte, 1991), but relatively little evidence exists to support the idea that teachers are active research partners.

A strong support system is needed if teacher-as-researcher programs are to be successful in the long term. Both schools and universities must sufficiently value the idea to provide the funds, time, and flexibility for teachers and researchers to interact professionally. Short of involving the teacher directly as a partner in research (i.e., teachers as researchers), teachers must be involved as "research users" throughout a given study. Teachers must be shown the value of doing action research in their classrooms, and university researchers must come to understand the value of having teachers as members of the education research community.

RECOMMENDATIONS

Because science education reform—especially if it intends to be interdisciplinary—casts a wide net, it is important to focus on a relatively small number of research themes; otherwise, the research effort will be as diluted and fragmented as the current education research picture. Teams of researchers across disciplines working on common research questions offer the promise of coordinated, longitudinal research projects. The teacher-as-researcher or research-partner concept must be developed to ensure both improved research and closer ties between research and practice.

Research should stay close to the subject matter content in *Benchmarks* and *Standards* that defines science literacy. Research questions should be related to the various content themes in *Benchmarks* so that findings bear directly on the outcomes defined as science literacy. Losing sight of the central focus of *Science for All Americans* would dilute research findings, making progress toward achieving science education reform goals more difficult.

Finally, a research agenda for science literacy should reflect the following general recommendations for how it should be conducted and what tools need to be developed to carry it out:

■ A coordinated, longitudinal research effort will be required.

■ A major research effort directed at developing or identifying assessment tools for *Benchmarks* and *Standards* should be initiated.

■ Clear connections among school science, mathematics, and social studies should be identified.

■ Research must be connected to teaching practice by having teachers on research teams and by expanding the teacher's role in research and development efforts.

In addition, the following specific areas of research have been raised in the chapter and are necessary to build the research base for reform in science education:

■ The role of natural language and other symbolic systems.

■ The nature of students' mental models about natural phenomena, linked to *Benchmarks* and *Standards*.

■ Curriculum and instruction that can provide equitable science learning opportunities.

■ Strands or themes that cut across many disciplines.

■ The role of misconceptions and the critical components of conceptual change.

■ The effects of college science teaching and subject matter knowledge on K-12 science teaching.

■ Case studies of schools that are implementing various forms of science education reform.

Successful science education reform needs a foundation of research-based standards, curriculum, and teaching. The grade level delineations in *Benchmarks* that show how learning develops across the grades are drawn from research on teaching and learning. This is a first step that can be extended. Science teachers should require that curriculum and performance frameworks, instructional materials and technology, teaching strategies, and assessments also be based upon research.

REFERENCES

American Association for the Advancement of Science. (1993). *Benchmarks for science literacy*. New York: Oxford University Press.

American Association for the Advancement of Science. (1989). *Science for all Americans*. New York: Oxford University Press.

Berger, C., Lu, C., Belzer, S., & Voss, B. (1994). Research on the uses of technology in science education. In D. Gabel (Ed.), *Handbook of research on science teaching and learning*. New York: Macmillan.

Cochran-Smith, M., & Lytle, S. (1993). *Inside/outside: Teacher research and knowledge*. New York: Teachers College Press.

Cole, M., & Griffin, P. (1987). *Contextual factors in education: Improving science and mathematics education for minorities and women.* Madison, WI: Wisconsin Center for Education Research.

Committee on Research in Mathematics, Science, and Technology Education. (1985). *Mathematics, science, and technology education: A research agenda.* Washington, D.C.: National Academy Press.

Gabel, D. (Ed.). (1994). *Handbook of research on science teaching and learning.* New York: Macmillan.

Good, R. (1994). *Project 2061 research blueprint.* Prepared for the American Association for the Advancement of Science, Project 2061, Washington, D.C.

Good, R., Trowbridge, J., Demastes, S., Wandersee, J., Hafner, M., & Cummins, C. (Eds.). (1993). *Toward a research base for evolution education: Report of a national conference.* Baton Rouge, LA: Louisiana State University.

Grouws, D. (Ed.). (1992). *Handbook of research on mathematics teaching and learning.* New York: Macmillan

Hickman, F., Patrick, J., & Bybee, R. (1987). *Science/technology/society: A framework for curriculum reform in secondary school science and social studies.* Boulder, CO: Social Science Education Consortium, Inc.

Ladson-Billings, G. (1994, April). *Creating a civic culture in a scientific world: A social studies research agenda.* Paper prepared for Project 2061's Blueprint Research Conference, New Orleans, LA.

Linn, M. (1987). Establishing a research base for science education: Challenges, trends, and recommendations. *Journal of Research in Science Teaching, 24,* 191–216.

Linn, M. (1994, April). *Establishing a research agenda for science education: Project 2061.* Paper prepared for Project 2061's Blueprint Research Conference, New Orleans, LA.

National Council of Teachers of Mathematics. (1989). *Curriculum and evaluation standards for school mathematics.* Reston, VA: Author.

National Research Council. (1996). *National science education standards.* Washington, D.C.: National Academy Press.

Romberg, T. (1992). Perspectives on scholarship and research methods. In D. Grouws (Ed.), *Handbook of research on mathematics teaching and learning.* New York: Macmillan.

Schon, D. (1990). *Educating the reflective practitioner.* San Francisco: Jossey-Bass.

Science Education Research Agenda Coalition. (1994, April). *Blueprint Research Conference papers.* Project 2061's Blueprint Research Conference, New Orleans, LA.

Shaver, J. (Ed.). (1991). *Handbook of research on social studies teaching and learning.* New York: Macmillan.

Shymansky, J., & Kyle, W. (1992). Establishing a research agenda: Critical issues of science curriculum reform. *Journal of Research in Science Teaching, 29,* 749–778.

Sowder, J. (Ed.). (1989). *Setting a research agenda: Research agenda for mathematics education.* Reston, VA: National Council of Teachers of Mathematics.

Steen, L. (1990). *On the shoulders of giants: New approaches to numeracy.* Washington, D.C.: National Academy Press.

Thompson, P. (1994, April). *Bridges between mathematics and science education.* Paper prepared for Project 2061's Blueprint Research Conference, New Orleans, LA.

Whyte, W. (1991). *Participatory action research.* Newbury Park, CA: SAGE.

BIBLIOGRAPHY

American Association for the Advancement of Science. (1993). *Benchmarks for science literacy.* New York: Oxford University Press.

American Association for the Advancement of Science. (1990). *The liberal art of science: Agenda for action.* Washington, D.C.: Author.

American Association for the Advancement of Science. (1989). *Science for all Americans.* New York: Oxford University Press.

Anderson, G.L, Herr, K. & Nihlen, A.S. (1996) What does practitioner research look like? *Teaching and Change, 3*(2), 173-206.

Anderson, R. & Mitchener, C. (1994). Research on science teacher education. In D. Gabel (Ed.) *Handbook of research on science teaching and learning.* New York: Macmillan.

Apple, M. (1971). The hidden curriculum and the nature of conflict. *Interchange, 2* (4), 27-40.

Atwater, M. (1994). Research on cultural diversity in the classroom. In D. Gabel (Ed.). *Handbook of research on science teaching and learning.* New York: Macmillan.

Basalla, G. (1988). *The evolution of technology.* Cambridge, MA: Cambridge University Press

Berger, C., Lu, C., Belzer, S., & Voss, B. (1994). Research on the uses of technology in science education. In D. Gabel (Ed.), *Handbook of research on science teaching and learning.* New York: Macmillan.

Bishop, B. & Anderson, C. (1990). Student conceptions of natural selection and its role in evolution. *Journal of Research in Science Teaching, 27,* 415-427.

Campbell, D. & Stanley, J. (1963). *Experimental and quasi-experimental designs for research.* Chicago, IL: Rand McNally.

Cherryholmes, C. (1991). Critical research and social studies education. In J. Shaver (Ed.), *Handbook of research on social studies teaching and learning* (pp. 41-55). New York: Macmillan.

Cochran-Smith, M. & Lytle, S. (1993). *Inside/outside: Teacher research and knowledge.* New York: Teacher College Press.

Committee on Research in Mathematics, Science, and Technology Education (1985). *Mathematics, science, and technology education: A research agenda.* Washington, D.C.: National Academy Press.

Confrey, J. (1994, April). *An agenda for equitable access to quantitative tools.* Paper prepared for Project 2061's Research Blueprint meeting, New Orleans, LA.

Cummings, H. (Ed.) (1956). *Science and the social studies.* Washington, D.C.: National Council of the Social Studies.

Demastes, S., Good, R. & Peebles, P. (1994, March 28). *Patterns of conceptual change in evolution*. Paper presented at the 1994 annual National Association for Research in Science Teaching meeting, Anaheim, CA.

Dewey, J. (1913). *Interest and effort in education*. Boston, MA: Houghton Mifflin.

Doran, R., Lawrenz, F., & Helgeson, S. (1994). Research on assessment in science. In D. Gabel (Ed.), *Handbook of research on science teaching and learning*. New York: Macmillan.

Elliott, J. (1991). *Action research for educational change*. Philadelphia, PA: Open University Press.

Fleischer, C. (1995). *Composing teacher-research: A prosaic history*. Albany, NY: SUNY Press.

Fraser, B. (1994). Research on classroom and school climate. In D. Gabel (Ed.) *Handbook of research on science teaching and learning*. New York: Macmillan.

Gabel, D. (Ed.), (1994). *Handbook of research on science teaching and learning*. New York: Macmillan.

Good, R., Trowbridge, J., Demastes, S., Wandersee, J., Hafner, M., & Cummins, C. (Eds.) (1993). *Proceedings of the 1992 Evolution Education Research Conference*. Louisiana State University: Baton Rouge, LA.

Hickman, F., Patrick, J. & Bybee, R. (1987). *Science/technology/society: A framework for curriculum reform in secondary school science and social studies*. Boulder, CO: Social Science Education Consortium, Inc.

Hofstein, A. & Yager, R. (1982). Societal issues as organizers for science education in the 80s. *School Science and Mathematics, 82*, 539-547.

Holton, G. (1993). *Science and anti-science*. Cambridge, MA: Harvard University Press.

Huberman, M. (1990). Linkage between researchers and practitioners: A qualitative study. *American Educational Research Journal, 27*, 363-391.

Hurd, P. (1984). *Reforming science education: The search for a new vision*. Washington, D.C.: Council for Basic Education.

Hutchinson, J. & Huberman, M. (1993, May). *Knowledge dissemination and use in science and mathematics education: A literature review*. Washington, D.C.: National Science Foundation.

Jackson, P. (1968). *Life in classrooms*. New York: Holt, Rinehart, & Winston.

Johnson, B.M. (1995). Why conduct action research? *Teaching and Change 3*(2), 190-104.

Kahle, J. & Meece, J. (1994). Research on gender issues in the classroom. In D. Gabel (Ed.) *Handbook of research on science teaching and learning*. New York: Macmillan.

Kaput, J. (1994, April). *Research for long-term reform: Strands instead of layers*. Paper presented at Project 2061's Research Blueprint Meeting, New Orleans, LA.

Kromhout, R. & Good, R. (1983). Beware of societal issues as organizers for science education. *School Science and Mathematics, 83*, 647-650.

Ladson-Billings, G. (1994, April). *Creating a civic culture in a scientific world: A social studies research agenda*. Paper presented at Project 2061's Research Blueprint Meeting, New Orleans, LA.

Linn, M. (1987). Establishing a research base for science education: Challenges, trends, and recommendations. *Journal of Research in Science Teaching, 24*, 191-216.

Linn, M. (1994, April). *Establishing a research agenda for science education: Project 2061.* Paper presented at Project 2061's Research Blueprint meeting, New Orleans. LA.

McGee-Brown, M. (1994, March 28). *Systematic reflective teacher research in educational reform in science literacy: Process and understanding.* Paper presented at the National Association for Research in Science Teaching annual meeting, Anaheim. CA.

McLean, James E. (1995). *Improving education through action research: A guide for administrators and teachers.* Thousand Oaks, CA: Corwin Press, Inc.

National Council of Teachers of Mathematics. (1989). *Curriculum and evaluation standards for school mathematics.* Reston, VA: Author.

National Science Teachers Association. (1982). *Science-technology-society. Science education for the 1980s.* Washington, D.C.: Author.

Pinar, W., Reynolds, W., Slattery, P. & Taubman, P. (1995). *Understanding curriculum.* New York: Peter Lang.

Popkewitz, T. (1984). *Paradigm and ideology in educational research: The social functions of the intellectual.* London: Falmer Press.

Romanish, B. (1983). Modern secondary economics textbooks and ideological bias. *Theory and Research in Social Education, 11*, 1-24.

Romberg, T. (1992). Perspectives on scholarship and research methods. In D. Grouws (Ed.), *Handbook of research on mathematics teaching and learning.* New York: Macmillan.

Schauble, L., Klopfer, L., & Raghavan, K. (1991). Students' transition from an engineering model to a science model of experimentation. *Journal of Research in Science Teaching, 28*, 859-882.

Schon, D. (1990). *Educating the reflective practitioner.* San Francisco, CA: Jossey-Bass.

Shaver, J. (Ed.). (1991). *Handbook of research on social studies teaching and learning.* New York: Macmillan.

Shulman, L. (1987). Knowledge and teaching: Foundations of the new reform. *Harvard Educational Review, 57*, 1-22.

Shymansky, J. & Kyle, W. (1992). Establishing a research agenda: Critical issues of science curriculum reform. *Journal of Research in Science Teaching, 29*, 749-778.

Sowder, J. (Ed.). (1989). *Setting the agenda for mathematics education.* Reston, VA: National Council of Teachers of Mathematics.

Steen, L. (Ed.). (1990). *On the shoulders of giants: New approaches to numeracy.* Washington, D.C.: National Academy Press.

Thompson, P. (1994, April). *Bridges between mathematics and science education.* Paper presented at Project 2061's Research Blueprint Meeting, New Orleans, LA.

Wandersee, J., Mintzes, J., & Novak, J. (1994). Research on alternative conceptions in science. In D. Gabel (Ed.), *Handbook of research on science teaching and learning.* New York: Macmillan.

Whitson, J. (1994, April). *Social and behavioral sciences: A Project 2061 research blueprint.* Paper presented at Project 2061's Research Blueprint meeting, New Orleans, LA.

Whyte, W. (1991). *Participatory action research.* Newbury Park, CA: SAGE.

Wolpert, L. (1992). *The unnatural nature of science.* Cambridge, MA: Harvard University Press.

PAUL KLEE, *der gefundene Ausweg (The Way Out Discovered)*, 1935.

PART II
The School Context

OTHER THAN PEOPLE AND FACILITIES, perhaps the most apparent parts
of a school system are its organization, curriculum, and instructional
materials and technologies. These are obviously interdependent, although
decisions regarding them are often made as though they were entirely
independent entities. In principle, time, space, and personnel are organized to accommodate students' learning a given curriculum. In practice, a curriculum is constrained by the availability of time, space, and
personnel. Similarly, materials and technologies are acquired to serve a
curriculum, yet the materials and technologies on hand often determine
what the actual curriculum will be. School organization (how time is
configured, space allotted, and staff hired and assigned) and instructional
technology (what learning materials and instruments of instruction will
be used) also have important interdependencies.

These three interrelated aspects of schooling (organization, curriculum,
and instructional materials and technologies) share the purpose of promoting learning. But do they actually do so? That is what the fourth
component of the school context, assessment, is designed to determine.
External assessments, which may or may not be matched to the local
curriculum, are intended to find out how well the system is working.
If either one of these two types of assessment shows that student performance does not meet standards, something needs changing—the
organization and conduct of instruction, the selection and use of learning
materials and teaching technologies, or the content and structure of the
curriculum. But that is too neat a picture.

For one thing, that picture implies that assessment, curriculum, and school organization function independently. In fact, each is often designed with the other in mind. For example, assessment content usually reflects the curriculum ("fair testing") and over time the curriculum content is modified to reflect the assessment ("teaching to the test"). And there are other interactions: because assessment takes time (a fixed and enormously valuable resource), a balance must be achieved between the time allotted to assessment at the expense of instruction, and vice versa; the sophistication of curriculum and assessment depends greatly on the number and quality of instructional and support staff; testing materials are often indistinguishable from instructional materials; and so forth.

And of course school organization, curriculum, materials and technologies, and assessment are all subject to local, state, and federal education policies which, in turn, are constrained by budget decisions. The reverse is also true to some substantial degree: policies are set and budgets determined to take into account decisions made on school organization, curriculum, materials and technologies, and assessment. Moreover, the school context is precisely where questions of equity come to the fore, because it is there that inequities play out—whether as biased tests, curricula that serve some groups better than others, higher quality learning materials in some schools than in others, or any number of other ways.

By the same token, what schools can do—or are pressed into doing—with regard to school organization, curriculum, materials and technologies, and assessment depends significantly on the support they receive from families, community leaders (including the media), business and industry, and higher education (especially teacher education and admissions policies), and the availability of trustworthy knowledge to inform decision making. These interactions are addressed in Part III: The Support Structure.

As in Part I, Project 2061 has framed questions related to each chapter. These questions are intended to initiate discussions of the interactions and components of the education system, with some attention to their bearing on the aims of Project 2061.

SCHOOL ORGANIZATION

1. Are there valid lessons to be learned about the organization of schooling from the organization of business and industry? Are policies dealing with the support given professionals, the utilization of modern technologies, the utilization of time, the assignment of decision-making responsibilities, performance assessment, and incentives transferable to the school context? If so, with what gains and at what costs?

2. Where should the locus of authority reside with regard to how time, space, and personnel will be deployed? The district or each school in the district? If authority is to be shared among these, can jurisdictional battles be avoided? On whose shoulders should the final responsibility for meeting student learning goals rest?

3. How can organizational fads be avoided? How can valid organizational reforms avoid being declared fads that will have their day and then go away? What research is needed to guide decisions on proposed organizational changes?

4. If radical changes in organization are to be considered, at what point should stakeholders and other interested parties be brought into the picture?

5. How can organizational changes simplify an already complex system and make it more effective? What changes have positive effects on teachers? On students? In what ways?

CURRICULUM CONNECTIONS

1. What does it take to align curricula with standards? What evidence can be adduced to support alignment claims? What if national standards and state or district frameworks are not themselves in accord?

2. What should be the balance in the curriculum between core requirements and elective ones (both remedial and for the gifted)? Between
discipline-based courses and subjects and those that are interdisciplinary
or otherwise integrated? Between traditional courses and non-traditional
structures, such as seminars, courses organized entirely around individual
and group projects, peer teaching, and independent study?

3. How can curricula accommodate the recommendations in *Science for
All Americans* for all students to gain understandings and skills that connect science (natural and social), mathematics, and technology? That
soften the boundaries among the sciences? That emphasize history,
philosophy, and cross-cutting themes? That call for science teaching to
be consistent with the nature of scientific inquiry and to reflect scientific values?

4. How can curricula respond effectively to the recommendations in
Benchmarks for Science Literacy for coherence and attention to cognitive
development? What steps can be taken to avoid either failing to treat
essential material often enough and sequentially enough or having
needless redundancy?

5. If "less is more" means reducing the number of topics covered in
order to gain time to invest in greater understanding, on what grounds
can decisions be made about what to eliminate? Who makes the decisions? What response can be expected from parents, the media, textbook publishers and test developers, and universities?

Materials and Technology

1. How can the claims publishers make to the effect that their textbooks and other instructional materials address *National Science
Education Standards* and *Benchmarks* be validated? Because publishers
respond to the market (often leading to topic-burdened, vocabulary-
intensive textbooks) and teachers seem willing to use such books, what
can be done to make "less is more" possible?

2. What needs to be done to realize the promise of computer-based information and communications technologies? What effect will their use have on the gap between the lowest-performing students and the highest-performing? Will the cost of obtaining new hardware, maintaining and updating it periodically, adding and changing software, training and retraining teachers, and paying Internet access charges be justified by the benefits realized? How can such cost-benefit judgments be made?

3. As computers are introduced, which functions (word processing, calculating, graphing, building and accessing databases, etc.) and purposes (drill, tutoring, testing, etc.) should take precedence? Should it vary by grade level? Subject matter? What computer skills will all teachers need in the future in order to do their job effectively? Are there ways—separate from their use to promote student learning—for computers to serve the professional needs of teachers?

4. Can teachers be expected to create their own courses? Should schools adopt courses rather than textbooks? In considering whether to adopt a course, no matter who developed it, should school authorities demand evidence from field testing that the course yields the learning outcomes it claims?

5. Which way will the spread of home computers and Internet access cut educationally? Will learning be enhanced or impeded? Will it depend more on school use or home use? Does loaning portable computers to students improve their learning? Improve communications with their families?

ASSESSMENT

1. How can schools best deal with the need to assess student performance for a variety of different purposes—to adjust instruction; to report to students and parents on progress; to create a record that will influence employment and college admission; to report on the effec-

tiveness of the curriculum; to compare a district, state, or country with other districts, states, or countries—without confusion? When do the time and financial costs of assessment outweigh the advantages?

2. What are the tradeoffs between relative objectiveness of multiple-choice tests (and their kin) and the relative subjectivity of assessment techniques such as performances? Who decides when to use which kind?

3. How can educators, parents, and others be sure that the assessment tools and techniques they use measure what they want them to? What components of the education system can and should be assessed periodically, and how?

4. How should mathematics and science education respond to calls for "first in the world" performance? What assessments or outcomes do we value in making such comparisons or in making important decisions about schooling?

5

School Organization

HOW SCHOOLS ARE ORGANIZED and how well they can accomodate change are critical to success in educational reform. This chapter discusses organizational changes in governance, curriculum, assessment and evaluation, students, time, staff, space, and instruction that can help educators to implement Project 2061's vision of science, mathematics, and technology education reform.

Organizational change, in order to be effective and sustainable, may need to be incremental, and it must accommodate the need to simplify complexity in schools and classrooms. We form organizations in part to manage the complexity of a disorganized world and to create stability and predictability where none exists naturally. Simplification is necessary to the health of an organization and the well-being of its members. In schools, where staff are responsible for large numbers of students and a variety of content subjects in the course of a day, the need to reduce complexity is especially important.

This chapter begins with a general analysis of lessons gleaned from the historical influences on school organization, followed by a discussion of how reforms might be implemented in the organization of governance, curriculum, assessment and evaluation, students, time, staff, space, and instruction. Finally, it examines the process of change at one of six School-District Centers where Project 2061 principles are being deliberately employed.

GUIDING PHILOSOPHY

The philosophical underpinnings of Project 2061 guide the possibilities for and characteristics of organizational change. Specifically, two educational perspectives are embraced that, in the past, have been viewed as mutually exclusive. One orientation involves structuring science teaching and learning around predetermined knowledge, skills, and attitudes that students are expected to master over the course of thirteen years of schooling. The other is that of a more child-centered, student-initiated, inquiry-based approach to teaching and learning that requires a less rigid and more improvisational form of pedagogy than is normally found in math and science classrooms.

Implicit in this second educational orientation is Project 2061's notion of reflective literacy as a key component of scientific literacy. Reflective literacy is the ability to know and understand a concept and to connect it meaningfully to other ideas when making decisions or interpreting information. For example, reflective literacy might lead a person to realize all the potential ramifications of logging a given tree, including the potential disruption of the tree's relationships with other organisms, the complexity of those relationships, the difficulty of predicting the ramifications of those disruptions, and so on.

Concern with reflective literacy suggests a break with accountability-based, outcome-oriented reform movements of the past such as competency-based education and mastery learning. Moreover, it is difficult to imagine that students will develop the habits of mind that promote this sort of deliberate thought process without opportunities to practice. And it is particularly difficult to imagine meaningful practice opportunities occurring in environments that are overly structured and teacher-directed, as is currently the case in many, if not most, classrooms.

Project 2061 is not simply a curriculum reform project but is committed to the reform of the entire educational system. Indeed, curriculum reforms in science and mathematics will inevitably die out quickly if they are superimposed upon the existing educational system. Consequently, many aspects of schools and school systems must be altered to realize this vision of reflective, long-term learning. Hence the need for examining the possible types of change with which this chapter is concerned.

LESSONS FROM HISTORY

Historical analysis alerts us to move cautiously when implementing change; to avoid change for the sake of change; and, when changes in school organization are deemed necessary, to be sensitive to the need to accommodate increased complexity. As demonstrated by Cuban (1995), there are similarities between early reform initiatives and the ideas now being advanced by Project 2061 and other science education reformers. Earlier initiatives, however, had a limited impact on practice over the long haul, largely because of the stability of the age-graded school,

Curriculum reforms in science and mathematics will inevitably die out quickly if they are superimposed upon the existing educational system.

which had been imported from Prussia in the 19th century. The age-graded school revolutionized the governance, structures, cultures, and practices of schooling and teaching. Embedded within the concept of an age-graded structure were a host of other organizational components: self-contained classrooms, curriculum divided into segments, time schedules for teaching subject matter and skills, tests to determine whether the knowledge and skills have been learned, promotion to the next grade for those who attain the minimum levels set for each grade, and remedial work for those who are left behind.

The age-graded school, in turn, helped to create other characteristics of schooling. Because the school building itself isolates teachers into self-contained classrooms, monitoring and supervision are complicated, as is collaborative work with peers. Age-graded schools also helped to create certain pedagogical and classroom organization commonplaces, including teacher-centered instructional practices such as whole-group instruction and arranging desks in rows, and teacher-established routines for students, such as hand raising. Other efficiency practices include lecturing, recitation, seat work, text-based homework and, more recently, weekly multiple choice or fill-in-the-blank tests. These practices are ingrained in teachers' belief systems about instruction: changing these accepted norms means changing a set of cultural beliefs.

Variation among school and classroom practices and norms does exist. However, the dominant tendencies in the school and classroom regularities described above are well documented, and their ubiquity and durability are well established. Not only do these commonplaces respond to the needs of a specific type of organization—contemporary American schools—they also accommodate certain needs common to all organizations, including the need to simplify complexity.

FACETS OF NEEDED CHANGE

Changes in the commonplaces of schools can occur. However, we should attempt only those changes that are essential to reform, and we should attempt them only if we are committed to finding ways to reduce any complexity that those changes introduce.

ORGANIZATION OF GOVERNANCE

Since the mid-1980s, the interrelated notions of site-based management and shared decision making have been central to many contemporary reform agendas. Indeed, most of the models produced by Project 2061's School-District Centers recommended some sort of shared decision making at the school site.

In contrast to this thinking, others are a bit more ambivalent about site-based management and shared decision making, although supportive of the aspirations underlying these concepts. They argue that a large amount of discretion on the part of teachers and site-based administrators seems essential for several reasons. First, the only viable generalization educational research has produced is that there are no generalizations which hold in all places, at all times, and for all students. Educators at the local site need discretion so they can respond to the idiosyncrasies they encounter in their work. Second, teaching and learning are ultimately human enterprises rather than mechanical processes. The enthusiasm of a teacher matters in the learning process, and one important way to generate teacher enthusiasm is to give teachers ownership over what they do. Third, schools are loosely coupled organizations. Often, hierarchical control from the top leads to little more than token compliance and procedural display at lower levels of the structure.

Beyond these general reasons for providing a great deal of school site discretion, there is also a reason related to science education reform. If reform aims to promote reflective literacy, and if more informed,

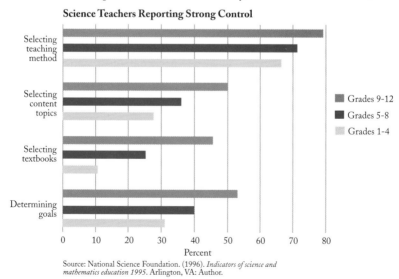

Science Teachers Reporting Strong Control

Source: National Science Foundation. (1996). *Indicators of science and mathematics education 1995*. Arlington, VA: Author.

locally contextual approaches to learning are required to develop reflective literacy, then teachers must engage in a flexible sort of pedagogy that cannot be choreographed from on high. They need freedom to respond to students' initiatives and to shape students' interests and concerns into educationally worthwhile activities. This kind of freedom requires some local discretion over issues such as budget, use of time, and grouping of students.

Teachers must engage in a flexible sort of pedagogy that cannot be choreographed from on high.

Although the goals of site-based management/shared decision making are important for education in general and science education reform in particular, the common means used to achieve their objectives—committees or teams—may need to be replaced. These committees generally consist of administrators, teachers, and sometimes parents. The empirical evidence about site-based governance teams is equivocal (David, 1989). Of particular concern, however, is that such structures—even those focused on curriculum and instruction—may violate the guiding principle related to complexity. Rather than simplifying schools, they add both organizational and political complexity by bringing school board politics down to the building level and making every principal a highly politicized quasi-superintendent.

Site-based management might be better realized by relying less on formally constituted site-based management teams and more on informal mechanisms. Specifically, this would mean, among other things, appointing administrators who practice democratic decision making. Models of democratic leadership and decision making are rooted in several principles: eschewing the use of power, whether in the form of brute force or the iron fist covered by a velvet glove; being open to ideas; welcoming criticism; and basing decisions on evidence and argument (Argyris & Schon, 1975).

It also may be better to rely less on bureaucratic mechanisms (rules and written policies) to run schools and school districts and more on cultural mechanisms (stories, myths, and rituals) that provide direction but also allow for greater discretion over how the belief system gets played out locally. Furthermore, when formal school and district policies must be written, these policies should not be so general as to be meaningless but also not so tightly defined as to provide no discretion for individual schools and individual teachers. This strategy is especially important in the area of curriculum organization.

ORGANIZATION OF CURRICULUM

State frameworks, district curricula, curriculum guidelines, textbooks, and other resources provide the basis for curriculum organization. Historically, curriculum documents either have been so general and vague that they have collected dust on office shelves and had little impact on classroom practice (often the fate of state and district curriculum guides) or they have provided a closely followed script which has choreographed, to a large extent, the teaching and learning process (the role frequently played by textbooks).

A commitment to reflective literacy requires that learners and teachers have frequent opportunities to structure the learning and teaching process.

If science education reform is to be successfully implemented, some middle ground between these two extremes must be found. On the one hand, the need to reduce complexity in the lives of teachers suggests the need for curriculum materials that are more than dust catchers. On the other hand, a commitment to reflective literacy, which in turn implies commitment to more student-centered learning and more inquiry-based teaching, requires that learners and teachers have frequent opportunities to structure the learning and teaching process. In addition, a successful curriculum should attend not only to science content itself, but also to assessment that is linked with instruction, allowing teachers to identify preconceptions and assess multiple areas and levels of student performance and literacy.

In all of this, an appropriate balance between direction and discretion must be struck. Some might argue that the *National Science Education Standards* (National Research Council, 1996) provide the proper balance in specificity. They serve a useful political function by creating a large tent under which many groups and individuals who hold conflicting views can gather. However, *Benchmarks for Science Literacy* (American Association for the Advancement of Science [AAAS], 1993) is a tool that educators can use to design a curriculum that makes sense to them and that supports the interdisciplinary, reflective literacy that Project 2061 promotes.

Reorganizing the curriculum around specific national, state, or local goals could, in the short term, introduce new complications for teachers. A greater and more effective use of computers and other technology might be one way to manage this added complexity. Technology's potential as a teaching tool is only beginning to be explored. Computers and other technology, for example, could allow students to do highly complex simulations and help teachers keep detailed records of performance. However, the fact that today's technology has a greater capacity to accommodate complexity than technologies used in the past, does not, in and of itself, mean that the person using the technology has acquired a similar sort of ability.

Although experimentation with relatively dramatic technological solutions to problems of curriculum organization may be useful, such experimentation should not preclude more modest and incremental explorations of the potential of existing technologies that support teaching. For example, new types of text material may be able to accommodate the ideas of science education reform and may even be a stimulus for change. The availability of selected individual modules and chapters could support teachers' efforts to implement interdisciplinary curricula and allow flexibility in meeting students' needs.

Assessment and Evaluation

The organization of assessment and evaluation is related to the organization of curriculum. Assessment and evaluation, after all, are often the tails that wag the curriculum dogs. In fact, they are one of the few effective means of promoting hierarchical control in what is generally a loosely coupled system. These topics are developed in *Blueprints'* Chapter 8: Assessment. Therefore, we merely wish to make the following interrelated points:

■ A clear, operational definition of what it means to be scientifically literate is necessary to assess the mastery of benchmarks and standards.

■ Although traditional, standardized paper and pencil assessment methods meet individuals' and organizations' inevitable need for simplification, they can steer the curriculum away from some of the teaching and learning opportunities envisioned by science education reformers.

■ Authentic, performance assessments can better accommodate standards and benchmarks, but may introduce greater complexity.

■ Even so-called authentic assessment may be inadequate to assess both whether students can display knowledge and skills when called on to do so and whether they will use their knowledge and skills spontaneously. Assessment of students' ability to use knowledge and skills almost always requires observation by external evaluators and teachers over time, which may not be feasible in large-scale assessments.

ORGANIZATION OF STUDENTS

If meaningful reform of classroom practice is to occur, changing internal commonplaces is at least as important as changing governance and curriculum. The grouping of students is the first of these internal, structural variables. At least two significant changes are possible for successful implementation of reform: teachers, or teams of teachers, could work with multiage groups, and teachers, or teams of teachers, could work with the same group of students for more than one year.

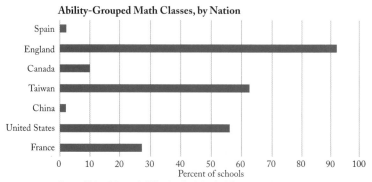

Ability-Grouped Math Classes, by Nation

Source: National Center for Education Statistics. (1991). *Education in states and nations.* Washington, D.C.: Author.

Using either or both of these strategies would result in *de facto* changes in instructional practice. For example, if the class were composed of students with a wide range of ages, it would be difficult to perpetuate the myth that all students in a class are or should be at the same developmental level in science. Consequently, teachers would be less likely to rely exclusively on whole group instruction and common assignments. Additionally, a teacher who works with students over prolonged periods of time may feel less pressure to unnaturally and inappropriately force students to master science benchmarks by the end of a specific curriculum unit. The teacher may, in other words, be less anxious about coverage and more likely to use the benchmarks as developmental markers rather than as competencies which must be mastered at a particular time. Finally, these ways of organizing students allow for blurring the sharp distinctions currently made between science subjects and between science and other subject areas, enhancing interdisciplinary learning.

Although both of these strategies add considerable complexity to the classroom, keeping students with teachers for more than one year should also simplify the teacher's work somewhat. This is particularly true in the beginning of the year when teachers usually must get to

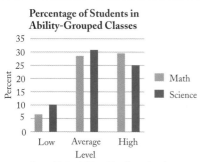

Percentage of Students in Ability-Grouped Classes

■ Math
■ Science

Source: National Science Foundation (1996). *Indicators of science and mathematics education 1995.* Arlington, VA: Author.

know a completely new class of students. Continuing students might also help by socializing new students. Still, even with these advantages, the added complexity associated with grouping strategies is great. To compensate, the age range assigned to any teacher may have to be limited.

Moreover, multi-age grouping and assigning students to a teacher for more than one year is likely to be unpopular with both students and their parents. These strategies break with tradition and disrupt people's images of what school is and what it ought to be. They also require that parents and students reassess the notion of learning as simply a linear, additive process and teaching as a process of disseminating information.

Although these concerns suggest that reformers proceed cautiously, the system must be shaken up at least somewhat if instructional practices are to change and certain goals of science education reform are to be achieved. Altering the way we group students may be one way of doing this.

ORGANIZATION OF TIME

Another organizational structure that could, and perhaps should, be altered is the 50-minute class period. It is difficult to see how teachers can engage in flexible teaching, and how students can design meaningful inquiry in the fractured school day that exists in most schools. Changes in school schedules could range from modest to relatively dramatic and include these three possibilities: double blocking, in which subjects remain discrete, but are taught in 100-minute periods for half a year rather than in 50-minute periods for the entire year; teaching, or team teaching, two or more subjects in a double period over the course of a year; and using a "mosaic" scheduling approach that combines longer and shorter blocks of time. These approaches have both potential benefits and costs. Double-blocking will broaden the repertoire of teaching strategies beyond lecturing, but increase the time devoted to seat work and teacher planning. Teaching two or more subjects in a double period will encourage curriculum integration, but demand greater content knowledge of teachers.

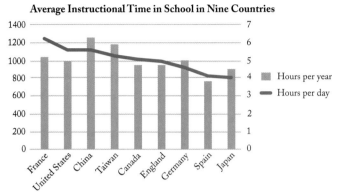

Source: National Center for Education Statistics. (1991). *Education in states and nations*, Washington, D.C.: Author.

The mosaic approach alters the existing organization of time in schools most radically. This might be considered a virtue, yet because it considerably complicates the school environment, its viability seems doubtful. In most schools, flexibility might be better provided by assigning a block of periods and a particular space to a group of teachers and their students rather than trying to implement the mosaic model schoolwide. Such a strategy creates schools within schools, providing flexibility without altering the traditional period organization.

ORGANIZATION OF STAFF

Creating relatively small units of teachers and students with large degrees of control over their use of time and space has several advantages. First, reducing the size of an organization reduces the number of variables that must be taken into account when scheduling, thus making more sophisticated use of time possible. Also, when size is limited, teams of teachers can develop schedules through face-to-face interaction, thus permitting more improvisation and negotiation.

Teaming also opens the door for more interdisciplinary work, which may be necessary simply to cover, in something other than a didactic way, the vast number of benchmarks. If responsibility for science literacy is limited to science and mathematics classes and an occasional class in technology, teachers may be overwhelmed by coverage anxiety and resort to didactic teaching and rote learning. Finally, teaming provides opportunities for mentoring and helps newcomers to develop professional practice in a supportive group.

Despite these potential advantages, teaming and schools within schools should not be viewed as panaceas. The idea of schools within schools has been around for some time, but in most places it has not taken hold. If science education reformers endorse the notion of teaming—and the emphasis on joint planning and commitment to making connections across disciplines and fields virtually requires a team effort—they must also realize that various supports are needed to make teaming work. Teachers, for instance, need substantial periods of time to work together—ideally a large block of time once a week—for planning. One way to create time during school is to engage students in community service, extracurricular activities, apprenticeships, independent projects, or similar activities one day a week. This strategy, of course, may add to the complexity of schooling because placements need to be arranged and students need to be monitored. Other activities, such as athletics, the arts, and library research, can be scheduled without a great deal of extra effort.

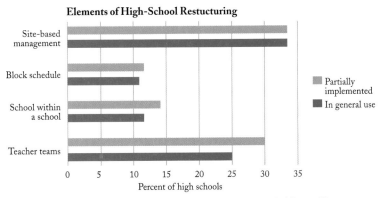

Elements of High-School Restructuring

Source: Cawelti, G. (1994). *High school restructuring: A national study.* Arlington, VA: Educational Research Service.

Team members also need training in handling conflict productively and in using planning time effectively. This means more than an occasional in-service session. Rather, coaches are required, at least during the beginning stages of team building and, ideally, beyond this point. Money currently devoted to formal staff development programs might be used to support this more informal approach to creating "learning organizations." University resources might be employed to support team-coaching programs. Other resources and professional networks may be needed in rural areas. However, the limited empirical information available from professional development schools suggests that these staff support and development activities also add complexity to school life.

ORGANIZATION OF SPACE

Altering physical space can be an effective agent of change. The way we organize space sets the stage for certain things to happen and sends important symbolic messages. Tearing down walls literally can lead to tearing down walls interpersonally. (Of course, in many architecturally open schools built in the 1960s and early 1970s, teachers simply built makeshift walls.) The following strategies may support science reform:

■ The science-mathematics-technology laboratory could become the center of the school much as the media center is now.

■ To emphasize connections across scientific fields, laboratories for the individual disciplines could be combined.

■ To encourage connections across mathematics and the sciences, these classrooms might be grouped together, and meeting space for teachers and students might be provided in that pod. Conversely, for more extensive interdisciplinary work, mathematics and science teachers could be dispersed throughout the building.

One other way to "shake things up" in schools from a space standpoint is to let students out into the community. Yet, opening school doors adds tremendous complexity to school organization. The monitoring of student attendance, for example—a traditional function of schools that is not likely to be abandoned—becomes considerably more difficult when students are spread throughout the community.

Even if we treat the process of opening up schools to the community more metaphorically than literally by bringing community members into the school, we still add complexity to school and classroom life. What is an administrator or biology teacher to do when the local association of fundamentalist ministers offers to teach a course in scientific creationism? Although school boards and other entities can limit potential conflicts, teachers and administrators will still spend considerable time negotiating varying agendas and other issues introduced by an open-door policy. Because of this potential, before a school or school system considers such reorganizations of space, it should weigh the costs along with the benefits.

SOME FIRST STEPS TOWARD CHANGE

As we have seen, the change process itself inevitably adds complexity to organizational life. Change disrupts organizational stability, and this disruption adds a degree of unpredictability to the already complicated process of schooling. It is as if we must transform a car into an airplane (or possibly a rocket ship) while still driving the car down the road. How can we manage such a process without crashing the vehicle? The experiences of Project 2061's San Francisco School-District Center illustrate some of the general principles of implementing reforms.

It is as if we must transform a car into an airplane while still driving the car down the road.

The district developed a technology of teaching called "challenge-based learning," which involved organizing units around a challenge to students such as building a kayak that would float a specified distance. (See *Blueprints'* Chapter 6: Curriculum Connections for a more detailed description of this challenge activity.) In short, challenge-based learning balanced direction and discretion.

There was a conscious effort to accommodate the varying interest levels of schools and teachers in the district. Not all teachers in the district were expected to implement challenge-based learning, for instance. Equally important, the district offered strategies to help teachers who might be persuaded to teach this way. Interested teachers could move incrementally toward this sort of teaching, beginning with kits and later moving on to create their own challenge-based learning units.

The director of the local initiative was amazingly patient and positive—the quintessential example of someone who waits for and makes the most of teachable moments. He truly believed that teachers would, in time, see the worth of reform ideas and, consequently, that they did not have to be manipulated into "buying in." The director was not, however, a totally passive change agent. He engaged in selling reform ideas to the district's teachers and administrators. He was, in fact, a consummate practitioner of cultural leadership.

The antithesis of a bureaucratic strategy was also employed to link science education reform with the many other initiatives going on in the San Francisco Unified School District. There was no attempt to bring these initiatives under one governance structure, undoubtedly an impossible task. Rather, attempts to coordinate the science education strategy with other district initiatives were characterized by informality, serendipity, and improvisation.

San Francisco's Project 2061 team was always recruiting new members, rather than having a small group of insiders run the project and risking resentment by other teachers in the district. The team continued to expand: new members joined as some older members took a sabbatical from direct involvement and other, older members opted back into direct participation. Programs such as summer school or special after school programs were used to increase involvement and bring in new members. Programs like these, outside the regular school day, provided opportunities to experiment with different ways of teaching without having to contend with many of the constraints of the regular school setting. This strategy, in short, was a way of minimizing complexity; it was, in a sense, another example of the district's gradual approach to change.

This sketch of one district's efforts to implement reforms is important because it provides evidence that Project 2061's ideas are beginning to take hold (albeit, quite slowly and less than completely). This is a viable model for how to drive the car while simultaneously trying to make it soar. The process is messy, slow, and incremental, but it illustrates a fundamental principle that cannot be ignored: the need to recognize and somehow accommodate the organizational complexity of schools.

RECOMMENDATIONS

This chapter has focused on the organization of governance, curriculum, assessment and evaluation, students, time, staff and instruction, considering how each might be altered to implement Project 2061's vision of science teaching and learning. Historical analysis alerts us to the need to simplify complexity in organizational life. This need has led to amazingly stable structures in schools—structures to which schools generally revert in the face of the increased complexity that reform efforts create. This does not mean that change in school organization is impossible, rather that reformers must move incrementally and acknowledge the need for simplification and resistance to change.

As reform progresses, recommendations for change will be developed. Among potential recommendations to support the vision of science education reform in the organization of science and mathematics education, in this chapter we have identified these:

ORGANIZATION OF GOVERNANCE
■ Rely on informal approaches that use democratic models of leadership and shared decision making.

■ Make use of cultural mechanisms that provide direction, yet allow for discretion in how details develop.

Organization of Curriculum

■ Materials (e.g., state frameworks, texts) must strike a balance between direction and discretion. Technological solutions to curriculum organization may support this balance, although textbooks that consider this need may be sufficient.

Organization of Assessment and Evaluation

■ Use performance-based assessments to better accommodate the vision of science literacy.

■ Understand that observation is a key component of assessing students' abilities to think critically and spontaneously.

Organization of Students

■ Use of multi-age grouping can lead to significant changes and deserves serious consideration; however, the age range for any individual teacher should be limited.

■ Have a teacher or team of teachers work with the same students for more than one year to foster long-term understanding and literacy.

Organization of Time

■ Allot a block of time periods and space to a group of teachers and students, providing flexibility to implement curriculum integration and student-centered learning.

Organization of Staff

■ Support team teaching by providing a large block of time once a week for planning.

■ Provide staff development focused on productive use of planning time, team building, and conflict resolution necessary for creating informal "learning organizations."

Organization of Space

■ Make the science-mathematics-technology laboratory the center of the school, focusing student learning activity there, much as current media centers do.

■ Combine laboratory space for biology, chemistry, earth science, and physics to emphasize connections across subjects.

■ Combine mathematics and science classrooms to encourage connections among them. Alternatively, intersperse science and mathematics classrooms throughout the building for more extensive connections to other disciplines.

■ Send students into the community or bring the community into classrooms, realizing that approaches need to be developed to reduce the inevitable complexity of doing so.

As noted previously, change naturally disrupts organizational stability and thereby adds a degree of unpredictability to the already complicated process of schooling. We must therefore move cautiously, avoid change for change's sake, and be sensitive to the need to simplify complexity. But change in school organization is possible—indeed it is necessary if the goals of science education reform are to be achieved.

REFERENCES

American Association for the Advancement of Science. (1993). *Benchmarks for science literacy*. New York: Oxford University Press.

American Association for the Advancement of Science. (1989). *Science for all Americans*. New York: Oxford University Press.

Argyris, C., & Schon, D. (1975). *Theory into practice: Increasing professional effectiveness*. San Francisco: Jossey-Bass.

Cuban, L. (1995). The hidden variable: How organizations influence teacher responses to secondary science curriculum reform. *Theory Into Practice, 34*(1), 4–11.

David, J. (1989). Synthesis of research on school-based management. *Educational Leadership, 46*(8), 45–53.

National Research Council. (1996). *National science education standards*. Washington, D.C.: National Academy of Sciences.

BIBLIOGRAPHY

American Association for the Advancement of Science. (1993). *Benchmarks for science literacy*. New York: Oxford University Press.

American Association for the Advancement of Science. (1990). *Science for all Americans*. New York: Oxford University Press.

Apple, M. W. & Beane, J. A. (1995). *Democratic schools*. Alexandria, VA: Association for Supervision and Curriculum Development.

Arcaro, J. S. (1995). *Teams in education: Creating an integrated approach*. Beach, FL: St. Lucie Press.

Argyris, C. and Schon, D. (1975). *Theory into practice: Increasing professional effectiveness*. San Francisco, CA: Jossey-Bass.

Baratta-Lorton, M. (1976). *Mathematics their way.* Menlo Park, CA: Addison-Wesley.

Belenky, M., et. al. (1986). *Women's ways of knowing.* New York: Basic Books.

Black, P. (1993). *Preference assessment and accountability: The experience in England and Wales.* Paper presented at the annual meeting of the American Educational Research Association, Atlanta, GA.

Blase, J. & Blase, J. R. (1994). *Empowering teachers: What successful principals do.* Thousand Oaks, CA: Corwin Press, Inc.

Borman, K. M. & Greenman, N. P. (1994). *Recapturing the past or inventing the future?* Albany, NY: State University of New York Press.

Brown, D. (1990). *Decentralization and school-based management.* New York: Falmer Press.

Carnegie Forum on Education and the Economy. (1986). *A nation prepared: Teachers for the 21st century.* New York: Carnegie Forum.

Carnoy, M. & MacDonnell, J. (1989). *School district restructuring in Santa Fe, New Mexico.* New Brunswick, NJ: Consortium for Policy Research in Education.

Castle, D. K. & Estes, N. (1995). *High-performance learning communities.* Thousand Oaks, CA: Corwin Press, Inc.

Clark, S. & Clark, D. (1987). Interdisciplinary teaming programs, organization, rationale, and implementation. In *Schools in the middle: A report on trends and practices.* Reston, VA: National Association for Secondary School Principals.

Clune, W.H. & White, P.A. (1988). *School-based management: Institutional variation implementation, and issues for further research.* New Brunswick, NJ: Rutgers University, Center for Policy Research in Education. (ERIC Document Reproduction No. ED 300 908).

Conley, S. & Bacharach, S. (1990). From school-site management to participatory school-site management. *Phi Delta Kappan, 71*(7), 539-544.

Conley, S. (1991). Review of research on teacher participation in school decision making. *Review of Research in Education, 17,* 225-266.

Cuban, L. (1995). The hidden variable: How organizations influence teacher responses to secondary science curriculum reform. *Theory Into Practice, 34*(1), 4-11.

Cuban, L. (1992). *The hidden variable: How organizations influence teacher responses to science curriculum reform, 1900-1990.* Background paper for *school organization blueprint.* Columbus, OH: The National Center for Science Teaching and Learning.

Cuban, L. (1989). At-risk students: What teachers and principals can do. *Educational Leadership, 46* (5), 29-32.

Dade County Public Schools. (1988). *School-based management: Shared decision making.* Miami, FL: Author.

David, J., with Purkey, S. & White, P. (1988, September). *Restructuring in progress: Lessons from pioneering districts.* Paper presented at the Annual Meeting of the National Governors' Association, Washington, D.C.

David, J. (1989). Synthesis of research on school-based management. *Educational Leadership, 46*(8), 45-53.

Donmoyer, R. and Kos, R. (1993). At-risk students: Insights from/about research. In R. Donmoyer and R. Kos (Eds.), *At-risk students: Portraits, policies, programs, and practices.* Albany, NY: State University of New York Press.

Donmoyer, R. (1995). The rhetoric and reality of systemic reform: A critique of the proposed national science education standards. *Theory Into Practice, 34*(1), 30-34.

Fairfax County Public Schools. (1986). *School-based management: A process for school improvement.* Falls Church, VA: Author.

Fullan, M. G. (1991). *The new meaning of educational change.* New York: Teachers College Press.

Kulik, P. (1991). *The interdisciplinary team in a nationally recognized middle school setting.* Unpublished doctoral dissertation, Ohio State University.

Maeroff, G. (1990). Getting to know a good middle school: Shoreham Wading River. *Phi Delta Kappan, 71* (7), 505-511.

Mager, R. (1984). *Preparing instructional objectives.* Belmont, CA: Pitman Management and Training.

Malen, B., & Ogawa, R.T. (1988). Professional patron influence on site-based governance councils: A confronting case study. *Educational Evaluation and Policy Analysis, 10*(4), 251-270.

Meyer, J. and Rowan, B. (1977). Institutionalized organizations: Formal structure as myth and ceremony. *American Journal of Sociology, 83,* 340-363.

Page, R. (1995). Who systematizes the systematizers? Policy and practice interactions in a case of state-level systemic reform. *Theory Into Practice, 34*(1), 21-29.

Popham, J. (1987). The merits of measurement-driven instruction. *Phi Delta Kappan, 68*(9), 679-682.

Shakeshaft, C. (1993). *Gender issues, school organization, and Project 2061.* Background paper for *School organization blueprint.* Columbus, OH: The National Center for Science Teaching and Learning.

Sharer, P. and Zajano, N. (1993). Direction with discretion: Reading recovery as an example of balancing top-down and bottom-up decision making. In R. Donmoyer and R. Kos. (Eds.). *At-risk students: Portraits, policies, programs and practices.* Albany, NY: State University of New York Press.

Sickler, J.L. (1988). Teachers in charge: Empowering the professionals. *Phi Delta Kappan, 69,* 354-358.

Slavin, R. & Madden, N. (1990). What works for students at risk: Research synthesis. *Educational Leadership, 47,* 4-13.

Smith, M. & O'Day, J. (1991). Systemic school reform. In S. Furhman & B. Malen (Eds.), *The politics of curriculum and testing: The 1990 yearbook of the Politics of Education Association* (pp. 233-267). Bristol, PA: Falmer Press

Villa, R. A. & Thousand, J. S. (1995). *Creating an inclusive school.* Alexandria, VA: Association for Supervision and Curriculum Development.

Wagstaff, J.C. (1995). Site-based management, shared decision making, and science and mathematics education: A tale of two districts. *Theory Into Practice, 34*(1), 66-73.

Weiss, C., Cambone, J. & Wyeth, A. (1992). Trouble in paradise: Teacher conflicts in shared decision making. *Educational Administration Quarterly, 28*(3), 350-367.

6

Curriculum Connections

THIS CHAPTER SEEKS TO ILLUSTRATE how standard K-12 curricula in the United States can foster the science learning called for in *Science for All Americans* (American Association for the Advancement of Science [AAAS], 1989). By recommending increased emphasis on connections between science and other disciplines—naturally occurring connections in the physical and biological world studied by scientists that traditional science curricula rarely emphasize—we suggest that educators can encourage students not only to know scientific facts but also to view the world scientifically.

This chapter provides rationale for connecting what students learn in school through interdisciplinary links, real-world connections, and connections to the world of work. We present five case studies of attempts to explore and define curriculum connections in those contexts and identify some principles that contribute to a well-coordinated curriculum consistent with the goals of Project 2061 and other science education reform efforts. This chapter does not offer teachers specific guidelines for implementing interdisciplinary curricula—our intention is to inspire rather than to prescribe the development of curriculum connections. Changing aspects of the school structure, such as the use of time and space in schools, as described in *Blueprints'* Chapter 5: School Organization, can help teachers to act on this inspiration.

THE CURRENT STATUS

Each day, children of all ages apply scientific principles or engage in scientific activities as part of their normal routine. An interest in the local baseball team leads thousands of youngsters to compute batting averages or to understand why the famous Chicago winds favor hitters at Wrigley Park one day and pitchers the next. A child who loves dancing gains new understandings of human biology and physiology and uses those understandings to develop an intuitive framework for understanding the physical world.

Unfortunately, these activities and interests are cultivated too infrequently in schools. Lessons or units have specified starting and ending times so students can move on to something else. In addition, the lessons and units are almost always presented in tidy packages in subjects such as Chemistry, Art, or History. Students are rarely asked to apply what they have learned to solve problems that they design or that are relevant to their lives. While *Science for All Americans* acknowledges the importance of disciplines for their ability to provide a conceptual structure for organizing research, it also recognizes that the divisions between disciplines do not necessarily match the way the world works and can skew learning and limit understanding.

As technology and the continuing communications revolution make our world ever smaller and more complex, individuals will increasingly need to synthesize multiple strands of information to make informed decisions about their lives and their communities. Because these strands of information will not come equipped with tidy labels of Chemistry, Art, or History, people will need to connect what they know to new information to construct new knowledge and craft better solutions. Individuals who succeed in making those connections and in understanding some of the ways in which mathematics, technology, and the sciences depend on each other will have achieved one facet of what *Science for All Americans* defines as science literacy.

> *Some important themes pervade science, mathematics, and technology and appear over and over again, whether we are looking at an ancient civilization, the human body, or a comet. They are ideas that transcend disciplinary boundaries and prove fruitful in explanation, in theory, in observation, and in design."* —SCIENCE FOR ALL AMERICANS

WEAVING CONNECTIONS

Fortunately for science education reformers, curriculum connections is an idea whose time has come. Available literature on the subject grows daily, and conferences publicizing interdisciplinary curriculum models attract significant numbers of participants. Nonetheless, even in schools that appear to be at the forefront of establishing interdisciplinary connections, the gulf between the humanities and the sciences often seems impassable. For example, the humanities and sciences are still taught in separate blocks in many schools that belong to the Coalition

of Essential Schools, a nationwide reform movement that stresses curriculum connections (Sizer, 1989).
Educators should work to bridge this chasm for two main reasons. First, to be science literate, citizens must be able to draw on knowledge inside and outside the fields of science and mathematics. Second, and on

Understandability of the World

This strand map shows an array of benchmarks that deal with the understandability of the world. Students in the grade levels indicated could be expected to understand these ideas.

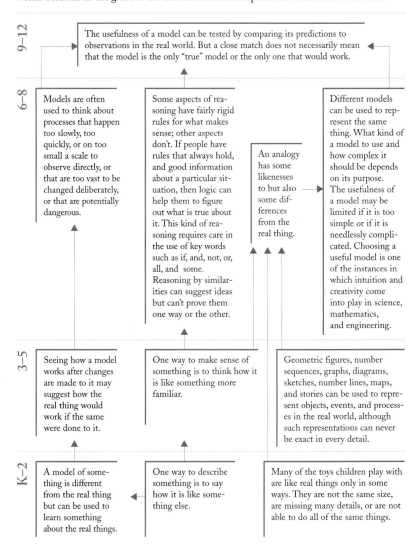

9–12
The usefulness of a model can be tested by comparing its predictions to observations in the real world. But a close match does not necessarily mean that the model is the only "true" model or the only one that would work.

6–8
Models are often used to think about processes that happen too slowly, too quickly, or on too small a scale to observe directly, or that are too vast to be changed deliberately, or that are potentially dangerous.

Some aspects of reasoning have fairly rigid rules for what makes sense; other aspects don't. If people have rules that always hold, and good information about a particular situation, then logic can help them to figure out what is true about it. This kind of reasoning requires care in the use of key words such as if, and, not, or, all, and some. Reasoning by similarities can suggest ideas but can't prove them one way or the other.

An analogy has some likenesses to but also some differences from the real thing.

Different models can be used to represent the same thing. What kind of a model to use and how complex it should be depends on its purpose. The usefulness of a model may be limited if it is too simple or if it is needlessly complicated. Choosing a useful model is one of the instances in which intuition and creativity come into play in science, mathematics, and engineering.

3–5
Seeing how a model works after changes are made to it may suggest how the real thing would work if the same were done to it.

One way to make sense of something is to think how it is like something more familiar.

Geometric figures, number sequences, graphs, diagrams, sketches, number lines, maps, and stories can be used to represent objects, events, and processes in the real world, although such representations can never be exact in every detail.

K–2
A model of something is different from the real thing but can be used to learn something about the real things.

One way to describe something is to say how it is like something else.

Many of the toys children play with are like real things only in some ways. They are not the same size, are missing many details, or are not able to do all of the same things.

a far more pragmatic level, as American students are called on to master an ever-expanding body of knowledge, using junctures across the curriculum will eliminate needless redundancies and enable teachers to use time more efficiently.

Interdisciplinary links are the most obvious way to approach curriculum connections. Whether by examining the mathematical structures of music or studying carbon dating while learning about Mayan culture, interdisciplinary connections make scientific principles tangible to a wide variety of students. Teachers can use them to streamline lesson planning and reinforce the content learned in several subjects at once. Learning in multiple and meaningful contexts enhances students' abilities to build knowledge and understanding of science and its relationship to other disciplines.

Providing a link to the student's own world through contextual learning can be a powerful motivating factor.

Linking science education to the real world offers another approach to curriculum connections. Providing a link to the student's own world through contextual learning can be a powerful motivating factor. *Blueprints'* Chapter 11: Family and Community addresses this issue. It encourages schools and parent organizations to help families recognize that they can make science education more relevant for students by nurturing their children's natural curiosity, posing questions, asking children to create hypotheses, and helping children recognize that science is an important part of their everyday lives. Doing science every day is one way of learning science, and young people should be encouraged to discover science in their homes, their backyards, and their communities.

Once students understand how science impacts their everyday lives, it becomes easier for them to see connections between science education and the world of work. Strengthening these connections is particularly valuable to those students who are oriented more toward the working world than to the academic world. This importance has been confirmed in reports such as the Secretary's Commission on Achieving Necessary Skills (SCANS) (U.S. Department of Labor, 1991), which suggests that many students are unable to find and hold good jobs because they are unable to apply what they learn in school to the world of work. Some scientists and other professionals graduate from higher education without knowing how scientific knowledge, concepts, and methods are applied to problem solving in larger systems—natural systems or design and production systems—that are addressed in the working world. The SCANS report calls for changes in our education system that will make learning more concrete and require that students be competent in problem solving, reasoning, and communication, which will ease their transition from school to work.

NEEDED CHANGES

Restructuring science curricula is an ambitious goal. It is unlikely that interdisciplinary approaches can simply be grafted onto existing curricula, most of which are noteworthy for their fragmentation. Project 2061, for example, calls for a complete rethinking of how we teach science in the United States. At the school site, this might result in blocking time for a fully integrated program, realigning a conventionally structured curriculum to highlight connections between disciplines, or any of the myriad alternatives that combine elements of both approaches. Many schools are already launching curricular revolutions to undertake this ambitious task. The next section describes alternatives developed at five of those special places

The following examples provide specific ideas for making the necessary changes to establish connected curricula. These projects are prototypes of the kinds of curriculum connections that address benchmarks and standards. They illustrate that all players—not just science educators—must be involved in planning and implementing reform, and they show that reform needs time to develop in order to address how children learn as well as what they learn.

INTERDISCIPLINARY CONNECTIONS: To Build a Kayak
Project 2061's San Francisco School-District Center works with six district schools to develop and implement K-12 curriculum models that achieve the learning objectives outlined in *Science for All Americans.* Although these educators work within the confines of the existing educational system, their emphasis on Project 2061's goals allows them to introduce some non-traditional activities into the curriculum. For example, several of the schools work with curricular models for interdisciplinary learning. Interdisciplinary units are often organized not around central themes but around imagination, curiosity and skepticism, or "challenges" to a belief or action. A tangible product, usually a project or presentation, is required as evidence that students have met each challenge.

While this type of activity may sound abstract to the layperson or to teachers who have seen more than their share of impractical educational theory, the San Francisco team has enjoyed several successes using these curricular models. One successful challenge involved nine teams of three middle school students who were charged with building a kayak in three weeks. The kayak—to be constructed with only plastic tape and cardboard—had to be sufficiently sound to carry a student on water. The need for students to integrate a variety of mathematical and scientific knowledge and skills to meet this challenge is obvious—it required familiarity with mass, volume, density, buoyancy, flotation, and water displacement, and it required students to engage in scientific inquiry to measure; compute areas, volumes, and ratios; and use their understanding of scale to construct a model.

Although many educators may have been satisfied with this meaningful integration of various science disciplines and mathematics, the San Francisco team saw a history in the kayak that connected it to many other disciplines. During the three-week unit, students studied the history of the kayak, examined the culture of the Aleutians and Inuits— decorating their boats with Inuit art—and learned the geographic relationship of the Bering Strait to the Arctic Ocean. They studied relations between the Aleutians and the Russians, reviewed the region's place in the Cold War, and discovered where their small experiment in boat building fit in the technological history of boats and transportation. When the students launched their boats for a 100-yard race at the end of the challenge, they were evaluated on team cooperation, boat design, and aesthetics; their understanding of the key science and mathematics concepts embedded in the experience; and, most importantly, the ability of the boat to float (all nine boats floated, with one clear winner).

This challenge addressed several benchmarks, including understanding the relationship between technology and design, knowing physical laws related to mass, and applying mathematics. In addition, designing and building the boats gave students the means to develop their ability to question, hypothesize, and solve problems—skills that *Science for All Americans* defines as key to science literacy.

REAL WORLD CONNECTIONS: TAKING AN URBAN SAFARI
The UCLA Science Project gives K-8 teachers in the Los Angeles County School District the opportunity to practice new strategies of science teaching during intensive two-week summer institutes. One of these institutes leads teachers on a safari in the urban landscape of Los

Angeles. The dual purpose of the urban safari is to overcome the lack of confidence that many teachers—especially elementary teachers—have in their ability to teach science and to challenge the misconception that science is an arcane discipline whose activities take place in a laboratory or other remote site.

Using only inexpensive and makeshift items such as empty tape cassette boxes (which, when dabbed with crumbs and sugar, were perfect for catching bugs), groups of teachers were sent to explore a vacant lot, a maintained yard, a parking lot, and a construction site. The groups were given questions to help guide their searches, such as, How do some plants adapt to growing through sidewalk cracks? How did the seeds get there? Is the animal life there self-supporting or supported by human intrusions such as garbage or gardens? Gathering air temperature and humidity data over concrete, grass, and puddles expanded teachers' experiences.

The participants' investigations were guided by the loose charge to pull together aspects of their study to illustrate one of the five themes in the California Science Framework: energy, evolution, patterns of change, scale and structure, and systems and interactions. Given this charge, the teachers saw the unlimited possibilities for investigation and realized that they could undertake the activity at various levels of depth and sophistication. They discussed replicating the exercise in their own communities, with many teachers noting that they could extend the experience by having students observe changes in one small site over the course of the school year.

The urban safari not only helps teachers overcome some of their fears about teaching science, it also offers them strategies for connecting science meaningfully to the world in which their students live. This exercise serves a wide range of objectives outlined in *Science for All Americans, Benchmarks for Science Literacy* (AAAS, 1993), and the *National Science Education Standards* (*Standards*) (National Research Council, 1996): understanding the physical setting (weather, erosion, water and rock cycles, and structure of matter) and the living environment (diversity of life, cells, food

Benchmarks for Science Literacy
Chapter 12: Habits of Mind
A. Values and Attitudes
B. Computation and Estimation
C. Manipulation and Observation
D. Communication Skills
E. Critical-Response Skills

Science for All Americans
"Taken together, these values, attitudes, and skills can be thought of as habits of mind because they all relate directly to a person's outlook on knowledge and learning and ways of thinking and acting."

cycles) and encouraging students to develop desirable habits of mind. This strategy, when combined with knowledge of the local environment and clearly-defined goals for a student-conducted safari, can be a powerful means for teaching science in the elementary grades.

CONNECTIONS TO THE WORKPLACE: CREATING A FUNCTIONAL ELITE

The humanities and fine arts curricula are strong at the Thomas Jefferson High School for Science and Technology. Design, writing, and performance are emphasized at this exclusive magnet school for the mathematics and science whizzes of northern Virginia. Graduating seniors are required to produce an intensive research project, often conducting their research under the guidance of industrial mentors in government and private laboratories.

Jefferson's curriculum is organized into a labyrinth of interdisciplinary blocks that produce such unconventional classes as a three-hour block called "Biology, English, and Introduction to Technology." The decision to integrate the core classes arose in part from a desire to replicate problem solving in a work setting. Along these lines, technology is considered a tool to be used for learning rather than the object of study itself and so is combined with other core classes (Barth, 1993).

Jefferson's innovative academic program has evolved in partnership with business and industry. The support of these partners is evident in both curriculum and facilities, including funding for the school's eleven technology labs. In the mentorship program, seniors interact with professionals from the scientific, engineering, technological, and industrial communities during their independent research project. Mentorships sponsored by Atlantic Research Corporation have assisted such student projects as "The Fabrication of a Gyro Utilizing Fiber Optic Technology," while BDM and Martin Marietta Gould have helped Jefferson seniors solve problems related to automation and robotic systems. Jefferson students are consistently recruited by top universities in science and engineering, and corporate interests view their participation as an investment paying off in future employees. Private funding and employee mentorships continue to flow to Jefferson as its graduates become known as the future work-force elite.

The success of Jefferson High School is due in large part to the curricular innovations that break down interdisciplinary barriers; the view that all academic work—the arts, humanities, and sciences—can be applied; and the direct involvement of field practitioners in providing educational services. The careful admissions screening process also contributes to the school's success. The exclusive nature of Jefferson's students has cast some doubt on the replicability of the program. While principal Geoffrey Jones admits that the quality of his students affords him a luxury of flexibility that many principals do not have, he believes that Jefferson's interdisciplinary approach and block scheduling could be used by all high schools. In addition, he insists that learning for students with lower achievement records as well as for Jefferson's self-starters should be driven by students' questions and their attempts to answer them. It is the same theory around which Henry Levin's Accelerated Schools (Levin, 1987) have had success at improving the learning of students labeled "at-risk."

The approach at Jefferson clearly matches the goals of Project 2061, which stresses the connections between disciplines as seemingly disparate as biology and English. While Jefferson's exclusivity allows its science curriculum to exceed the guidelines for science literacy outlined in *Science for All Americans*, the curricular structure of its program, the emphasis on student-generated problems, and the mentorships could be adopted by schools seeking to implement new frameworks for science, mathematics, and technology. In addition, if schools can convince businesses that their aims should be to make all schools like Jefferson (or at least to encourage all schools to aspire to that goal), they would be well on their way to gaining crucial political and, perhaps, financial support.

CONNECTING THE DISCONNECTED

In stark contrast to Jefferson stands Middle College High School, on the campus of LaGuardia Community College in Queens, New York. For eighteen years Middle College High has opened its doors to students identified by their junior high counselors as chronic underachievers or as having emotional or behavioral problems. Principal Cecilia Cullen explains that the key to keeping these students in school is to pique their interest quickly, and she has turned to nontraditional methods to do so.

Middle College was initially established as a New York City "alternative school." Six years ago it joined Ted Sizer's Coalition of Essential Schools (CES), a reform endeavor that often stresses, in addition to student-centered learning, a schedule that blocks time for interdisciplinary courses. While many CES schools offer one block of interdisciplinary classes in the sciences and another in the humanities, Middle College High is leading the move towards linking the two.

One of Middle College's most successful attempts at forming these linkages is a 13-week unit called "The Motion Program," in which seniors explore the concept of motion through the study of literature, mathematics, physics, and physical education. The physical education component of the program, Project Adventure, calls for such activities as the "Spider's Web," where an entire group of students moves through a giant nylon web without touching the web material. The school principal credits Project Adventure with a large share of the school's success in reaching its students and with developing their problem-solving capabilities.

The literature strand of the unit examines the ideas of motion, movement, and change through fiction, nonfiction, and poetry. In addition to their reading assignments, students are asked to write a play scene applying Newton's laws to the interaction of people. Physics and mathematics are combined and team-taught, emphasizing collaborative experimentation that leads students to a fundamental understanding of motion, especially of phenomena that may seem counterintuitive to them.

Career education is the central and integrative experience at Middle College High. The Avon Corporation and local hospitals are the stalwarts of a long-running internship program in which more than 350 public and private sector organizations participate. All students are required to take three internships over the course of a four-year career. While teachers admit that the quality of internships varies—interns may be animal behavior lab assistants at a museum or they might be performing clerical tasks in the mailroom—all emphasize the overall success of integrating internship with school activities.

The average combined SAT scores of Middle High graduates have risen by 200 points since the school joined the Coalition of Essential Schools. In addition, about 85% of Middle High students—once targeted as likely drop-outs—graduate from high school. Almost 80% of graduates attend two- or four-year colleges. Internship sponsors provide positive feedback and many organizations participate in the program year after year.

The school principal noted that many Middle College teachers initially resisted developing interdisciplinary curricula or cooperating with their colleagues. Only a handful of teachers are still resistant, but science education reformers should acknowledge the potential for difficulties when implementing an integrated curriculum.

Middle College High is undoubtedly a work in progress. The school recently launched a process to articulate academic goals for its students that will serve as the framework for further design and assessment.

Adding formal learning goals will clarify the purpose of the interdisciplinary units at Middle College and ensure that student learning is foremost. In addition, it may define expectations for the uneven internship program, especially if outcomes are linked to better means of assessing student performance off campus. It is noteworthy that *Benchmarks* would fit neatly within Middle College's structure; its well-defined learning goals could bring needed coherence to a program that has already accomplished much.

CONNECTIONS ALL AROUND:
FIRST...YOU GET A CABOOSE

Located directly across the Susquehanna River from Harrisburg, Pennsylvania, the Susquenita Public School District serves just 2,500 students with one high school, one middle school, and one elementary school. Superintendent Steven Messner and colleague Thomas Campbell were early converts to the cultural literacy movement, believing that public school may be their students' only exposure to art and literature. Their first step was to introduce famous paintings into the entire school curriculum. When told by a science department chair that there was no art in science, Campbell produced a *National Geographic* article about the painstaking and often scientific process of renovating paintings in the Sistine Chapel. Soon, Susquenita students were learning about art with their chemistry.

The real breakthrough in integrating the district's curriculum occurred when the schools restored a railroad caboose. The caboose was to be a standing testimonial to this railroad community's history, serve as a working science and technology lab for students to gain tangible experience with the abstractions they learn in the classroom, and provide regional artists and storytellers with a means to keep local culture alive.

Most of the preliminary work involved coordinating the caboose's move from the railyard to an interim home near the high school. With Conrail (the caboose's donor), the city, and volunteer crews, high-school students planned the move while the rest of the student body researched railway technology, probed the local rail culture, researched drawings to prepare for renovations, and even cannibalized rail yards for authentic parts. The senior class documented the move to demonstrate the mathematical and scientific concepts applied in this task alone.

Messner and Campbell wanted a section of the track where the caboose would ultimately rest to curve. The geometry teacher assigned the problem to her students, who gave the work crew the arc for the rail on the day the track was to be laid. On examining the plans, the crew offered the class the opportunity to stake out the curve according to the design they had made. When they ran into difficulty, the class received an impromptu geometry and history lesson as the carpenter staked out a center arc and made parallel lines with string.

Although secondary students were the most active in the plans and negotiations, the younger students got involved by learning about trains and train culture. First-graders were not merely told how trains run on rails, but were given wooden block models with which they could design a plan to keep their own "train" on its "tracks." They tried to pull wooden blocks along lengths of 2x4s without having them fall off. For weeks, Campbell had children in the lower grades greet each other with a secret handshake: interlock cupped fingers and pull. Children were thrilled to find when they visited the caboose that their secret hand-shake mimicked the way rail cars fit together.

Although Susquenita's endeavor may seem haphazard, the spontaneity of the activity made the schools exciting places where students were encouraged to explore, follow connections on their own, and develop their own solutions to problems. And the caboose theme provided for-tuitous links to technology, cultural literacy, and scientific and mathe-matical principles. While Messner and Campbell cannot point to a traditional measure of the project such as test scores, they do indicate that the number of students pursuing postsecondary education has increased during their tenure. Also, students and the community have surely benefited from so much effort and hard work. Sometimes what has value cannot be easily measured.

MAKING CONNECTIONS

The examples in the previous section are initial attempts, works in progress. They do not necessarily define what we believe are comprehen-sive models for integrated curriculum. And although they were not all designed to meet the learning goals of *Benchmarks* and *Standards*, they do represent important first steps toward the type of learning and teach-ing that is advocated by Project 2061. Other examples of this kind of work, including full curriculum projects, are becoming available (see the May 1996 issue of *Educational Leadership* for descriptions of some of these curricula). Each of the case studies and other exemplars of inter-disciplinary curricula has unique characteristics. It is possible, however, to draw from them some general principles about connecting curricula:

■ *The most effective curriculum connections are designed at the school by people directly involved with the school.*
Stamped-out curricula tied to written-to-formula textbooks have served teachers and students notoriously poorly in the past. Even if we disregard the growing sentiment that teachers and administrators must be given the freedom to design instruction relevant to their students, the resistance of many teachers to top-down mandates implies that those implementing science education reform must drive its local design and application. This is not necessarily to say that all the designers must be educators; Jefferson High, Middle College High and the Susquenita district all effectively involve community representatives. Projects such as those, however, must ultimately be created through the collective effort of the school staff.

■ *Curriculum connections need a focus.*
Whether it's a theme, a San Francisco-style challenge, something physical like the caboose, or a particular object, each interdisciplinary unit needs to have obvious and tangible connections for students to build from the concrete to the abstract. Teachers also report that having a focus eases their task of developing connections to other subjects.

■ *Curriculum connections should not be forced.*
Connections should not be sought for the sole purpose of developing an interdisciplinary unit. Individual science disciplines did not develop out of a perverse desire to make school tedious and disconnected. Each discipline has unique features that sometimes dictate the necessity for discrete instruction. Scientific inquiry differs from historical inquiry, for example, and students should learn both. Understanding that mathematics in the abstract has a beauty of its own is as important as understanding that mathematics has important real-world applications. There is no magical formula for finding the balance between discrete instruction in subjects and integrating them. Teachers who understand both the content and students' needs will be able to strike the appropriate balance for each situation.

■ *Connections should be linked to something worth knowing.*
While there might be great debate even among teachers in the same school about what is "worth knowing," benchmarks and standards will provide specific learning goals on which to base curriculum connections. As states and districts move to adopt content standards and develop

their own frameworks, science educators should move to ensure that those frameworks reflect the content that is most central to achieving science literacy.

NEXT STEPS

Developing interdisciplinary curricula is one of the most daunting tasks teachers face in the current wave of reform. In many cases, however, it is taking place almost by default. Teachers indicate that the standards developed by the National Council of Teachers of Mathematics (1989), which are consistent with the mathematics content of *Benchmarks*, have influenced them to teach in ways they never before imagined, such as having children use mathematics to solve problems in social studies and science. These reports come primarily from elementary and middle school teachers, many of whom are still guided by state-mandated curricula and textbooks and prescribed time allotments. Even so, elementary schools offer the advantage of classrooms that are managed primarily by one teacher. Therefore, they still offer the easiest environment in which to develop curriculum connections. Science education reformers should work to support state policies that encourage these endeavors at all levels.

Though team teaching and the interdisciplinary approach in middle schools are experiencing the growing pains typical of any change in methodology, an increasing number of middle schools seem to be moving in that direction. Secondary teachers are generally the most resistant to developing curriculum connections. Because high schools are organized along fairly rigid disciplinary lines, secondary teachers have more invested in their disciplines than other K-12 teachers. Teachers at Middle College High were resistant to the idea of interdisciplinary teaching at first, but the insistence and nurturing of the principal moved them toward it. Many now report a boost in their sense of professionalism and a more valuable experience for their students. Still, the effort to attain the literacy called for in *Science for All Americans* will be hampered until more schools realize the necessity of building connections into the school curriculum.

WARNING FLAGS FOR CURRICULUM CONNECTIONS
The resistance of a school administrator, especially a principal, can doom most school-site reforms, and science education reform is no different. In addition, teachers themselves can impede change. For

instance, during the interviews for this chapter, many stories were related of algebra teachers who would not sit down with physics teachers and earth science teachers who would not talk to biology teachers. Trying to cross disciplinary lines between the sciences and the humanities proves even more difficult, and sometimes impossible.

Many teachers already have the knowledge and ability to think and plan connections, but they need the opportunity, the time, and the sometimes some not-so-gentle nudging to get them to try. In general, a few enthusiastic visionaries lead the charge to integrate curricula. To those who might see themselves as the potential visionaries in their school but feel overwhelmed by their task, this chapter offers one simple piece of advice: start small and start smart. Rather than tackling the whole curriculum, start with well-planned connections for two or three subjects.

EXTERNAL INFLUENCES

Ostensibly, schools are locally controlled in the United States. But districts and states exert great control over schooling through mandated tests, required courses, or disbursement of earmarked funds. All of these factors can influence science education reform. As mentioned previously, however, many states are beginning to adopt agreed-on standards to provide schools with the foundation to design curriculum suited to the needs of their students. Science education reformers should support these efforts in every way possible.

As science educators prepare their standards, goals, and objectives for public display, they must be aware that interdisciplinary connections can be a hard sell. Many parents have been vocal critics of the concept, uncomfortable that their children may not be learning algebra if they are not enrolled in a class called Algebra. Educated parents have sometimes balked as their children's schools move toward an interdisciplinary framework because they worry that colleges will not accept transcripts that lack references to traditional disciplines.

Educators wishing to institute an interdisciplinary curriculum must above all communicate openly and effectively about the proposed change. In public education especially, working in secret is usually a recipe for failure. At some early point and in some capacity, the public must be involved. An excellent method for accomplishing this is to show parents something tangible. For example, the San Francisco team recruited parent volunteers for the kayak race and later displayed the winning kayak before the Board of Education. These efforts were key in securing public and political support for the team's approach.

RECOMMENDATIONS

An integrated view of science literacy that encompasses natural and social sciences, mathematics, and technology requires connections with areas not traditionally thought of as relevant to the sciences. A curriculum that meets those needs cannot simply be substituted for an existing science or mathematics program; connections have to be made throughout the curriculum. We close with some overall recommendations that are critical if curriculum connections are to be widely adopted.

■ *Public outreach.* *Science for All Americans* and *National Science Education Standards* need to become household words. The public, especially educators and parents, needs to understand and demand that their schools adopt the goals put forth in these documents. As described in *Blueprints'* Chapter 11: Family and Community, the public does not readily embrace educational change, no matter how deep the concern about the current quality of education. Therefore, a widespread informational campaign should be undertaken.

■ *Resources and materials.* The availability of high-quality materials can be a great catalyst for change, and their absence a great inhibitor of change. For example, a current lack of materials for environmental education courses has forced many teachers to rely on resources developed either by advocacy groups or the energy industry, both of which have opposite, but clear, agendas to promote. Careful and comprehensive analyses of books, software, and other resources that describe accurately how well they represent benchmarks and standards would help assure quality and validity of materials.

■ *Research dissemination.* To design effective curriculum, teachers need access to new findings about the cognitive development of children. It is important to know, for example, at what stage children begin to understand the concept of scale, or what ideas seem counterintuitive and how teachers can get students to understand them. While the benchmarks are written to accommodate many of these issues, it is important for teachers to have continual access to research on teaching and learning so that they may consider it in designing curriculum.

■ *Professional development.* Making interdisciplinary connections will require that science and mathematics teachers have a deep understanding of their subjects and how those subjects relate to the external world. Clearly, a rethinking of how teachers are taught is in order, especially developing opportunities for them to learn and teach science through interdisciplinary courses and activities. Stronger links among colleges of science, humanities, and education will be needed in planning teacher education programs, as discussed in *Blueprints'* Chapter 9: Teacher Education and Chapter 10: Higher Education.

Unlike the rest of the world, American schools have never embraced interdisciplinary approaches to learning. Some of the reasons, as pointed out in *Blueprints'* Chapter 5: School Organization, are historical, having to do with the way our schools have long been organized. But in order to achieve science literacy, as well as to prepare students who will work in an increasingly interdisciplinary world, it is time for a change that many educators have already recognized. A great deal of work remains for connections in the curriculum to become a normal and commonplace part of science education. The ideas in *Science for All Americans*, along with the examples, principles, and recommendations in this chapter, provide a good place to start.

REFERENCES

American Association for the Advancement of Science. (1993). *Benchmarks for science literacy*. New York: Oxford University Press.

American Association for the Advancement of Science. (1989). *Science for all Americans*. New York: Oxford University Press.

Barth, P. (1993, January). To make a good scientist. *Basic Education*, 1–4.

Levin, H. (1987, March). Accelerated schools for disadvantaged students. *Educational Leadership, 44*(6), 19–21.

National Research Council. (1996). *National science education standards*. Washington, D.C.: National Academy Press.

National Council of Teachers of Mathematics. (1989). *Curriculum and evaluation standards for school mathematics*. Reston, VA: Author.

Sizer, T. (1989). Diverse practice, shared ideas: The essential school. In H. Walberg & R. Lane (Eds.), *Organizing for learning: Toward the 21st century*. Reston, VA: National Association of Secondary School Principals.

U.S. Department of Labor. (1991). *What work requires of schools*. The Secretary's Commission on Achieving Necessary Skills (SCANS) Report. Washington, D.C.: Author.

BIBLIOGRAPHY

American Association for the Advancement of Science. (1993). *Benchmarks for science literacy*. New York: Oxford University Press.

American Association for the Advancement of Science. (1989). *Science for all Americans*. New York: Oxford University Press.

Barth, P. (1994, February). Taking an urban safari. *Basic Education*, 14-16.

Barth, P. (1993, January). To make a good scientist. *Basic Education*, 1-4.

Borko, H., Brown, C., Underhill, R., Eisenhart, M., Jones, D., & Agard, P. (1990). *Learning to teach mathematics for understanding*. College Park, MD: University of Maryland.

Donmoyer, R. (1993, September). *School organization blueprint*. Prepared for the American Association for the Advancement of Science, Project 2061, Washington, D.C.

Drake, S.M. (1993). *Planning an integrated curriculum: The call to adventure*. Alexandria, VA: Association for Supervision and Curriculum Development.

Elmore, R.F. (1993, June). *The development and implementation of large-scale curriculum reforms*. Background paper prepared for the American Association for the Advancement of Science, Project 2061, Washington, D.C.

Fogarty, R. (1991). *The mindful school: How to integrate the curricula*. Palatine, IL: IRI/Skylight Publishing, Inc.

Mitchell, R. (1993). *Interdisciplinary standards and curriculum: Promises and perils for the K-12 educational system*. Unpublished paper prepared for the Bauman Foundation, New York, NY.

Mitchell, R. (1992). *Testing for learning: How new approaches to evaluation can improve American schools*. New York: The Free Press.

Moore, J., Bridgman, T., Rohner, S. J., & Watson, C. A. (1993). Integrating language arts and math in the primary curriculum. In S. Tchudi (Ed.), *The astonishing curriculum: Integrating science and humanities through language*. Urbana, IL: National Council of Teachers of English.

Nehring, J. (1992). *The schools we have, the schools we want: An American teacher on the front line*. San Francisco, CA: Jossey-Bass Publishers.

Nelson, D., Joseph, G. G., & Williams, J. (1993). *Multicultural mathematics: Teaching mathematics from a global perspective*. Oxford, England: Oxford University Press.

Sizer, T. R. (1989). Diverse practice, shared ideas: The essential school. In H. Walberg & J.J. Lane (Eds.), *Organizing for learning: Toward the 21st Century*. Washington, D.C.: National Association of Secondary School Principals.

Toch, T. (1991). *In the name of excellence*. New York: Oxford University Press.

Tyson, H. (1988). *A conspiracy of good intentions: America's textbook fiasco*. Washington, D.C.: Council for Basic Education.

U.S. Department of Labor. (1991). *What work requires of schools*. The Secretary's Commission on Achieving Necessary Skills (SCANS) Report. Washington, D.C.: Author.

West, P. (1993). Skeptics questioning the accuracy, bias of environmental education. *Education Week*, June 16, p.1.

7

Materials and Technology

PERHAPS AT NO TIME in the history of schooling in the United States has the use of technology[1] in schools been more widely hailed as a crucial ingredient for quality education. There seem to be countless potential uses for satellite-linked classrooms, for CD-ROMs that hold previously unimagined amounts of information, and for an "information superhighway" whose power has just begun to be tapped. Educators and the general public are eager to see some of those potential uses put into practice.

Likewise, science and mathematics education reformers are eager to see technology used effectively in American classrooms. However, while we believe wholeheartedly in the power of technology to make a positive impact on education, we urge educators, policymakers, and the public at large to approach educational technologies with an eye towards their educational value first and their technological glamour second.

Previous technology reforms have almost always been hardware-driven and have largely ignored the content and structure of the curriculum they deliver. Therefore, the use of many technologies with potentially great educational value has followed a similar pattern: first, they are introduced with great fanfare and anticipation of the powerful impact they will have on student learning; then they are eagerly and hurriedly introduced into classrooms with little emphasis ever having been placed on examining their content or defining their role, and even less emphasis on training teachers to properly use them; and finally, their weaknesses are soon revealed to students, teachers and parents, and they are shelved permanently, their potential power forever wasted.

---

[1] The use of the term "technology" in this chapter refers to computers, video and audio systems, calculators, print production, and other hardware and software used as tools to support instruction and learning in the sciences and mathematics. It does not address the important issues involved in the study of technology as described in *Science for All Americans*, Chapter 8: The Designed World.

TECHNOLOGICAL LITERACY

The social need to be technologically literate grows more urgent every day. One can no longer go through life without being aware of and able to use technology. While many of the issues of learning about technology are beyond the scope of this chapter, it is important here to point to using technology both to access information and as a learning tool. Increasingly, much science learning, both in and outside of school, occurs through interaction with sophisticated media. This technology used to consist of measuring instruments and books. Today's media are not only more widespread, but also more sophisticated and complex. They require knowledge and skills to select and use them, as well as critical thinking skills to interpret them.

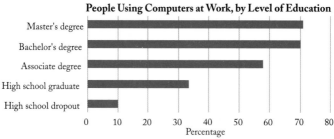

People Using Computers at Work, by Level of Education

Source: National Center for Education Statistics. (1996). *Digest of education stastics, 1996.* Washigton, D.C.: Author.

In spite of attempts to make computers, video equipment, and other technology user friendly, the skill and knowledge required to use them increases continually. It is no longer thinkable to be computer phobic. Nearly everything, from ignition systems to cash registers, has programmed chips that require, at the least, knowledge that they exist. Adjusting a carburetor or spark plugs the "old-fashioned way" can lead to major engine damage in a new car. And technology is also largely responsible for the well-known information explosion. New sources of information on the Web, cable TV, and public access media are not edited or prepared, bringing with them the responsibility for broader knowledge and critical thinking in all areas, including science. As the boundary between school and out-of-school learning blurs and technology becomes an integral part of the curriculum, these literacy issues will become increasingly important.

Technology and media innovation in American schools has been characterized by cyclic fads and a failure to use the sound tools and processes of science to systematically and progressively improve the qual-

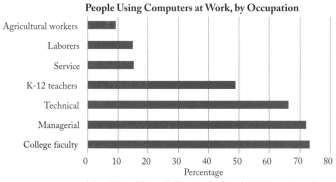

People Using Computers at Work, by Occupation

Source: National Center for Education Statistics. (1996). *Digest of education stastics, 1996.* Washigton, D.C.: Author.

ity of instruction. As we enter the 21st century, technology has become a far too powerful and valuable learning tool to allow this pattern to repeat. This chapter aims to help prevent just such repetition. The first section analyzes current and past practice in the use of technology in American schools, the second introduces an ideal vision for using technology in the classroom of the future, and the final section explores ways to close the gap between current practice and the ideal vision.

THE CURRENT STATUS

Hardware-driven vs. Content-driven Reform

For decades, cutting-edge technologies have been touted as ground-breaking boons to American education. But despite the optimism that frequently accompanies the introduction of new technologies into American classrooms, research on their use in schools has found a pervasive cycle of inappropriate use followed by disappointment and abandonment (Cuban, 1986). Perhaps the main reason for the repetition of this cycle is that when instructional "innovations" that use new technologies are introduced, the focus has centered on the lure of the new hardware and its ability to process or deliver information faster, in greater quantities, and from greater distances, rather than on the quality of instruction that the hardware carries or supports. These are hardware-driven, rather than content- or instruction-driven, reforms.

Hardware-driven reforms are doomed for three major reasons. First, they assume that technology alone will improve student learning, ignoring how it might actually produce affective and cognitive results. Second, because the hardware is assumed to make the difference (as

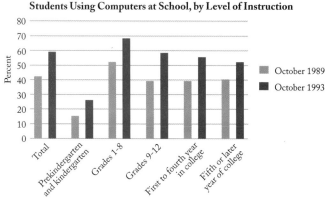

Students Using Computers at School, by Level of Instruction

Source: Published on the U.S. Department of Commerce, Bureau of the Census World Wide Web site at http://www.census.gov/

opposed to the teaching or the quality of its software), new hardware tends to be introduced into classrooms hurriedly on a wave of enthusiasm and public support, but with little time and few resources devoted to training teachers to integrate the hardware into their curriculum. Third, because technology is often hurriedly introduced, its role and purpose in instruction is usually left undefined. These severe problems cannot be solved without drastic changes in current practice by the producers and marketers of hardware, in the research on educational technology, and in the ways schools select and implement hardware.

STUDENT OUTCOMES

The lessons from history tell us that if technologies, media, and materials are to be productive, the curriculum content and pedagogy that are implemented through them must have promise and value in their own right. Some of the technologies in schools today are being introduced without attention to how they actually affect student performance. For example, computer-assisted instruction (CAI) is still one of the more popular forms of technology used in schools. However, most CAI programs are highly individualized, a method that has been criticized for increasing the gap between high- and low-achieving students (Hativa, 1988). A simple but crucial question is: How effective was the original instructional approach (in this case, highly individualized instruction) before mediation in the form of computer-assisted instruction? This factor is critical, especially when the approach has high acquisition and maintenance costs as CAI does.

These costs are important to keep in mind when considering the

Students per Computer in Public Schools

School year

Source: Published on the QED World Wide Web site at http://www.infomall.org/Showcase/QED/

role student outcomes should play in selecting technology for use in the classroom. For example, if a $2,000-per-student, computer-based program intended to raise achievement does only as well as an existing program, then the technology has failed in terms of cost-effectiveness. On the other hand, if technologies are selected for their ability to save money, educators must make sure student learning does not suffer.

Of course, not all uses of technology produce poor results. There are numerous examples of substantive advantages of technology over comparison programs. In some cases, technology-based programs delivered their results at one-tenth the cost, for wide ranges of student ability, and in content understanding that transferred to new situations (see for example, Thorkildsen & Lowry, 1990; Woodward, 1994). Although technology was important for providing access, these results were attributed in large part to the specific combination of pedagogy and curriculum organization in the program content.

STAFF DEVELOPMENT

Many educators contend that the major issue with the dissemination of technology-based instructional programs and materials is one of equitable access for all students. It is true that many American schools, especially in disadvantaged areas, are not designed or equipped for technology-based instruction. However, even if technology is available, a program can't work unless we know how to provide sufficient training to the teachers who will use the technology with students.

In the past, and in many current technological reforms, the dissemination of technology-based materials has not been accompanied by staff development that is substantive, program specific, or sus-

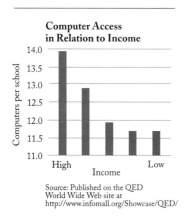

Computer Access in Relation to Income

Source: Published on the QED World Wide Web site at http://www.infomall.org/Showcase/QED/

tained long enough to be effective. Teachers are, therefore, put in an extraordinarily difficult position. They are often charged with designing instructional materials to accompany technologies that they are not familiar with and whose educational purpose is often ill-defined. On the occasions when staff development does take place, methods for teaching with a new technology are often prescribed by individuals far removed from the classroom, and they have little relevance for the unique needs of each teacher's classroom. The result of poor staff development, loosely defined goals, and traditional methods of implementation is that gains of time and efficiency rarely materialize. Instead, we find loss of teacher control, understanding, and autonomy (Callister & Dunne, 1992).

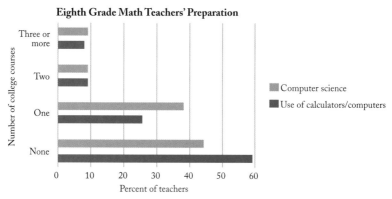

Eighth Grade Math Teachers' Preparation

Source: Nelson, B.H., Weiss, I.R., and Conaway, L.E. (1992). *Science and mathematics education briefing book; Volume III.* Chapel Hill, NC: Horizon Research, Inc.

Those who would send instructional technology and materials down the information highways of the future must recognize that teachers are the most important link in the chain that connects technological innovation with improved student performance.

Technology's Role in the Classroom

Whenever a new technology is introduced into classrooms, its role should be clearly defined before it is used. Too often, it is assumed that the role of a certain technology is understood by students, teachers, administrators, and marketers of the product alike. Few educational administrators work with teachers and others to clarify how technology will be used in the classroom, and few marketers of technological hardware determine the unique needs of specific districts or schools in which their products are to be sold.

Failure to define technology's role can have several adverse consequences. For example, if a technology-based program is to be the entire curriculum, then a certain set of evaluation criteria apply for assessing its worth. If this same program is to serve as a tool to support the learning of some other curriculum goal, an entirely different set of evaluation criteria apply. A spreadsheet program, for example, might be the focus of a curriculum unit or an entire course in which the goal is to teach students how to use a spreadsheet program. This same program might be used in a chemistry class because the teacher believes that using spreadsheets improves the quality of students' data collection, analysis, and reporting in laboratory experiments. Used for these two purposes, the same spreadsheet program has vastly different roles. If those roles are not clearly defined, it is impossible to determine how effective a technology is, apart from the specific instructional contexts in which it is used.

THE ROLE OF INDUSTRY

Needless to say, if technological innovations in the classroom have a history of mediocrity, administrators and teachers are not alone in taking the blame. Industry salespeople are likely to emphasize the unique contribution to science learning of a piece of hardware and less likely to stress that the machine alone makes no significant contributions to student performance. Not only does this create an obvious temptation for the manufacturer to exaggerate the benefits of a specific piece of hardware over and above all others, it also ignores the fact that any hardware is likely to be obsolete within four or five years, or less. This is no small consideration for schools, most of which run on extremely tight budgets.

Finally, educators are often frustrated with unfulfilled promises about hardware and software. Among the examples are hardware and software that are not compatible, the never-ending requirement for more memory capacity and speed, poorly written manuals, and difficulty with installations and upgrades. Given the level of technical assistance available to teachers and the cost of continual upgrades, the truly user-friendly technology always seems just beyond reach.

The Role of Research and Evaluation

The educational research community also shares responsibility for the failure of many technological reforms. According to Clark (1992), for decades researchers have studied whether one mechanical or electronic medium produced more student learning than another, with little reference to the educational context or pedagogical or curricular content of these media. Much of this research is confounded by uncontrolled variables, rendering it invalid and not replicable. A reasonable first step in future research would be to move away from comparing technologies or methods and begin to describe carefully the science teaching and learning situations in which technology has an impact on student performance and behavior. This research-based focus on observation, analysis, and synthesis of approaches that work would at the same time meet the need to tie technology to science content and provide science teachers with specific information about how to implement technology successfully.

Because the greatest attention in many program evaluations is focused on the final results, educators often overlook the need for data to provide midcourse corrections.

Because the greatest attention in many program evaluations is focused on the final results, educators often overlook the need for data to provide midcourse corrections that will improve the program. When evaluations are planned, reported, or read, it is important to think not only about the question "How well does a finished program work?" but also, and perhaps more usefully, "What must be done to create and progressively refine the program?"

Improving the nature of evaluation research on the use of technologies in schools is valuable not only in and of itself. Unless evaluation results are valid, reliable, and transportable to contexts other than the specific situation studied, it is impossible to use those results to define the goals of technology more clearly, or to provide teachers with a framework for using technology effectively in their classrooms.

NEEDED CHANGES

Effectively used technology would have three simple distinguishing characteristics. First and foremost, technologies should provide quality education to students. There are numerous examples of effective applications of technology that not only are better than traditional approaches, but also offer unique learning opportunities. Collaboration via the Internet, real-time data collection, computer modeling, and image analysis are all examples of science learning that is either impossible or cumbersome without technology. An important distinguishing characteristic of these applications is that they focus on the specific combination of teaching and curricular organization resident in the content of the program, and on the subsequent benefits to students, rather than on the hardware that carries the application. In these examples, technology can be integrated fully into the curriculum so that all students gain an understanding of its nature, power, and limitations.

Second, teacher competency would be treated as the most important and most potent variable in implementing programs. State or district leaders, with input from science teachers, would set broad but clearly defined goals for the use of specific materials or technology. Only then would highly targeted, field-based, site-specific staff development take place to provide teachers with the knowledge and support necessary to effectively use the new materials or technologies in their classrooms.

Finally, educators, researchers, and marketers of materials and technology would combine forces to stress that the hardware, the curriculum content, and the instructional context form an indivisible package. Researchers and evaluators would examine the processes that make technology-based programs work, and draw their conclusions solely from the results on student learning; marketers would stress the flexibility of their product to adapt to many different instructional packages; and educators would base their selections of materials and technology on the results of high-quality, replicable research and the cost-effectiveness of their purchase. This ideal situation appears to be a long way from current practice. In the following section, we explore some approaches to bringing current practice closer to this ideal vision.

We strongly endorse the idea to analyze, describe, and disseminate reports on science, mathematics, and technology curriculum materials that can help students achieve science literacy as spelled out in the *National Science Education Standards* (National Research Council, 1996) and in *Benchmarks for Science Literacy* (American Association for the Advancement of Science, 1993). This process is being developed by Project 2061 as part of *Resources for Science Literacy*.[2] Curriculum

---

[2]Project 2061 has developed a procedure for analyzing science curriculum materials whose content and pedagogy match benchmarks and standards, and is training teachers and others to analyze materials. A small set of science curriculum materials has been analyzed; work is underway to analyze more materials and develop a greater capacity for training people to do the analysis.

materials that are aimed at the singular goal of having student outcomes match benchmarks and standards can serve as tangible teaching tools that will bring the visions for science reform into the classroom.

These curricula can also provide a framework around which to focus staff development efforts, helping to define the role that technology, media, and materials can play in a school's reformed science curriculum. Once staff development has passed its formative stages, the curricula can provide teachers with the content of their instruction, thus removing from them the burden of having to design instructional materials on their own.

Finally, in order to ascertain that curricula are effective, they will have to be accompanied by an associated body of assessments that gauge their effectiveness. Designers of these assessments should refer not only to *Benchmarks*, but also to *Blueprints'* Chapter 8: Assessment, which describes assessment practices and procedures that match the goals for reform. The assessments will need to undergo the same rigorous analysis procedure as the curriculum in order to describe how they meet benchmarks and standards.

Educated science teacher "consumers" will expand the market for curricula that actually can be used to teach benchmarks.

This cycle of design and independent analysis of science curriculum and assessment not only builds teachers' expertise in judging and using science materials, it also leads to curriculum development that is standards-driven rather than market-driven. Educated science teacher "consumers" will expand the market for curricula that actually can be used to teach benchmarks, driving out materials and technology that are attractive for other reasons.

In designing and implementing the most effective science curricula, one approach is to follow the guidelines of the U.S. Department of Education Program Effectiveness Panel (PEP) for designing and validating educational programs, judging whether those programs are effective in meeting their goals, and assessing whether similar results are likely to be attained by others who use the program. Backed by a wealth of practical and theoretical expertise, PEP suggests that any educational program measure its effectiveness by the following three criteria:

■ Evaluation design. A credible evaluation design assures that the results of assessments are appropriate for the program (in this case, a science curriculum) and that the program clearly produces the desired results.

■ Meaningful results. The results of the program are meaningful only if the goals are important and the impact on student learning is strong.

■ Potential for replication. The program must be transportable to other sites at reasonable cost in dollars and effort, with the expectation of similar results.

Ralph and Dwyer (1988) discuss the PEP criteria in more detail and offer a practical look at the problems involved in integrating the principles of program development with the everyday realities of public schools.

STAFF DEVELOPMENT

One of the keys to successful program change is a focus on staff development. The use of facilitators at the state, regional, or district level can provide the link between those who develop educational programs and their prospective clients, namely, schools and teachers. A large portion of resources should go to support highly qualified trainers who work directly with schools to plan, develop, and deliver intensive, program-specific, long-term instruction to teachers and administrators. Although this type of program is extremely effective, the cost of sending thousands of highly qualified trainers to school sites to train staff in specific science and technology programs makes it impractical as a vehicle for large-scale reform. A more cost-effective method is to use the growing power of communications networks to support quality training. Professional associations, curriculum developers, local alliances, universities, and regional centers can form networks of expert resources and clearinghouses for

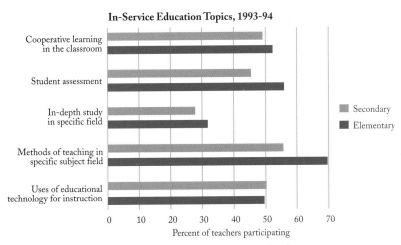

In-Service Education Topics, 1993-94

Cooperative learning in the classroom

Student assessment

In-depth study in specific field

Methods of teaching in specific subject field

Uses of educational technology for instruction

Secondary
Elementary

0   10   20   30   40   50   60   70
Percent of teachers participating

Source: National Center for Educational Statistics. (1996). *Condition of education 1996.* Washington, D.C.: Author.

information about how to implement specific science programs and technologies, providing tailored on-site help as needed.

The science and mathematics knowledge needed for new curricula and technology is an important focus for staff development. However, simply taking more courses is not the answer, because researchers have found little, if any, correlation between a teacher's understanding of a subject (as measured by the number of college courses taken) and student outcomes (Ball, 1991). Instead of more mathematics and science knowledge, teachers need more "context-specific case knowledge" that blends subject matter and pedagogical knowledge (Brophy, 1991). For example, teachers need to know how to use their knowledge of molecules to ask questions that guide sixth graders through experiments on whether sugar dissolves faster in hot water or cool water. For this reason, highly targeted, program-specific staff development deserves far more attention than it has received in the rhetoric of reform.

The Role of Industry

Just as science and mathematics curriculum analysis may serve to refocus the use of technology toward improving student outcomes, it can also provide industry with an understanding of what schools truly need from technology. Hardware and software that can be adapted to a variety of science instructional programs that meet benchmarks and standards is much more useful than technology that might make a unique contribution to one component of science learning.

Considering technology, media, and materials as independent tools and resources has two distinct advantages: it places the emphasis on the content of the educational products that will be delivered through the technology rather than solely on the media, and it ensures that a piece of hardware will adapt to a variety of different instructional programs—an important consideration in the rapidly changing, high-tech field of software development and design.

An independent technology base must be capable of storing and presenting instructional content in an elegant and user-friendly form, and must ensure the highest quality and greatest generalizability across present and future media forms. At present, a highly generalizable media base could include a broadcast-quality, 30-frames-per-second video, and text and graphics that can be reproduced in black and white and color. Promising tools are the laser video disc, with high-quality motion and still-video storage, and CD-ROM formats, which hold more than 60 minutes of quality, compressed, full-motion video. The CD-ROM is moving from 600 megabytes to more than 6 gigabits of storage and can store text and graphics files in digital form along with the still and motion video. This provides an "off-line" or "on-line" vehicle for print, audio, and analog video information that is now stored on laser video-disks. At present, stiff competition is driving down prices in the hardware industry. This reality is likely to make manufacturers more amenable to working with science educators to develop products on their terms.

THE ROLE OF RESEARCH AND EVALUATION

The most important way in which research on the use of technology can support science education reform is to make student outcomes the primary measure of a program's effectiveness. Observations of teacher behavior, costs, and physical and social infrastructure are important in assessing a technology's worth, but they are nonetheless secondary to that technology's ability to produce positive changes in cognitive and affective student performance.

Vital to the success of any effort to make better use of technology in science education is the increased use of formative evaluation in testing program effectiveness.

Another factor vital to the success of any effort to make better use of technology in science education is the increased use of formative evaluation in testing program effectiveness. The process of formative evaluation has great potential to limit or prevent unintended negative consequences because it involves intense, sometimes even intrusive, monitoring of student reactions. Formative evaluation allows researchers and teachers to decide whether their ideas are having negative consequences before they are irreversible. This is an especially important consideration given the growing diversity of the American school population and the respect for diversity that is found in the goals of science education reform. For children without a support system outside of school to supplement their education, it is unconscionable to experiment full-scale before doing pilot testing and formative evaluation. By examining the effects of a specific science program on students before it is fully implemented at a school or district level, educators can ensure that it has the desired effects in a variety of classrooms.

For any formative evaluation to be effective, teachers must be included in its design and implementation. Although for many teachers it is too burdensome to design, implement, and evaluate their own science programs, they can still be instrumental. For example, at the Far West Laboratory, teachers were heavily involved in reviewing the design of the curriculum, as well as the formative and summative testing of the program's qualities (Borg & Gall, 1989).

Finally, formative evaluation must become an institutionalized part of all educational program development. In rigorous science, significant time is devoted to the formative stages of a research project's development. But much educational research is constrained by the timed nature of grants, meaning that researchers often must select problems with known solutions, spending relatively little time in the formative stages of program development. Barbara Flagg's *Formative Evaluation for Educational Technologies* (1990) blends the general principles of program development and formative evaluation with the rapidly changing range of educational technology alternatives, and can serve as an invaluable guide to researchers and science teachers who wish to make formative evaluation a key part of program development efforts.

RECOMMENDATIONS

If technology and media are to play a crucial role in implementing science education reform, visible leadership must be cultivated to carry this vision forward. Designers and supporters of science education reform, an enlightened sponsor, and a national media platform could serve as a powerful voice for significant progress. It is a voice that is currently missing, but one that is vital if science education reform is to gain widespread acceptance.

This chapter has set out to identify, exemplify, and recommend a course of action for addressing the teacher enhancement and instructional materials envisioned by reformers. This course of action would require all involved parties to collaborate in the following actions:

■ Adopt the most important science literacy goals that have value to the individual and the nation.

■ Apply theories of instructional design to provide educational elegance to science materials and technology and to give practical and pervasive form to the theme of "less is more" in science education.

■ Use validated and replicable analyses to identify and describe science curriculum materials—including those that use technology and media—that meet *Benchmarks* and *Standards* requirements.

■ Make the considerable investment necessary for formative and summative program evaluation and for revision activities to ensure that the needs of all learners are addressed.

■ Develop an approach to science program dissemination and teacher enhancement that ensures high fidelity in the widest possible range of instructional settings, using appropriate technology to achieve economy of fiscal and personnel resources.

As the information age dawned, several observers accurately predicted the classroom implications and called for a "technology of instruction" that would support the teacher and enhance instruction. The following quote by Peter Drucker thoughtfully and accurately summarized and predicted the issues now faced by reform in science, mathematics, and technology:

> Learning and teaching are going to be more deeply affected by the new availability of information than any other area of human life. There is a great need for a new approach in new methods, and new tools in teaching, man's oldest and most reactionary craft. There is a great need for a rapid increase in learning. There is above all, great need for methods that will make the teacher effective and multiply his or her efforts and competence. Teaching is, in fact, the only traditional craft in which we have not yet fashioned the tools that make an ordinary person capable of superior performance. (Heinrich, 1970, p. 56)

REFERENCES

American Association for the Advancement of Science. (1993). *Benchmarks for science literacy*. New York: Oxford University Press.

Ball, D. (1991). Research on teaching mathematics: Making subject-matter knowledge part of the equation. In J. Brophy (Ed.), *Advances in research on teaching* (Vol. 2, pp. 1–48). Greenwich, CT: JAI Press.

Borg, W. R., & Gall, M. D. (1989). *Educational research*. New York: Longman.

Brophy, J. (Ed.). (1991). *Advances in research on teaching* (Vol. 2). Greenwich, CT: JAI Press.

Callister, T. A, Jr., & Dunne, F. (1992). The computer as doorstop: Technology as disempowerment. *Phi Delta Kappan, 74*(4), 324–326.

Clark, R. E. (1992). Six definitions of media in search of theory. In D. P. Ely & B. B. Minor (Eds.), *Educational media and technology yearbook* (Vol. 18, pp. 65–76). Englewood, CO: Libraries Unlimited.

Cuban, L. (1986). *Teachers and machines: The classroom use of technology since 1920*. New York: Teachers College Press.

Flagg, B. (1990). *Formative evaluation for educational technologies*. Hillsdale, NJ: Lawrence Erlbaum.

Hativa, N. (1988). Computer-based drill and practice in arithmetic: Widening the gap between high- and low-achieving students. *American Educational Research Journal, 25*(3), 366–397.

Heinrich, R. (1970). *Technology and the management of instruction.* Washington, D.C.: Association of Educational Communications and Technology.

National Research Council. (1996). *National science education standards.* Washington, D.C.: National Academy Press.

Ralph, J., & Dwyer, M. C. (1988). *Making the case: Evidence of program effectiveness in schools and classrooms.* Washington, D.C.: U.S. Department of Education, Office of Educational Research and Improvement and RMC Research.

Thorkildsen, R., & Lowry, W. (1990). *The effects of a videodisk program on mathematics self-concept: Research report.* Logan, UT: Utah State University, Center for Persons with Disabilities.

Woodward, J. (1994). Effects of curriculum discourse style on eighth graders' recall and problem solving in earth science. *Elementary School Journal, 94*(3), 299–314.

BIBLIOGRAPHY

American Association for the Advancement of Science. (1989). *Science for all Americans.* New York: Oxford University Press.

Anderson, R. C. (1988, September 8). Comments submitted to the California State Board of Education at a public hearing in Sacramento, CA.

Baker, D. P. (1993). Compared to Japan, the U. S. is a low achiever . . . really: New evidence and comment on Westbury. *Educational Researcher, 22*(3), 18-20.

Ball, D. L. (1991). Research on teaching mathematics: Making subject-matter knowledge part of the equation. In J. Brophy (Ed.), *Advances in research on teaching* (Vol. 2, pp. 1-48). Greenwich, CT: JAI Press.

Bangert, R. L., Kulik, J. A., & Kulik, C. C. (1983). Individualized systems of instruction in secondary schools. *Review of Educational Research, 53*(2), 143-158.

Bateman, B. (1992). *Academic child abuse.* Eugene, OR: International Institute for Advocacy for School Children.

Begle, E. G., & Geeslin, W. (1972). *Teacher effectiveness in mathematics instruction* (National Longitudinal Study of Mathematical Abilities Reports, No. 28). Washington, D.C.: Mathematical Association of America and National Council of Teachers of Mathematics.

Bishop, A. J. (1990). Mathematical power to the people. *Harvard Educational Review, 60*(3), 357-369.

Block, J. H. (1980). Success rate. In C. Denham & A. Lieberman (Eds.), *Time to learn* (pp. 95-106). Washington, D.C.: U. S. Department of Education, National Institute of Education.

Borg, W. R., & Gall, M. D. (1989). *Educational research.* New York: Longman.

Brophy, J. (Ed.). (1991). *Advances in research on teaching,* Volume 2. Greenwich, CT: JAI Press.

Buchmann, M. (1986). Role over person: Morality and authenticity in teaching. *Teachers College Record, 87*(4), 529-543.

Bunge, M. (1991). A critical examination of the new sociology of science, Part I. *Philosophy of the Social Sciences, 21*, 524-60.

Callister, T. A., Jr., & Dunne, F. (1992). The computer as doorstop: Technology as disempowerment. *Phi Delta Kappan, 74*(4), 324-326.

Carnine, D. (1993a). *The development of educational tools—for scientific literacy, instructional technology, media, and material* (Research Report). Eugene, OR: National Center to Improve the Tools of Educators, The University of Oregon.

Carnine, D. (1993b). *Process for selecting and implementing valid educational approaches.* Eugene, OR: National Center to Improve the Tools of Educators, The University of Oregon.

Cherryholmes, C. H. (1992). Notes on pragmatism and scientific realism. *Educational Researcher, 21*(6), 13-17.

Clark, R. E. (1992). Six definitions of media search of a theory. In D. P. Ely & B. B. Minor (Eds.), *Educational media and technology yearbook* (Vol. 18, pp. 65-76). Englewood, CO: Libraries Unlimited.

Clark, R. E. (1985). Confounding in educational computing research. *Journal of Educational Computing Research, 1*(2), 137-147.

Clark, R. E. (1983). Reconsidering research on learning from media. *Review of Educational Research, 53*(4), 445-59.

Clark, R. E. (1982). Antagonism between achievement and enjoyment in ATI studies. *Educational Psychologist, 17*(2), 92-101.

Clark, R. E., & Salomon, G. (1986). Media in teaching. In M. Wittrock (Ed.), *Handbook of research on teaching* (3rd ed., pp. 464-478). New York: Macmillan.

Clifford, G. J. (1973). A history of the impact on research on teaching. In R. M. W. Travers (Ed.), *Second handbook of research on teaching.* Chicago: Rand McNally & Company.

Cochran-Smith, M. (1991). Word processing and writing in elementary classrooms: A critical review of related literature. *Review of Educational Research, 61*(1), 107-155.

Cohen, D. K., Peterson, P. L, Wilson, W., Ball, D., Putnam, R., Prawat, R., Heaton, R., Remillard, J., & Wiemers, N. (1990). *Effects of state-level reform of elementary school mathematics curriculum on classroom practice* (Research Report 90-14). East Lansing, MI: The National Center for Research on Teacher Education and The Center for the Learning and Teaching of Elementary Subjects, Michigan State University.

Columbro, M. N. (1964). Supervision and action research. *Educational Leadership, 21*, 297-300.

Commission on Instructional Technology. (1970). *To improve learning. A report to the President and the Congress of the United States.* Washington, D.C.: Author.

Cronbach, L. J., & Snow, R. E. (Eds.). (1977). *Aptitudes and instructional methods.* New York: Irvington/Neiburg.

Cronbach, L. J. (1963). Course improvement through evaluation. *Teachers College Record, 64*(8), 672-683.

Cuban, L. (1989). The "at-risk" label and the problem of urban school reform. *Phi Delta Kappan, 70*(10), 780-784.

Cuban, L. (1986). *Teachers and machines: The classroom use of technology since 1920.* New York: Teachers College Press.

Engelmann, S., & Carnine, D. (1991). *Theory of instruction: Principles and applications.* Eugene, OR: ADI Press.

Feynman, R. P. (1985). *Surely you're joking, Mr. Feynman.* New York: W. W. Norton & Co.

Finn, J. D. (1993). *School engagement and students at risk.* Buffalo, NY: State University of New York at Buffalo.

Flagg, B. N. (1990). *Formative evaluation for educational technologies.* Hillsdale, NJ: Lawrence Erlbaum Associates.

Fulton, K. (1993, Autumn/Winter). Teaching matters: The role of technology in education. *ED-TECH Review,* 5-10.

Grint, K. & Gill, R. (1995). *The gender-technology relation.* Bristol, PA: Taylor & Francis, Inc.

Hannifin, M. J. (1985). Empirical issues in the study of computer-assisted interactive video. *Educational Communications and Technology Journal, 33*(4), 235-47.

Hasselbring, T., Sherwood, R., Bransford, J., Fleenor, K., Griffith, D., & Goin, L. (1987-88). An evaluation of a level-one instructional videodisc program. *Journal of Educational Technology Systems, 16*(2), 151-169.

Hativa, N. (1988). Computer-based drill and practice in arithmetic: Widening the gap between high- and low-achieving students. *American Educational Research Journal, 25*(3), 366-397.

Heinich, R. (1970). *Technology and the management of instruction.* Washington, D.C.: Association for Educational Communications and Technology.

Hodgkinson, H . L. (1957). Action research: A critique. *Journal of Educational Sociology, 31,* 137-153.

Hodson, D. (1988). Toward a philosophically more valid science curriculum. *Science Education, 72*(1), 19-40.

Hofmeister, A. M. (1993). Elitism and reform in school mathematics. *Remedial and Special Education, 14*(6), 8-13.

Hofmeister, A. M. (1992). Multimedia overview: An educator's perspective. In *Stimulate learning with DVI multimedia* (pp. 4-6). Atlanta, GA: International Business Machines (IBM).

Hofmeister, A. M. (1990). Individual differences and the form and function of instruction. *The Journal of Special Education, 24*(2), 150-159.

Hofmeister, A. M. (1989). Teaching problem-solving skills with technology. *Educational Technology, 29*(9), 26-29.

Hofmeister, A. M., & Thorkildsen, R. (1989). Videodisc levels: A case study in hardware obsession. *Journal of Special Education Technology, 10*(2), 73-79.

Hofmeister, A. M. (1984). *Microcomputer applications in the classroom.* New York: Holt, Rinehart, and Winston.

Hofmeister, A. M. (1973). Audio-tutorial programming with exceptional children. *Educational Technology, 13*(12), 50-52.

Hooper, S., & Hannifin, M. J. (1991). Psychological perspectives on emerging instructional technologies: A critical analysis. *Educational Psychologist, 26*(1), 69-95.

House, E. R. (1991). Realism in research. *Educational Researcher, 20*(6), 2-9, 25.

Hughes, M. M. (1955). Iron County teachers study their problems scientifically. *Educational Leadership, 12,* 489-495.

James, R. K., and Francq, E. (1988). Assessing the implementation of a science program. *School Science and Mathematics, 88*(2), 149-159.

Kameenui, E. J. (1993). Diverse learners and the tyranny of time: Don't fix blame; fix the leaky roof. *The Reading Teacher, 46*(5), 376-383.

Komoski, K. (1992, March 18). A testimony given by Kenneth Komoski, Director of the Education Products Information Exchange, to the U.S . Congress Select Committee on Education, Washington, D.C.

Kozma, R. B. (1991). Learning with media. *Review of Educational Research, 61*(2),179-211.

Long, J. L. (1989, November 14). *Judge of the Superior Court. Statement of Decision, No. 361906, Dept.* 14. Sacramento. CA: Superior Court of the State of California, in and for the County of Sacramento.

Maddux, C. D. (1989). Logo: Scientific dedication or religious fanaticism in the 1990s? *Educational Technology, 29*(2), 18-23.

Mann, L. (1979). *On the trail of process.* New York: Grune & Stratton.

Martin, M. (1979). Connections between philosophy of science and science education. *Studies in Philosophy and Education, 9,* 329.

Multimedia Monitor. (1993). IBM Corporation offers print-on-demand service. *Multimedia Monitor, 11*(10), 6.

National Council of Teachers of Mathematics. (1991). *Professional standards for teaching mathematics.* Reston, VA: Author.

Nicholls, J. G. (1989). *The competitive ethos and democratic education.* Cambridge, MA: Harvard University Press.

Nicholls, J. G. (1979). Development of perception of own attainment and causal attributions for success and failure in reading. *Journal of Educational Psychology, 71,* 94-99.

Nicholls, J. G. (1978). The development of the concepts of effort and ability, perception of own attainment, and the understanding that difficult tasks require more ability. *Child Development, 49,*800-814.

Orleans, J. S. (1952). *The understanding of arithmetic processes and concepts possessed by teachers of arithmetic* (Publication Number 12). New York: Office of Research and Evaluation, Division of Teacher Education, College of the City of New York.

Ralph, J., & Dwyer, M. C. (1988). *Making the case: Evidence of program effectiveness in schools and classrooms.* Washington, D.C.: U. S. Department of Education, Office of Educational Research and Improvement and RMC Research.

Ross, S. M., & Morrison, G. R. (1990). In search of a happy medium in instructional technology research: Issues concerning external validity, media replications and learner control. *Educational Technology Research and Development, 37*(1), 19-33.

Salomon, G., & Gardner, H. (1986). The computer as educator: Lessons from television research. *Educational Researcher,* 13-19.

Schoen, H. L. (1976). Self-paced instruction: How effective has it been in secondary and post-secondary schools? *The Mathematics Teacher, 69,* 352-357.

Sewall, G. (Ed.). (1992). *Social studies review #9.* New York: American Textbook Council.

Shulman, L. (1987). Knowledge and teaching: Foundations of the new reform. *Harvard Educational Review, 57*, 1-22.

Shumsky, A. (1956). Cooperation in action research: A rationale. *Journal of Educational Sociology, 30*, 180-185.

Slavin, R. E. (1989). PET and the pendulum: Faddism in education and how to stop it. *Phi Delta Kappan, 70*(10), 752-758.

Snider, W. (1988). "Small changes won't do," says California panel: Cites failure to serve diverse student body. *Education Week, 7*(37), 1, 12.

Strahler, A. N. (1992). *Understanding science: An introduction to concepts and issues.* Buffalo, NY: Prometheus Books.

Tetenbaum, T. J., & Mulkeen, T. A. (1984). Logo and the teaching of problem-solving: A call for a moratorium. *Educational Technology, 24*(11), 16-19.

Thorkildsen, R., & Lowry, W. (1990). *The effects of a videodisc program on mathematics self-concept.* Logan, UT: Utah State University, Center for Persons with Disabilities.

Thorkildsen, R. (1986). *Development and testing of videodisc systems for main streaming.* Final Report to U.S. Department of Education, Office of Special Education Programs (Grant No. G008402242). Logan, UT: Utah State University, Center for Persons with Disabilities.

Toch, T. (1993). The perfect school. *U. S. News & World Report, 114*(1), 46-60.

Tyson-Bernstein, H., & Woodward, A. (1991). Nineteenth century policies for twenty-first century practice: The textbook reform dilemma. In P. G. Altbach, G. P. Kelly, H. G. Petrie, & L. Weis (Eds.), *Textbooks in American society* (pp. 91-104). Albany, NY: State University of New York Press.

Tyson-Bernstein, H. (1988). *A conspiracy of good intentions: America's text book fiasco.* Washington, D.C.: The Council for Basic Education.

Vitale, M., & Romance, N. (1992). Using videodisc instruction in an elementary science methods course. *Journal of Research in Science Teaching, 29*(9).

Westbury, I. (1993). American and Japanese achievement . . . again: A response to Baker. *Educational Researchers, 22*(3), 21-25.

Wilson, J. (1990). Integrated learning systems: A primer. *Classroom Computer Learning, 10*(5), 22-23, 27-30, 34, 36.

Woodward, J. (1994). Effects of curriculum discourse style on eighth graders' recall and problem solving in earth science. *Elementary School Journal, 94*(3), 299-314.

Worthington, R. M. (1963). Action research in vocational education. *American Vocational Journal, 38*(1), 18-19, 38.

8

Assessment

ASSESSMENT OF STUDENT PERFORMANCE exerts extraordinary influence on every level of the United States education system, from state house to classroom. For this reason, many argue that assessment is an impediment to meaningful reform, while others contend just as forcefully that it is perhaps the most crucial catalyst for effecting change in educational practice. In either case, the power that assessments exert on education is unlikely to wane. Therefore, any effort at nationwide science education reform must include reform of student assessment as a major goal.

This chapter explores how student assessment in American schools might be redesigned to match the goals of science education reform that are exemplified in efforts such as Project 2061's *Benchmarks for Science Literacy* (American Association for the Advancement of Science [AAAS], 1993) and the *National Science Education Standards* (*Standards*) (National Research Council [NRC], 1996). The chapter is divided into three sections that describe current assessment practice in the United States, suggest changes that are needed in order for science reform goals to be implemented, and explore possibilities and recommendations for closing the gap between current practice and a more ideal vision of science assessment.

In reading this chapter, it is important to keep in mind two often overlooked facts. First, although many people immediately associate the term "assessment" with standardized, group-administered, multiple-choice tests, assessment actually includes an enormous range of procedures used to gather information about what a student knows, believes, or can do. Student-focused assessment procedures—for example, judging students by a compiled portfolio of work on a range of performances rather than by an average of individual test scores—are currently being developed and used effectively by many educators, meaning that the rich variety of assessment procedures is likely to increase.

Second, assessments are not used only to assign grades to students or rankings to schools. Assessments have several goals, which are classified as either "internal purposes" or "external purposes." Internal purposes for assessment include:

- conveying to students expectations about what is important to learn,
- providing information to students and parents about student progress,
- helping students learn to judge their own learning,
- guiding and improving instruction, and
- classifying and selecting students.

External purposes serve the needs of those on the outside of the school looking in and include:

- providing information for accountability systems;
- guiding policy decisions on funding, staff development, and so on;
- gathering information for program evaluation; and
- sorting and classifying people for admissions, certification, or hiring.

Though assessments have long had a significant impact on educational policy and practice in the U.S., in recent years mandated assessments—especially at the state level—have grown in their influence and breadth of use. This chapter acknowledges that influence and offers suggestions for student assessment that will help promote the goals of science, mathematics, and technology education reform.

CURRENT STATUS

The decentralized system of schooling in the United States ensures great variation in the way assessment takes place from school to school, district to district, and state to state. On the whole, however, the assessment techniques that would be ideally compatible with the goals of science education reform are not widely practiced in American schools. This section presents a brief overview of current assessment practice and policies at three levels: classroom, district and state, and national. District, state, and national assessments are especially relevant to reform because of their increasing dominance of student and teacher time and their visibility to the public in displaying achievement levels in mathematics and science.

CLASSROOM ASSESSMENT

Classroom assessment remains a major influence on students' day to day learning. Teacher-designed tests for an individual class can serve the needs of individual students to a far greater degree than statewide or

The assessment techniques that would be ideally compatible with the goals of science education reform are not widely practiced in American schools.

nationwide standardized skills tests. However, research suggests that teacher-made tests are often as limited in measuring student thinking as their standardized counterparts (Stiggins & Conklin, 1992). First, teacher-made tests are mostly short-answer or matching items that place far more emphasis on student recall than on student thinking ability. Second, evidence suggests that because teachers do not receive proper training in effective assessment methods, they tend not to change the methods they use as assessment needs change. Different assessments are needed to measure performance, effort, and achievement, for instance, but teachers tend to use the same type of assessment to measure all three. Third, because of time constraints, teachers often use the assessments that are found at the end of textbook chapters or included in the textbook publisher's package. These assessments contain mainly short answer questions that require only low-level thinking skills and simple recall of factual knowledge (Center for the Study of Testing, Evaluation, and Educational Policy, 1992). Many newer science and mathematics curriculum projects and textbooks, however, include assessments that address an array of valued outcomes and show promise for improving classroom assessment if teachers are trained in using them.

Even if teachers receive the training, time, and resources that would allow them to broaden their science assessment practices, students themselves may be a barrier. Students, especially high school students who have become test-wise, sometimes object to the more labor-intensive format of assessments that require performing tasks, answering essay questions, or providing possible solutions to open-ended problems. Parents also have become accustomed to report cards that contain letters and percentages and may question new approaches that are not clearly explained and justified.

Finally, there are logistical and technical reasons why prevailing practice persists. Standardized, machine-scored tests are efficient and cost-effective. In addition, they provide quantifiable results that are easily understood by both internal actors—teachers and students—and external actors—legislators, policymakers and the lay public. Issues such as assessing individual contributions in group activities or determining how to address student absenteeism during multiple-day tasks are quite real and require further time and effort by teachers and others.

District and State Assessments

Nearly every state has some type of statewide assessment in place. Some of these assessments have been developed specifically to align with state curriculum frameworks in science and mathematics, and a few use performance tasks and open-ended items. However, many statewide and most districtwide tests are inconsistent with the goals of science reform. They are "off-the-shelf," standardized, multiple-choice tests that are not well-aligned with standards or benchmarks and do not allow students to develop their own solutions to problems or to analyze, synthesize, and present information on their own. The tests are often chosen for the content of their mathematics and reading sections rather than their science content, and their results are seldom used to improve science instruction.

State and district tests have high stakes for both students and schools. For students, some states require passing scores on the state assessment in order to graduate from high school; school districts often use the tests as a factor in decisions about student placement into remedial, regular, or honors classes. High-stakes tests usually place students in a passive, reactive role rather than allowing them to develop ideas or to solve problems. For schools, the consequences of these high-stakes tests are also serious. The pressure on administrators and teachers to improve test scores is enormous, overshadowing other educational concerns. Local newspapers often publish the test averages of individual schools. In some states and districts, funding decisions are based on student performance on standardized tests: those doing well get bonuses. In a few cases, school districts have been placed under state control because of poor student performance on tests.

There is considerable evidence suggesting that high-stakes tests can have negative consequences for instruction (Darling-Hammond, 1995).

State Assessment Characteristics

Component	Number of States*
Includes mathematics assessment	45
Tests in grade 4	33
Tests in grade 8	40
Tests in grade 11	32
Used for school accountability	30
Used for student accountability	26
Aligned with state curriculum standards	23**

*45 states have statewide assessment systems
**21 states in the process of doing alignment

Source: National Education Goals Panel. (1996). *Profile of 1994-95 state assessment systems and reported results.* Washington, D.C.: Author.

These tests force students and teachers to emphasize test-taking skills over and above other educational concerns, and they exclude many kinds of knowledge. Fairness and freedom from bias—particularly in large-scale assessments—continue to be issues, especially for females and minority students and those with disabilities or English as a second language. Unfair testing is especially troubling because the test results may be used for purposes as varied as tracking students, making promotion or hiring decisions, and allocating rewards or imposing sanctions.

Despite the many negative consequences that may result from overemphasizing the importance of standardized test results, assessment used appropriately can be a powerful factor in science education reform. It is a widely accepted claim in educational circles that what is tested is what gets taught. Therefore, poorly designed assessments are an enormous barrier to reform. At the same time, state and district science assessments that are designed with the goals and philosophy of *Science for All Americans* (AAAS, 1989) in mind could help produce results that are at least somewhat akin to the goals that science education reformers envision.

NATIONAL AND INTERNATIONAL ASSESSMENTS

The public concern over a perceived decline in the quality of education in the United States has largely been fueled by student performance on three tests—the National Assessment of Educational Progress (NAEP), which measures student achievement within the United States; the International Evaluation of Achievement (IEA); and the International Assessment of Educational Progress (IAEP). The latter two assessments compare student achievement among countries. NAEP, commonly known as the "nation's report card," regularly assesses a broad sample of U.S. students in various subjects.

NAEP mathematics and science scores declined from the time of the test's introduction in 1969 until the mid-1980s, when they began to improve slightly. The results of international tests and comparisons have been equally dismal. For example, in a 1994-95 IAEP study, U.S. 8th graders ranked 28th out of 41 countries in mathematics (Beaton et al. 1996). More detailed analyses of curriculum, time spent in and out of the classroom, and other variables reveal that these rankings provide just a small part of the picture. For example, U. S. achievement has more to do with the nature of the curriculum and how mathematics is taught than the time spent in classrooms. Recent comparisons between countries and individual states have revealed that using over-

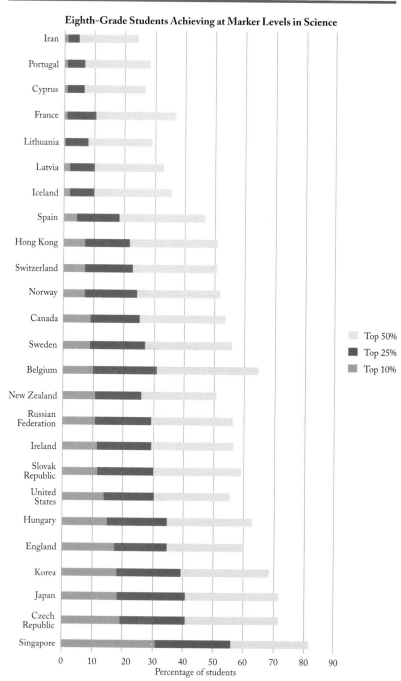

Eighth-Grade Students Achieving at Marker Levels in Science

Legend:
Top 50%
Top 25%
Top 10%

Percentage of students

Source: Beaton, et al. (1996). *Science achievement in the middle school years: IEA's third international mathematics and science study.* Chestnut Hill, MA: Boston College.

all U.S. averages gives a too simplistic picture. For example, the mathematics achievement averages for many states compare well with the top countries in the world (National Science Foundation, 1996). With these scores fueling public outrage over the quality of American education, and with Goal 4 of the President's "Goals 2000" plan for American education calling for U.S. students to be first in the world in science and mathematics by the year 2000, the tests are likely to become even more high-stakes in the near future. An IEA assessment is planned for the year 1999, and teachers and administrators are likely to place increasing emphasis on improving exam scores as this date approaches. And while earlier calls for national achievement tests in all subjects have diminished, the National Education Goals Panel has been formed to monitor states' performances in mathematics and reading achievement, issuing annual reports of progress toward Goals 2000 (National Education Goals Panel, 1996).

Again, it is worth noting that while high-stakes standardized exams have extreme limitations and potentially negative consequences in their current design, national goals in science and mathematics reflecting *Benchmarks* or *Standards* would have an enormous, positive impact on the way these subjects are taught in American schools. *Standards* and *Benchmarks* are similar in their calls for greater depth of understanding in fewer topics. Still, there are differences in content, tone, style, and grade-level focus in these two sets of standards, which could pose a problem in implementing united efforts to improve science education through common assessments.

NEEDED CHANGES

Several important aspects of student assessments need to change in order to support reforms such as those envisioned by Project 2061. They include assessment philosophy and practice, assessment and instruction, teacher preparation in assessment, and external assessments.

ASSESSMENT PHILOSOPHY AND PRACTICE

Communicating the goals of science education reform and the philosophy of science literacy outlined in *Science for All Americans* presents perhaps the greatest challenge to science education. Teachers, educational administrators, local board members, and state department of education officials are working to develop science frameworks and standards that reflect Project 2061's *Science for All Americans* and *Benchmarks for Science Literacy* and the National Research Council's *Standards* (Blank & Pechman, 1995). To translate these state frameworks into district policy and classroom practice, an extensive communication effort is needed to promote the goals of science education reform. If reformers hope to have a wide and substantive impact, they must work to influence and support state-level efforts to set and implement science learning goals through curriculum frameworks and related assessments:

■ State frameworks—By late 1996, 45 states had curriculum frameworks in science and mathematics. Many of these frameworks have been heavily influenced by the curriculum content described in *Science for All Americans*, *Benchmarks*, and *Standards*. More work is needed at the state level to support and encourage implementation by local districts, ensuring equitable and appropriate access to improved science instruction.

■ State assessments—Because what is tested is what gets taught, science education reformers could have great impact by trying to influence the nature of statewide testing for students in science and mathematics. In addition to having science included as an area for regular state-level assessment, clear attention is needed to using assessments that reflect reasoning, inquiry, and conceptual understanding in science.

Above all, assessments must be fair to all students.

Above all, assessments must be fair to all students. Many standardized assessment procedures used in schools and districts do not provide a wide enough variety of techniques for showing science and mathematics competence. Worst of all, these same assessments are used to track students, creating a system where some students are forced completely out of science and mathematics courses solely because of their poor performance on tests. Assessments need to be examined for bias in language and content, recognizing that current assessments are unfair to students who have not had the same learning opportunities as their peers (FairTest, 1991). Science educators must support research on this issue, and must also make it a priority in their efforts to influence the design of new state assessments.

Many states now test every student several times—typically at grades 4, 8, and 11 or 12—as a part of their accountability system. This type of widespread testing argues for inexpensive, easily scored tests that report quantitative scores. Because the multiple measures needed to reflect science literacy are expensive and because student-centered approaches require further development to make them reliable, there is a direct conflict between current accountability needs and the interests of science education reformers. Some possibilities for overcoming this conflict are described in "Recommendations."

In designing any assessment process, it is necessary to specify several factors: the type of data needed (e.g., achievement, attitude, performance), the way it is collected, who will use it, and for what purpose it will be used. Remembering that assessments have both internal and external purposes, science education reformers can influence policymakers to keep these factors in mind. For example, assessments of science achievement to monitor the effects of state frameworks may not require testing every student in the state. Sampling and in-depth approaches such as observations and interviews could minimize the importance placed on a single high-stakes exam and the influence of such exams on teaching practice.

For internal purposes, assessments can be changed from tools that force students to learn to instruments that encourage student reasoning, scoring the student on the rigor of her or his argument; examine the quality of work samples; base results on observations of behavior over long periods of time; and support students in developing their own judgments of the quality of their work. This type of philosophy is likely to blur the boundaries between instruction and assessment and to reflect the broad goals of science literacy described in *Science for All Americans*.

There are barriers to changing assessment philosophy and practice, but also some possible strategies for overcoming those barriers. Teachers need to know how to design and use new assessment methods. Students also must become accustomed not only to the idea of new assessments but also to taking some responsibility for assessing their own science learning. If teachers are comfortable with new testing procedures, student opinions are likely to follow.

Policymakers, administrators, and the constituents to whom they answer may resist seemingly "soft," nonquantifiable assessments. Such procedures might not seem like "real testing" to those who were taught using traditional multiple-choice and short-answer exams. Efforts are needed to show the skeptics that new assessments are anything but "soft" and that they measure the development of higher-order thinking skills. These are the skills that education policymakers and the media insist will be needed for Americans to live healthy, productive lives in our increasingly technological world. At the same time, business leaders insist that tomorrow's workers must be prepared to be flexible thinkers in order to perform in a workplace constantly transformed by technology.

Science education reformers should emphasize that higher-order thinking skills cannot be measured by machine-scored, multiple-choice tests. In fact, development of those skills may be hampered by such tests. By casting new assessments in this light, science educators may find political allies where they otherwise would have found opponents.

ASSESSMENT AND INSTRUCTION

Currently, assessment and student testing are not included in *Science for All Americans* or *Benchmarks*. Project 2061 avoids dictating assessment techniques to teachers, reasoning that teachers are better able to design flexible assessments that measure whether their individual students have reached the respective benchmarks. Nonetheless, teachers have little time to develop multiple assessments in science, especially given the effort necessary to design assessment activities that are valid and reliable. Although it may not be appropriate for Project 2061 to design assessments to accompany the benchmarks, a set of criteria for such assessments, complete with detailed examples, would help to bring reform goals into the classroom. Such a guide would surely play a major role in encouraging classroom implementation and would provide an additional layer of structure and depth to reform.

Testing practice in the United States, especially at state and district levels, still relies a great deal on short-answer tests that emphasize

---

Characteristics of Good Classroom Assessments

- They produce measurable evidence of learning.
- They are relevant to the student and to the learning goal.
- They involve close transfer of learning gained through the curriculum.
- They accommodate a variety of development levels and intelligences.
- They account for prior knowledge about the task context, or provide pre-assessment activities to familiarize all students with the content.
- They give students and teachers options to have tasks completed individually or cooperatively.
- They allow students to select the best approach to the task.
- They assess tasks consistently.

Adapted from: Lawrence Hall of Science. (1994). *Authentic assessment tools & shining examples.* Berkeley, CA: Author.

reflexive rather than reflective thinking on the part of students. Classroom science assessment—used by teachers and students to diagnose difficulties, plan instruction, give feedback on progress, make improvements in learning activities, and monitor attitudes—can use a variety of tasks and methods.

New, multiple methods of assessing science knowledge and reasoning have the potential to greatly increase our ability to promote higher-order, critical thinking skills among students. New assessments can also improve equity by measuring a wider variety of student abilities and skills in science than current methods. Accommodations for individual differences and the use of tools beyond pencil and paper can make assessments more valid and useful than traditional tests, which tend to reward those students with great recall ability over those who have other academic strengths like creativity or clarity of expression.

Testing remains distinct from learning in the minds of most American students and teachers. A typical scenario, especially in secondary school, is to read the text, listen to lectures, perhaps do some lab work, and then be tested on the week's work on Friday. This process is not unlike assessment procedures in most colleges and universities. Classroom science instruction and assessment can be brought together through observations and checklists of students' performance in activities such as solving problems and conducting lab experiments, assessment of individual and group projects using several criteria, and the use of portfolios that reflect student growth and achievement on a variety of activities over time. In all of these, students can have a role in selecting the criteria for evaluating their work, in making choices about what will be assessed, and in making improvements on performances.

To help break the cycle that maintains the status quo, the recommendations of this chapter should be implemented in concert with those in *Blueprints'* Chapters 9: Teacher Education and 10: Higher Education, so that prospective science teachers will learn about and experience improved assessments in their own science learning. Changing teacher preparation programs and improving teacher development will go a long way to helping educators rethink how they assess student performance in science classrooms.

TEACHER PREPARATION IN ASSESSMENT
Teachers continue to rely on traditional short-answer tests for three main reasons. First, they do not feel confident that new assessment techniques will be accepted for accountability purposes by school

administrators and the public at large. (This reminds us that until administrators approve, teachers are unlikely to use new assessments, even if they know how.) Also, many teachers have not yet learned how to develop and use new assessments in their classrooms. Finally, many new assessments take more time to develop or to administer than traditional tests. All of these reasons point to a great need to illustrate the role of new assessments and to train teachers and administrators to use those assessments.

Achieving this goal will require a cooperative effort between schools, colleges and universities, and state science education leaders. Teachers' fears that new assessments will not meet accountability needs could be mitigated by encouraging them to follow state science and mathematics curriculum frameworks and by providing state- and district-sponsored staff development that reflects those frameworks. States that have used *Benchmarks* or *Standards* to guide their science and mathematics framework would need to rethink their methods of statewide assessment, lending further support to teachers who wish to align classroom assessments with science literacy goals.

Both teacher preparation and staff development can focus on assessment along with other components of science instruction. Rather than ignoring assessment or keeping it as a separate course or workshop, as has been done in past work with teachers, professional development can integrate work on assessment with work on instruction and materials. Teachers can also learn how to analyze existing assessments in the same way they analyze curricula to determine how well they meet benchmarks and standards. These experiences would provide a natural way for science teachers to think about fusing these functions in their classrooms.

EXTERNAL ASSESSMENTS

Science education reformers can make great strides by including open-ended questions and other performance-based tasks in district, state, and national exams. However, teachers cannot be expected to change their assessment procedures only to be judged on the students' performance on standardized, multiple-choice exams. Realizing this, some states have brought together test publishers, state education officials, the reform community, and school personnel to create new forms of assessment. As other states implement frameworks that are based on *Benchmarks* and *Standards*, they will need to align assessments with these new goals.

Michigan Educational Assessment Program
Multiple Assessment Tasks Included in Statewide Assessment

I. *Multiple choice items.* The items require "using," "constructing," and "reflecting on" science knowledge.

II. *Cluster Problems.* Real world scenarios described in words, pictures, and diagrams followed by a cluster of five to six items, one of which is constructed response. The items require "using," "constructing," and "reflecting on" science knowledge.

III. *Text Criticisms.* Present a short passage involving science from the popular press or a trade book followed by five to six items. The items require "using," "constructing," and "reflecting on" science knowledge.

IV. *Investigations.* Students perform an investigation in the weeks before the test. During the test, they complete five to six items, based on the investigation, that require "using," "constructing," and "reflecting on" science knowledge.

Source: Michigan Department of Education. (1994). *Assessment frameworks for the Michigan high school proficiency test in science.* Lansing, MI: Author

Perhaps the greatest barrier to moving away from machine-scored tests is that they are efficient and cost-effective. It is hard to imagine the time and effort that would be required to judge and score open-ended responses and the performance of an entire state's students at several grade levels. As assessments change to reflect the goals of standards-based reform, states will need to rethink the uses of their assessments. State must consider seriously the ideas of sampling and of returning the responsibility for monitoring student progress and setting graduation requirements to local districts. It is critical that these issues be recognized and discussed, and that a viable solution be found.

RECOMMENDATIONS FOR IMPROVED ASSESSMENT

The previous section presented the needed changes in assessment to implement reform in science education. This section describes characteristics of ideal student assessment and recommends some steps toward this ideal.

ASSESSMENT AND SCIENCE CONTENT
Ideally, the content of assessment activities, both for internal and external purposes, should reflect the content of *Benchmarks* and *Standards*. State and district frameworks for science and mathematics education

should embrace these documents, and assessment programs should be linked to those frameworks.

■ In designing assessments, educators should refer to *Benchmarks* and *Standards*, but the statements in those documents should not be used as criteria for rote memorization. The student who can merely recite the benchmarks is not necessarily progressing toward science literacy, but the student who understands the concepts that the benchmarks describe is.

■ The link between *Benchmarks* and *Standards* and assessment practice can be further strengthened by using these documents as clear criteria for accountability at all levels. Science assessments designed to match the content in *Benchmarks* can help parents, legislators, educators, and interested taxpayers to determine whether the students in their schools, their districts, or their states are learning science.

ASSESSMENT PHILOSOPHY

Any assessment program designed for use in science classrooms should frequently test student familiarity with and comprehension of systems; models; constancy; and patterns of change, evolution, and scale. Assessments should also focus on students' habits of mind—curiosity, openness to new ideas, and skepticism—as described by Project 2061. This emphasis on themes rather than on bits of information—on habits of mind rather than on recall—means that assessments should stress reflective thinking rather than reflexive thinking.

■ The assessment program should be flexible and easily modified as new ideas are developed, reflecting the recognition that reform is an evolutionary and time-consuming process.

Teachers should be presented with the outcomes they are expected to achieve—contained in frameworks based on *Benchmarks* and *Standards*—and then be free to design their own methods of instruction and assessment. This allows for flexibility in the design of science curricula and assessment, for collaboration between and empowerment of teachers, and for curricula and assessments to better serve the needs of individual students.

■ States can serve their accountability needs without testing every student.

An important philosophical issue is how to justify states' accountability-based need to test every student several times during the K-12 grades in light of the negative impact this can have on classroom mathematics and science instruction. States should consider using sampling, similar to the NAEP approach, to provide more in-depth and comprehensive reports on student science achievement. Sampling would allow assessment of student task performance and collection of data on important variables that affect the opportunity to learn, such as types of science activities, the nature of the curriculum, types of classroom assessments, and students' attitudes toward science. Assessment systems that allow such in-depth investigation would be far more productive than inexpensive testing methods for every student.

ASSESSMENT STRATEGIES

Assessment strategies and activities should be available for each science curriculum unit used by teachers. These curriculum units—and the assessments that are used with them—should be analyzed using a valid, comprehensive, and standardized procedure that describes their alignment with *Benchmarks* and *Standards*.[1]

■ Teachers and students should use a variety of science assessment techniques that require students to use higher-order thinking skills.

■ In addition to good multiple-choice items, assessments should include open-ended items, essays, projects, portfolios, exhibits or displays, and other strategies that test students' ability to generate answers and support their contentions rather than simply recall data or select responses from several options.

■ Science assessments should also blur the boundaries between classroom learning and real-world living. For example, students working in groups over a period of days or weeks might examine the causes of pollution in a nearby pond or lake by taking water samples and observing runoff from nearby farmland. After the investigation, they might make a recommendation for correcting the problem.

■ Because science produces questions more frequently than absolute "right" and "wrong" answers, students should be assessed on their abilities to make accurate measurements, to use mathematics and data analysis to solve problems, and to be creative in designing experiments and solving mathematical or scientific problems, as well as on the rigor of their methodology and the quality of the questions they pursue.

---

[1]Project 2061 has developed a procedure for analyzing how well the content and pedagogy of science curriculum materials match *Benchmarks* and *Standards*, and is training teachers and others to analyze the materials. A small set of science curriculum materials has been analyzed; work is underway to analyze more materials, develop a greater capacity for training people to do the analysis, and develop a procedure for analyzing assessment activities.

ASSESSMENT AND LEARNING

Science assessment activities can also be occasions for learning. Rather than setting aside time for the testing of memorized facts, teachers and students together can design assessments that are integrated into the curriculum.

■ Students should be measured on their understanding of the nature of science and the world rather than on their ability to regurgitate facts.

■ Students should collaborate in assessment design and scoring to increase their sense of responsibility and motivation for learning and get feedback on their learning process.

For example, a ninth-grade biology class might be given a newspaper article that describes the results of a recent scientific study. Students should be scored on their ability to recognize possible flaws in the study and to suggest creative ways to make it more rigorous, and on their willingness to be skeptical about newspaper articles and other information sources.

APPROPRIATE AND FAIR ASSESSMENT

Assessment procedures must be appropriate and fair for all students. Techniques that aim to promote equity—to ensure that all American school students have an equal opportunity to learn science—will emphasize student accomplishment rather than document failure (Malcom, 1991).

■ Standards for good work should be discussed with students and used consistently in the evaluation process.

■ Students and teachers should recognize that there is more than one path to success. This idea is consistent with equitable and fair assessment, which focuses on helping students develop scientific habits of mind rather than producing pat answers.

TEACHER PREPARATION

Pre-service programs should ground future science teachers in a variety of assessment techniques. All teachers should be well prepared to understand and use effective and varied ways to judge student performance and to develop effective methods for blurring the line between testing and teaching.

Although state and district policies should emphasize assessment, teachers should be prepared to distinguish between assessments designed to meet state and district accountability needs and the richer, more comprehensive science assessments they use for instruction.

EXTERNAL ASSESSMENTS

District, state, and national level examinations should be based on the content of *Benchmarks for Science Literacy* and the *National Science Education Standards*. Because of content and student sampling considerations and time limitations, multiple-choice items may be used on these exams, but the tests should also include tasks that are similar to those used for internal purposes—open-ended questions, essays, or performance tasks. The format of the exams should be familiar to students to avoid jeopardizing the validity of inferences drawn from test results.

■ Significantly less time per student should be spent on external examinations than is currently the case. Time and resources should be devoted to helping districts and teachers to identify, analyze, or develop assessments that are integrated with their own science curriculum and that provide direct opportunities for student learning.

■ External examinations should provide external audiences with information used for accountability, program evaluation, and future policymaking. They should not be used to make decisions about individual students, teachers, or schools.

ASSESSMENT STANDARDS

Assessment techniques for both internal and external purposes should meet acceptable standards of validity, reliability, feasibility, and equity. The National Research Council's *National Science Education Standards* (1996) includes a set of standards for assessment in science education, and the National Council of Teachers of Mathematics has published *Assessment Standards for School Mathematics* (1995). Both of these documents are good starting points for addressing criteria that should be used to judge science assessments at all levels—classroom, district, state, or national. In addition, the American Educational Research Association, the American Psychological Association, and the National Council for Measurement in Education have established standards for testing, and several books and journals are devoted to the quality of tests.

■ Science assessments should be as rigorous as those sanctioned by these national organizations.

■ Science teachers should be trained to identify or develop reliable and valid assessments in which the intended effects of an assessment activity are achieved.

REFERENCES

American Association for the Advancement of Science. (1993). *Benchmarks for science literacy.* New York: Oxford University Press.

American Association for the Advancement of Science. (1989). *Science for all Americans.* New York: Oxford University Press.

Beaton, A.F., Martin, M.O., Mullis, I.V.S., Gonzalez, E.J., Smith, T.A., and Kelly, D.L. (1996). *Science achievement in the middle school years: IEA's third international mathematics and science study.* Chestnut Hill, MA: Boston College.

Blank, R. K., & Pechman, E. M. (1995). *State curriculum frameworks in mathematics and science: How are they changing across the states?* Washington, D.C.: Council of Chief State School Officers.

Center for the Study of Testing, Evaluation, and Educational Policy. (1992). *The influence of testing on teaching math and science in grades 4–12.* Boston, MA: Author.

Darling-Hammond, L. (1995). Equity issues in performance-based assessment. In M. T. Nettles & A. L. Nettles (Eds.), *Equity and excellence in educational testing and assessment* (pp. 89–114). Boston, MA; Kluwer Academic.

FairTest. (1991). *Statement on proposals for a national test.* Cambridge, MA: National Center for Fair & Open Testing.

Malcom, S. M. (1991). Equity and excellence through authentic assessment. In G. Kulm & S. M. Malcom (Eds.), *Science assessment in the service of reform.* Washington, D.C.: American Association for the Advancement of Science Press. (Now published by Lawrence Erlbaum).

National Council of Teachers of Mathematics. (1995). *Assessment standards for school mathematics.* Reston, VA: Author.

National Educational Goals Panel. (1996). *Profile of 1994–95 state assessment systems and reported results.* Washington, D.C.: Author.

National Research Council. (1996). *National science education standards.* Washington, D.C.: National Academy Press.

National Science Foundation. (1996). *The learning curve.* Washington, D.C.: Author.

Resnick, L. B., & Resnick, D. P. (1989). *Tests as standards of achievement in schools. The uses of standardized tests in American education.* Princeton, NJ: Educational Testing Service.

Stiggins, R. J., & Conklin, N. F. (1992). *In teachers' hands: Investigating the practices of classroom assessment.* Albany, NY: State University of New York Press.

BIBLIOGRAPHY

Baker, E.L., and Webb, N. (1993, April). *Implications of collaboration on the measurement of student achievement.* Paper presented at the annual meeting of the American Educational Research Association, Atlanta, GA.

Baron, J.B. (1991). Performance assessment: Blurring the edges of assessment, curriculum, and instruction. In G. Kulm and S.M. Malcom (Eds.), *Science assessment in the service of reform.* Washington, D.C.: American Association for the Advancement of Science. (Now published by Lawrence Erlbaum).

Black, P. (1993, April). *Performance assessment and accountability: The experience in England and Wales.* Address to the annual meeting of the American Educational Research Association, Atlanta, GA.

Blank, R. and Dalkilic, M. (1992). *State policies on science and mathematics education.* Washington, D.C.: Council of Chief State School Officers.

Carter, K. (1984). Do teachers understand the principles of writing tests? *Journal of Teacher Education, 35*, 57-60.

Council of Chief State School Officers. (1993). *State student assessment program database, 1992-93.* Washington, D.C.: Author.

Darling-Hammond, L., and Lieberman, A. (1992, January 29). The shortcomings of standardized tests. *The Chronicle of Higher Education,* B1-B2.

Davis, A. & Armstrong, J. (1991). State initiatives in assessing science education. In G. Kulm and S.M. Malcom (Eds.), *Science assessment in the service of reform.* Washington, D.C.: American Association for the Advancement of Science. (Now published by Lawrence Erlbaum).

Dorr-Bremme, D.W., and Herman, J.L.(1986). *Assessing student achievement: A profile of classroom practices.* Los Angeles, CA: Center for the Study of Evaluation, University of California, Los Angeles.

Educational Testing Service. (1990, August). Testing in the schools. *ETS Policy Notes, 2*(3).

Educational Testing Service. (1990, Summer). Growth through school. *ETS Policy Notes, 5*(3).

Educational Testing Service. (1990). *The education reform decade.* Princeton, NJ: Author.

FairTest. (1991). *Statement on proposals for a national test.* Cambridge, MA: National Center for Fair & Open Testing.

Fleming, M. & Chambers, B. (1983). Teacher-made tests: Windows on the classroom. In W.E. Hathaway (Ed.), *Testing in the schools: New directions for testing and measurement.* San Francisco, CA: Jossey-Bass.

Gong, B., LaHart, C., & Courtney, R. (1991). *Current state science assessments: Is nothing better than something?* Princeton, NJ: Educational Testing Service.

Gullickson, A.R & Ellwein, M.C. (1985). Post hoc analysis of teacher-made tests: The goodness-of-fit between prescription and practice. *Educational Measurement: Issues and Practice, 4*, 15-18.

Haertel, E., et al. (1984, April). *Testing in secondary schools: Student perceptions.* Paper presented at the annual meeting of the American Educational Research Association, New Orleans, LA.

Harmon, M. (1991). Fairness in testing: Are science education assessments biased? In G. Kulm and S. M. Malcom (Eds.), *Science assessment in the service of reform.* Washington, D.C.: American Association for the Advancement of Science. (Now published by Lawrence Erlbaum).

Hein, G. E. (1990). *The assessment of hands-on elementary science programs.* Grand Forks, ND: University of North Dakota Press.

Hein, G. E. & Price, S. (1994). *Active assessment for active science: A guide for elementary school teachers.* Portsmouth, NH: Heinemann.

Interview on assessment issues with Lorrie Shephard. (1991, March). Research News and Comment, *Educational Researcher, 20,* 21-23, 27.

Kulm, G. (1994). *Mathematics assessment: What works in the classroom.* San Francisco, CA: Jossey-Bass.

Kulm, G. & Malcom, S. M. (Eds.) (1991). *Science assessment in the service of reform.* Washington, D.C.: American Association for the Advancement of Science. (Now published by Lawrence Erlbaum).

Kulm, G. (Ed.) (1990). *Assessing higher order thinking in mathematics.* Washington, D.C.: American Association for the Advancement of Science. (Now published by Lawrence Erlbaum).

Lebert, K. (1991). Math: The tool we use to study science. In G. Kulm and S.M. Malcom (Eds.), *Science assessment in the service of reform.* Washington, D.C.: American Association for the Advancement of Science. (Now published by Lawrence Erlbaum).

Linn, R.L. (1993). Educational assessment: Expanded expectations and challenges. *Educational Evaluation and Policy Analysis, 15,* 1-16.

Linn, R.L., & Baker, E.L. (1992, Fall). Portfolios and accountability. *The CRESST Line, 1,* 8-9.

Madaus, G.F., et al. (1992). *The influence of testing on teaching math and science in grades 4-12.* Boston, MA: Boston College.

Madaus, G.F. (1988). The influence of testing on the curriculum. In L.N. Tanner (Ed.), *Critical issues in curriculum, 87th yearbook of the National Society for the Study of Education.* Chicago, IL: University of Chicago Press.

Malcom, S.M. (1991). Equity and excellence through authentic science assessment. In Kulm, G. & S. M. Malcom (Eds.) (1990). *Assessing higher order thinking in mathematics.* Washington, D.C.: American Association for the Advancement of Science. (Now published by Lawrence Erlbaum).

Mathematical Sciences Education Board. (1993). *Measuring up: Prototypes for mathematics assessment.* Washington, D.C.: National Academy Press.

Mathematical Sciences Education Board. (1993). *Measuring what counts: A conceptual guide for mathematics assessment.* Washington, D.C.: National Academy Press.

McColsky, W. & O'Sullivan, R. (1993). *How to assess student performance in science.* Greensboro, NC: Southeast Regional Vision for Education.

Messick, S. (1989). Validity. In R.L. Linn (Ed.), *Educational measurement* (3rd ed.). New York: Macmillan.

National Assessment of Educational Progress. (1987). *Learning by doing: A manual for teaching and assessing higher-order thinking in science and mathematics.* Princeton, NJ: Educational Testing Service.

National Commission on Testing and Public Policy. (1990). *From gatekeeper to gateway: Transforming testing in America.* Chestnut Hill, MA: Boston College.

Resnick, L.B. & Resnick, D.P. (1989). Tests as standards of achievement in schools. *The uses of standardized tests in American education.* Princeton, NJ: Educational Testing Service.

Rezba, R. J., Sprague, C., Fiel, R. L. & Funk, H. J. (1995). *Learning and assessing science process skills, Third Edition.* Dubuque, IA: Kendall/Hunt Publishing Company.

Rothman, R. (1995). *Measuring up: Standards, assessment, and school reform.* San Francisco, CA: Jossey-Bass.

Spauling, S. (1989). Comparing educational phenomena: Promises, prospects, and perils. In A.C. Purves (Ed.), *International comparisons and educational reform.* Alexandria, VA: Association for Supervision and Curriculum Development.

Stetz, F. & Beck, M. (1979, April). *Comments from the classroom: Teachers' and students' opinions of achievement tests.* Paper presented at the annual meeting of the American Educational Research Association, San Francisco, CA.

Stiggins, R. J. & Conklin, N. F. (1992). *In teachers' hands: Investigating the practices of classroom assessment.* Albany, NY: State University of New York Press.

U.S. Department of Education. (1991). *America 2000: An education strategy* Washington, D.C.: Author.

Walker, R. (1992, February). *The philosophy of the Illinois goal assessment program in science.* Paper presented at the annual meeting of the American Association for the Advancement of Science, Chicago, IL.

Welch, W. & Anderson, R. (1993, April). *The performance of performance testing in a large-scale assessment of computer education.* Paper presented at the annual meeting of the American Educational Research Association, Atlanta, GA.

Welch, W. W. (1995). Student assessment and curriculum evaluation. In B.J. Fraser &, H.J. Walberg (Eds.), *Improving science education: What do we know?* Chicago, IL: National Society for the Study of Education.

Wolf, D., et al. (1991). To use their minds well: Investigating new forms of student assessment. *Review of Research in Education, 17,* 31-74.

DAVID SMITH, *Cubi I, 1963.*

PART III
The Support Structure

SCHOOLS REFLECT THE SOCIETY in which they exist. This is true for neighborhood schools and for the entire education system of the United States. Indeed, education can be thought of as a subsystem of a social-political-economic system. In *Blueprints* we turn that around and look at aspects of the larger system as components of the education system. These four chapters examine the roles of families and communities, business and industry, higher education, and teacher education in relation to K-12 science and mathematics education.

While the main role of families, communities, businesses, and universities may be to "support" the K-12 education enterprise, it is certainly not their only one. These entities often play a major part in actually *shaping* the education enterprise. They do so by pressing the schools to establish policies they favor and discontinue ones they dislike, and by taking a hand in setting financial and other constraints for the schools to observe. What complicates matters is that in the United States the "they" of parents, communities, etc., is extremely diverse and rarely of a single mind. Moreover, control over the policies, finances, and operation of "the education enterprise" they wish to support or shape is widely and confusingly dispersed. Understanding education as a system would seem to require exploring its interactions with the social system in which it is embedded.

The first two chapters of this section might well have been one. On the face of it, higher education subsumes teacher education. But not all teacher education—in preparation or ongoing staff development—is sponsored by higher education or conducted by professors. Project 2061 commissioned separate reports in order to be sure to highlight the paramount importance of teacher education to reform. Also, the project wanted to be sure that sufficient attention was paid to all of the functions of colleges and universities that have an impact on K-12 education. Still, the reader may want to reassemble these chapters conceptually.

As direct influences on the policies and practices of individual school systems, teacher education and higher education can be as important as family, community, and business. However, while university-school partnerships of one kind or another are not unknown, they are neither numerous nor enduring. More commonly, the influence of higher education on K-12 schools is indirect. For example, the admissions standards of a college apply to the graduates of all high schools, not just to the schools in its immediate vicinity, and a school district can hire any teachers who meet state licensing requirements, no matter where they trained. This indirect influence can be strong (school districts everywhere pay attention to Ivy League admissions standards) as well as dynamic (there is a strong relationship between state universities that produce large numbers of teachers and the school districts around them). Finally, the important role of community colleges and historically Black universities should be carefully studied, not only as models of how to meet the needs of a changing undergraduate population, but as partners in meeting our goal of a more diverse science and mathematics teaching force.

Chapters 11 and 12 deal with individuals and groups that have an interest in the policies, budgets, and practices of particular schools or school systems. These include:

■ adults whose children attend schools, who pay close attention to what happens in the schools, and who make their wishes known;

■ citizens, with or without school children, who follow school issues and attend school board meetings; vote; join special interest groups; or run for the school board, city council or state legislature;

■ business organizations that provide schools with direct help such as computers and consultants, lobby school boards and state legislatures in behalf of education, and take positions on proposed tax measures;

■ philanthropic organizations that support education through scholarships and funding for ongoing programs; and

■ newspapers and radio and television stations that cover education issues regularly.

Clearly there is considerable overlap among these individuals, groups, and organizations, but their stories are told in two chapters: "Family and Community" and "Business and Industry." Each discusses reform in science and mathematics education from its own perspective. By considering the two chapters at the same time, readers may appreciate the complexity, and perhaps gain some insight into the inevitable clashes as well as the areas of potential cooperation and support by these important clients of the schools.

Again, the following questions are intended to initiate discussions of components of the education system and their interactions, with some attention to their bearing on the aims of Project 2061.

Teacher Education

1. If everyone should acquire the knowledge and skills recommended in *Science for All Americans*, doesn't it follow that all teachers and school administrators should also do so? What can be done to bring current and future educators up to that standard? What distinctions should be made between the preparation of elementary and secondary teachers?

2. Given the amount to be learned and the technical skills to be developed, how long should pre-service education take? Five years? More? Do economic and social realities limit the possibilities, such as raising certification standards dramatically or reducing the number of teacher education institutions by half or more, so that those that

remain can be more selective? What would be the effect of instituting rigorous entry tests to teaching, modeled after those in other professions? What are the likely benefits and costs of such tests?

3. How would the teacher training picture change if it became possible (at least in principle) to reduce the size of the certified teaching force necessary to operate the schools and still meet high standards of student learning? Would teacher salaries and status rise? Would the nature of the job change radically? Would new specialties arise?

4. Are there steps that can be taken to reduce the parochialism of education? Would it help if the top 100 or so professional development schools, like the top medical schools, deliberately drew their students from every section of the country? Is national certification a possibility? A combination of state and national certification?

5. Should the growing number of professional development schools (which are designed to be to the education of teachers as university-affiliated hospitals are to the education of physicians) become the norm and model for teacher education? How should the faculties of such training institutions be assembled? What should be required in the way of prior knowledge and experience to compete for admission? What evidence of competence should be required for graduation?

Higher Education

1. What can be done to get science, mathematics, and engineering departments in colleges and universities to work together to assure science literacy for all their graduates (many of whom will later influence education policy as legislators and business leaders)? What steps can be taken to improve the cooperation between academic departments and schools of education?

2. Because many teachers attend community colleges before transferring to teacher training institutions, what can be done to build coherent teacher education programs that reach across the full range of

higher education institutions? Can more coherence among institutions help to build a pipeline that would increase the proportion of minority teachers of science and mathematics teachers in the nation's schools?

3. How can universities set admissions in order to motivate K-12 institutions to produce science literate graduates? Because few colleges and universities in America have entrance examinations at all, what might they use as a reasonable substitute?

4. How can science and mathematics instruction at colleges and universities be improved? Are standards and incentives for faculty necessary? How can professional societies support this effort?

5. How can higher education faculty be encouraged to work with schools to improve the K-12 science and mathematics curricula, and to participate in the development of learning materials for the schools? To provide science research, laboratory, and field experience opportunities for K-12 teachers?

FAMILY AND COMMUNITY

1. How do and how should schools respond to the changing nature of family structure and life? Is there evidence to suggest that particular family arrangements are deleterious to learning? Are there responses to family circumstances that are educationally effective?

2. What are the educational consequences of having substantial numbers of either poverty-stricken or wealthy families in a community? Where do ideas such as school choice, charter schools, and school-based councils fit into this picture? What does research have to say about the effects of socioeconomic issues and about the programs to deal with them?

3. What is the place of out-of-school learning? How can all students have access to museums and informal science learning? How can families help to foster and support high expectations and achievement?

4. What ways have been found effective to secure the support of families for standards-based learning, such as that recommended in *Science*

for All Americans and *Benchmarks*? Does it vary according to family structure and circumstances? Cultural background? If the school and the families it serves are at odds on this, what steps have proven to be helpful in reaching a workable compromise?

5. What are the responsibilities of parents, community health agencies, state and federal governments, and the schools in safeguarding the health of all school-age children? Where do the issues of drugs, drinking, teenage pregnancy, and other health-related issues that are value-laden, fit into the education policy mix?

BUSINESS AND INDUSTRY

1. Does the reform of American industry in the 1980s and 1990s provide a model—or anti-model—for education? If not a model, are their some particular lessons to be learned for the operation of school systems? For the education of students for employment in those industries?

2. How can school systems enlist the political influence of large corporations on policy and financial issues at state and national levels? Likewise, how can teachers and administrators gain the support of smaller businesses in their communities? When the interests of business and education are in conflict, as in tax matters, what's to be done?

3. Which kinds of business-school interactions pay off? What are the short and long-term effects of contributions to the schools in the form of materials and consultants, grants, career information, scholarships or business-site experience for teachers and school administrators? Do they come and go, or are they generally sustained for years and decades?

9

Teacher Education

TEACHER EDUCATION plays an important role in science education reform. Some reformers say that changing teacher education is the first step to dramatic change in science education. Equipping teachers to bring about science literacy for all is certainly an intellectual and practical challenge of great societal importance. But sweeping reform of the teacher education system requires the same tremendous level of effort as reforming other components, such as standards, curriculum, and assessment.

Building on the visions and principles of the Holmes Group (1990), many colleges and universities are beginning to respond to this challenge. Partnerships between colleges and K-12 schools, in forming professional development schools, show promise. Another promising initiative is the Science and Mathematics Teacher Education Collaborative Program, which addresses the broad, systemic work needed from teacher educators, scientists, and schools (National Science Foundation, 1995). However, we are still a long way from implementing effective models in the thousands of teacher education programs across the country.

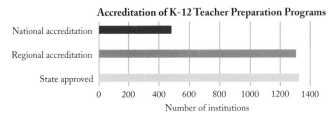

Accreditation of K-12 Teacher Preparation Programs

Source: National Association of State Directors of Teacher Education and Certification. (1996). *Manual of certification and preparation of educational personnel in the United States and Canada.* Dubuque, IA: Kendall/Hunt Publishing.

This chapter suggests ways to reform the education of prospective teachers and the continuing education of practicing science, mathematics, and technology teachers. It examines the conditions under which teachers currently develop and carry out their practice and suggests several factors that teacher educators need to consider to design better programs.

Immediately below, recommendations are made for restructuring undergraduate education in four areas: preparing teachers in subject matter, preparing them for diverse students, preparing them to teach, and recruiting science teachers. These recommendations are followed by suggestions for improving 1) teaching by college faculty and 2) the continuing education of science teachers. Finally, we propose guiding principles and suggestions for the professional education of teachers. Although this chapter focuses on teacher education, the importance of continuing education for administrators should also be recognized. Administrators will surely have to change their roles if they are to lead schools like those envisioned by reformers in science education.

NEEDED CHANGES IN UNDERGRADUATE TEACHER EDUCATION

Although the kind of teaching currently called for by science reformers has been advocated for decades, it has rarely been implemented successfully. Teacher education institutions must find ways to provide a lasting foundation upon which teachers can build the dispositions, skills, and knowledge required by the *National Science Education Standards* [*Standards*] (National Research Council, 1996) and *Benchmarks for Science Literacy* [*Benchmarks*] (American Association for the Advancement of Science, 1993). Teacher educators need to consider many factors when redesigning programs for teacher education; they also need to evaluate alternatives at every stage of the change (Wilson & Daviss, 1994). The appraisal, following, of the current state of undergraduate teacher education is meant to provoke discussion of needed changes.

PREPARING PROSPECTIVE TEACHERS IN SCIENCE

Addressing students' personal conceptions of scientific phenomena is one of the challenges in science teaching. It requires excellent knowledge of science, along with deep understanding of science learning. In response to everyday experiences with natural phenomena, children—including future teachers—construct their own theories and explanations to interpret the world around them. Some of these constructions have limited usefulness in and can interfere with learning about scientific phenomena. For example, many people come to believe that the seasons result from Earth's changing distance from the sun. Because ideas like this can account for personal observations and explain local phenomena, they are difficult to change. And because traditional test questions can be answered using these ideas, often science teachers in both K-12 and higher education do not detect them. The result is that even some college science majors continue to believe, for example, the incorrect reason for the seasons' changing. To be effective, most science teachers need a deeper and more generalized understanding of complex and often counterintuitive scientific principles than they currently have.

It is essential that all science teachers are literate enough in science to implement the goals presented in *Benchmarks* and *Standards*. The intensive study of a discipline increases the likelihood that future teachers will be able to understand science at a deep, conceptual level and to reflect on important ideas, theories, and applications. For this reason, most educators agree that all high school science teachers—and probably middle grades teachers as well—should have a major in science.

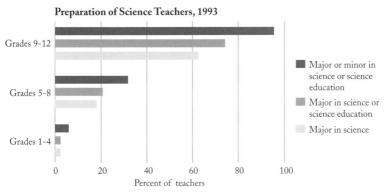

Preparation of Science Teachers, 1993

Grades 9-12

Grades 5-8

Grades 1-4

0   20   40   60   80   100

Percent of teachers

■ Major or minor in science or science education

▨ Major in science or science education

░ Major in science

Source: National Science Foundation. (1996). *Indicators of science and mathematics.* Arlington, VA: Author.

Most science and mathematics in the elementary grades is taught by generalists who majored in elementary education. Although it is impractical and perhaps inadvisable to suggest that all science and mathematics instruction at the elementary school level be taught by specialists, all elementary school teachers should have a deep understanding of some discipline, along with preparation in science content. Experts disagree about just what science content is most important for elementary teachers to understand. The answer may depend on whether elementary schools are organized departmentally or as self-contained classrooms, and on the role of K-6 science or mathematics specialists in the school. Colleges and universities can work closely with schools to develop programs in science and mathematics education that prepare their graduates to teach school science. For example, an urban or suburban area may opt for a program that allows for K-12 majors or specializations in science; a rural area may require broader science knowledge.

PREPARING PROSPECTIVE TEACHERS FOR DIVERSE STUDENTS

Effective teachers understand their students in ways not emphasized by traditional teacher education programs. Today's science teachers work with increasingly diverse student populations and are challenged by student attitudes and behaviors—cheating, questioning authority, and apathy—that reflect larger societal problems. Often, teacher education simply presents science teachers with summary characteristics of different groups without establishing their relevance to effective teaching. This can intensify, rather than reduce, hidden prejudices and stereotypes (Kozol, 1991). Therefore, prospective science teachers should be introduced to literature that helps them to understand the different issues faced in science classes by females, minorities, children with disabilities, and low-income students. They should work as undergraduates under careful direction in schools whose student population reflects this nation's growing diversity and with teachers who are effective in working with students of varied backgrounds.

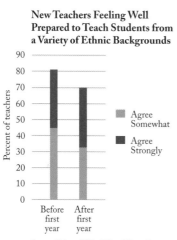

New Teachers Feeling Well Prepared to Teach Students from a Variety of Ethnic Backgrounds

Agree Somewhat

Agree Strongly

Source: Nelson, B.H., Weiss, I.R., and Conaway, L.E. (1992). *Science and mathematics education briefing book, Vol. III.* Chapel Hill, NC: Horizon Research, Inc.

PREPARING PROSPECTIVE TEACHERS TO TEACH

Science-teacher education must engage students in discussions about substantive issues of teaching and learning closely connected with the everyday work of teaching. This work should take place in K-12 schools where the best science teaching practice is in place. In addition, to narrow the gap between general principles of teaching learned in college classrooms and specific classroom situations, teacher education programs should adopt principles from Professional Development Schools (see

Blueprints' Resources for a description). This nationwide program integrates course work in teacher education with opportunities to assume various classroom responsibilities throughout the teacher education program. These experiences should not be concentrated at the end of the program in a full-time student teaching assignment.

Teacher education programs should expose their students to other cultural belief systems, controversies about the nature of science, and science from a feminist perspective.

To sustain these programs, faculty in schools of education and science must remain in close contact—through extended research, observation, or regular teaching—with the realities of the schools and classrooms where their students are teaching. Education faculty must also remain current on national professional standards for teacher education programs.

In addition to the assumptions, purposes, and discourse of science, teacher education programs should expose students to other cultural belief systems, discussions of controversies about the nature of science, and contributions to science from a feminist perspective. Students can also gain appreciation for the informal knowledge developed by people who live or work outdoors through long periods of observation. Finally, teachers can study approaches to developing and legitimizing knowledge, learning what counts as a good idea and what evidence can be used to decide what constitutes meaningful knowledge.

Field Experience. First-hand experiences in schools, teaching and mentoring experiences, and fieldwork with scientists must come early in the teacher education program. These experiences prepare prospective teachers for the content of their education courses and serve as living laboratories for formal course work. Although most prospective teachers have observed teaching either formally or informally, they rarely witness the extraordinary efforts teachers must undertake to educate themselves in their subject matter; to develop effective strategies for cultivating attitudes, skills, and knowledge of science in students; and to assess the success of their teaching and their students' learning. Field experiences allow experienced teachers to make these "hidden acts" of teaching more visible to prospective teachers. By creating and supporting professional discussions, teacher educators can give prospective science teachers a foundation for building habits of reflective teaching.

Teaching Practice. Teachers often do not see the relationship between the events they experience in their own classrooms and the generalizations about teaching and learning they are taught in universities. Many teachers report that they learned little of value about teaching until they began to teach. This finding challenges teacher education programs to create more effective ways to help prospective and experienced teachers connect general principles of teaching and student learning to specific problems and events in classrooms.

Schools should encourage team teaching and view individual teachers as specialists in various areas, including science. Organizing daily schedules to provide time during the school day for team planning and professional development is critical. At least one teacher on each team with strong science preparation can lead science study and lesson planning groups, demonstrate lessons, and provide special resources. These activities promote a belief in the value of increasing teamwork and professional interaction among teachers (Abell, 1990). In this environment, teachers can engage in continual learning about science and mathematics. In the "team specialist" model, every teacher would have expertise in at least one area, a liberal arts education, and a subject matter major. The team approach is an important departure from many current elementary generalist programs that assume a little science knowledge for teachers is better than no knowledge at all, and from many secondary programs that are highly departmentalized.

Novice teachers are often overwhelmed by the demands of teaching. Without opportunities to observe and be observed and to discuss issues with colleagues or a mentor, teachers find ways to meet these demands in the short term. These may include approaches to keeping students "on

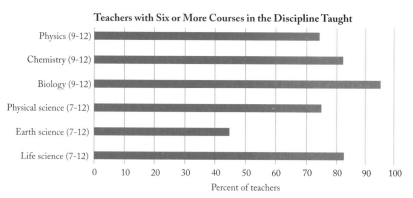

Teachers with Six or More Courses in the Discipline Taught

Source: National Science Foundation. (1996). *Indicators of science and mathematics, 1995.* Arlington, VA: Author.

task" that may not foster the type of learning promoted in *Benchmarks* and *Standards*. By forming teacher teams and other networking and leadership opportunities, school leaders can help teachers to develop habits of reflective practice, leading to their increased understanding of science, mathematics, and technology teaching and learning.

RECRUITING NEW TEACHERS

Because all levels of the educational system in the United States are decentralized, it is almost impossible to gather hard evidence on trends in the supply of new science teachers. However, some general patterns are clear. Physics teachers are generally in short supply, while the number of life sciences teachers sometimes exceeds available jobs. Too few students of color choose majors in science or mathematics education. Elementary teachers are abundantly available, but too few of them have strong subject matter preparation in science and mathematics. Uncertainties in school funding, a negative work environment, and generally low salaries often inhibit the most successful science majors from choosing science teaching as a career.

To strengthen and broaden the pool of science teachers, universities need to aggressively recruit and support able, high-achieving minority students to become teachers of science, mathematics, and technology. Science professionals and others with strong scientific backgrounds can also be recruited into teaching if universities adjust their programs to match the capabilities and experience these individuals bring, and if feasible and innovative career change opportunities are available.

To broaden science learning opportunities within and beyond the classroom, members of the scientific community can be recruited to participate in K-12 education as observers, guest speakers, tutors, and consultants. Scientists will need to become aware of the needs of teachers and students, but in the long run, their participation can enrich college and university classrooms and help K-12 teachers and scientists better understand each other.

Profile of the Eighth-Grade Science Teacher

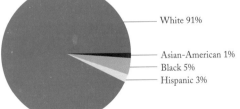

White 91%

Asian-American 1%
Black 5%
Hispanic 3%

Source: Nelson, B.H., Weiss, I.R., and Conaway, L.E. (1992). *Science and mathematics briefing book, Vol.III.* Chapel Hill, NC: Horizon Research.

NEEDED CHANGES IN COLLEGE
AND UNIVERSITY TEACHING

Even science majors in college often have serious deficiencies in fundamental ideas of science. It is no wonder that many science teachers enter classrooms without the kind of understanding called for by *Benchmarks* and *Standards* (Gallagher & Treagust, 1994; McDermott, 1990). Teaching in undergraduate science courses should change more systematically to emphasize central ideas and underlying themes that help students, including prospective teachers, to apply scientific principles in solving real problems. College curricula should also illustrate the relationships between science, mathematics, technology, and society. Integration does not need to occur in every course and throughout the curriculum, but connections cannot be left for students to conceptualize on their own.

Teachers rely far more on the teaching styles they have experienced as learners than on the theory or even the practical knowledge they encounter in teacher education programs (Grossman, 1991). Because lecture-based science and mathematics teaching is common in colleges and universities, higher education should heed this reality. Future secondary teachers who are successful science majors experience lecture approaches in college, leading them to believe that lectures are effective for all students. Teacher educators must be concerned with preparing future teachers to implement reform by exposing them in their own formal science learning to teaching styles that support reform.

Teaching and learning for understanding take time, desire, and ability. Faculty and students—especially in large introductory science classes—feel the "content crunch" of covering material in a limited amount of time. Science education for future elementary teachers is often limited to these introductory courses, giving them little opportunity to interact with faculty, write about and discuss science concepts, or engage in

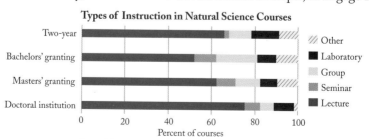

Types of Instruction in Natural Science Courses

Source: National Science Foundation. (1996). *Indicators of science and mathematics, 1995.* Arlington, VA: Author.

hands-on activities that would help develop science knowledge and understanding. As a result, they sometimes begin their teaching careers with negative attitudes toward science and without the skills to implement learning goals such as those outlined in *Benchmarks* and *Standards*.

Because most K-12 science teachers do not conduct research, they must be induced to read scientific journals and other sources of new scientific knowledge, and learn to interpret and evaluate data. Colleges can also use teaching methods that involve interactive participation, group work, and inquiry—especially in introductory courses taken by future elementary and secondary teachers. Finally, colleges can integrate the study of science with the study of and preparation for teaching to build on the widely held knowledge that the true understanding of a subject comes from teaching it.

Promising Approaches

While examples of excellent college teaching exist, serious shortcomings in science and mathematics teaching remain at many colleges and universities. University culture rewards faculty for research and provides little incentive to broaden their often limited repertoire of teaching and assessment methods. Several changes can focus attention on undergraduate teaching and learning: departments can help promote good teaching by holding faculty seminars and discussions on ways to improve teaching and assessment, by making the quality of a faculty member's teaching an influential factor in deciding on tenure and promotion, by developing the teaching competence of graduate students who teach much of the undergraduate coursework in many large universities, and by rewarding, fruitful innovations in university teaching.

Universities need to find ways to bring the extensive body of research on teaching, learning, and assessment in science and mathematics to the forefront in discussions of higher education. In addition, students should be allowed to become active learners, have first-hand experience with making connections between their own ideas and the knowledge they develop in courses, and participate in classes where faculty model a teaching style that is conducive to active learning. Even large lecture classes can be organized to promote active learning (Bonwell & Eison, 1991). When universities increase the number of science courses that allow students to become active learners, they increase the likelihood that future teachers and scientists will experience the excitement and satisfaction of designing inquiries and collecting and analyzing data to explore those inquiries.

NEEDED CHANGES IN PROFESSIONAL DEVELOPMENT

Perhaps the most important reason for continuing professional education for science, mathematics, and technology teachers is that it allows them to develop the special expertise related to their work. Specialized knowledge becomes a source of authority for setting policies and making curricular decisions. A second reason is that pre-service education is simply not long enough or intense enough for teachers to master all the skill areas they need. Third, as knowledge in the fields of both science and teaching continues to expand, and as our society and its demands continue to change, teachers themselves must grow and develop. Finally, when teachers engage in long-term professional development, they build relationships with a wider community of peers, which improves teaching quality.

A central problem with the current system of incentives for professional development is that teachers are rewarded for completing college credits or a degree rather than for mastering a subject and how best to teach it. Master's degree programs in education offer in-depth study but lack science content and strong ties to classroom practice. Professional development workshops lasting one or two days do little to improve teachers' understanding of their subject matter. Teachers are taught in "make it, take it" sessions how to conduct a particular set of activities or lessons, or they are taught to work with a curriculum package that has been adopted by the school or the district.

Neither of these approaches is satisfactory. Schools must be changed to reflect a view of teachers as intellectuals rather than technicians (Giroux, 1988). To support science instruction with activities tied to specific standards and benchmarks, professional development work must address more directly the curricular issues of sequences and connec-

Staff Development for Eighth-Grade Science Teachers per Year

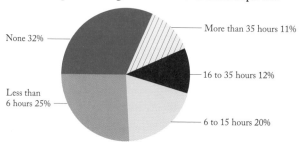

- None 32%
- Less than 6 hours 25%
- More than 35 hours 11%
- 16 to 35 hours 12%
- 6 to 15 hours 20%

Source: Nelson, B.H., Weiss, I.R., and Conaway, L.E. (1992). *Science and mathematics briefing book, Vol.III.* Chapel Hill, NC: Horizon Research.

tions among benchmarks and standards. The chances for successful reform will be enhanced by a focus on standards-based professional development that builds the scientific and instructional knowledge necessary for real curricular and instructional change.

The current work on systemic reform in many states, urban districts, and rural areas, and in the science and mathematics teacher education collaborative projects, has begun to yield models of long-term, active involvement of science and mathematics teachers in professional development activities. Sustained emphasis on professional development will ensure wider implementation of these models. In designing professional development activities, reformers must make a connection between increased knowledge in science and learning, and teachers' current concerns or teaching practice.

Principles for Change in Teachers' Professional Development

Our understanding of how teachers learn and of the opportunities for development suggest the following principles to guide the redesign of teachers' continuing education:

- Higher education and professional associations should strengthen their connections to professional development, providing greater coherence.
- An emphasis on science learning tied to local school context should replace the focus on general teaching skills.
- Activities should provide the curricular and practical skills for teachers to weave standards and benchmarks into an instructional sequence.
- Cadres of teachers should assume leadership responsibilities.
- Activities should promote learning for all school professionals, including administrators.

These principles imply a rethinking of the way teachers' time is organized, the way current staff development funds are used, and the level of staff development support that is necessary to implement and sustain reform.

By strengthening links with higher education and professional associations, teachers can begin to bring some coherence to the currently disjointed system of professional development. At the same time, these organizations are flexible enough for teachers to avoid creating a highly centralized system of professional development that is unresponsive to local needs. Teachers increase their use of research knowledge if they have sustained interaction with researchers (Huberman, 1983). This interaction also gives researchers a chance to present their work in ways that fit local circumstances. Similarly, professional associations and teachers' unions have the infrastructure in place to help teachers share knowledge with each other, although little is known now about the effects of membership in these organizations on teachers' development.

Learning must become an integral part of the entire school—not just for students but also for teachers and administrators. Teachers' professional development must be viewed as standard operating procedure.

Novice teachers need opportunities to develop craft skills such as classroom management.

One goal of reform is to increase teachers' capacity to learn what practices work best in their local situation for a given cohort of students. Thus, professional development should focus on helping teachers to inquire into their own practice and make connections to their own learning. Novice teachers need opportunities to develop craft skills such as classroom management. With experience and confidence, teachers gain greater interest in student learning, implying the importance of professional development in shifting to teaching strategies and assessment approaches that focus on the learner.

Teachers may also need specialized help in integrating the science curriculum and connecting it with technology. Although science learning should be tailored to the needs of each unique classroom or even each unique individual, it is clearly unrealistic for teachers to devise new activities for each topic. Teachers will need opportunities to learn how to integrate learning activities that support connected learning.

To keep focused on the goals of science education reform, groups of teachers might be organized to keep abreast of developments in science teaching and learning, to provide models of teaching, and to build a network of teachers who continually develop their own expertise. Finally, because administrators and other professional staff in schools and districts exert great power over science education, promoting their continued learning is crucial to change.

IMPLICATIONS FOR SCHOOL ORGANIZATION

The vision posed here for science teaching and teacher development substantially affects school organization and management. Schools should be organized to foster increased interdependence, coordination of specialization, and cultures that support innovation and experimentation. Organizations that employ large numbers of professional persons and high-technology firms, where much work is nonroutine, have begun to create these types of organizational structures. Levin's Accelerated Schools (1987)—described in *Blueprints'* Resources—demonstrate several aspects of this model.

The school is a learning organization that encourages continuous growth. Novices are inducted into school culture through close participation and joint responsibility with universities. Schools can create cultures that support teacher inquiry and reflection and develop a shared language to describe and analyze teaching practice. By creating time schedules that encourage shared planning and interdisciplinary approaches to school-wide curriculum development, and by providing regular opportunities for teachers to observe and discuss teaching and learning with a collegium of peers, schools can actively support their teachers through a lifetime of learning.

RECOMMENDATIONS

The recommendations below begin to suggest a new vision of reform and the necessary steps to implement that vision. Groups of faculty and administrators, professional organizations, government agencies and others need to find strategies appropriate to their own settings. Using the following ideas as guiding principles may help the process.

■ *Convey a broad vision of scientific literacy.*
Teacher education should be designed to produce science teachers who are committed to increasing understanding of connections between science, mathematics, and technology as well as understanding of the social, historical, and philosophical contexts of scientific knowledge. All teachers should be able to concentrate their teaching on essential ideas of their fields, limiting the use of technical vocabulary to what is required for clear thinking and effective communication.

■ *Emphasize the profession of teaching.*
Teacher education programs should develop the attitudes, knowledge, and understanding that enable prospective teachers to apply theories and principles in devising strategies and classroom activities that are responsive to the needs and backgrounds of particular students. This kind of teaching—called reasoned, principled, or reflective practice—is a defining characteristic of professional teachers. New standards and

curricula require teachers to have a deep understanding of their subjects rather than to be technicians adept only at delivering prepared educational products produced by curriculum specialists and other "experts"outside the classroom. To this end, teacher education must be redefined as a career-long endeavor. Teacher preparation programs should work with school districts to create schools in which critical inquiry and discussion are defined as part of the routine organization of the work of teaching.

■ *Enable teachers to teach science to all Americans.*
Teachers should be aware that science is not just a body of knowledge, but a paradigm through which to see the world. Prospective and practicing teachers should study and work with experienced teachers, researchers, and teacher educators who effectively teach science to students from different backgrounds. New teachers must be sensitive to student differences and understand how individual characteristics and special needs can affect engagement and achievement.

■ *Improve university instruction.*
Colleges and universities should draw the faculty's attention to available research in teaching, learning, and assessment that can be used to develop more effective undergraduate teaching. Undergraduate institutions should encourage and support faculty who strive to improve their courses and should hold seminars and discussions on ways to improve teaching. In addition, these institutions should work to develop more explicit guidelines about what constitutes effective teaching and incorporate these guidelines into policies on promotion and tenure. The large universities should focus on helping graduate students develop their teaching competence and on developing alternatives to the large lecture courses that dominate undergraduate education in science.

■ *Enhance teacher learning.*
It is crucial for teacher education programs to offer prospective teachers opportunities to observe, experience, and participate in activities that emphasize student-centered and hands-on learning. Teacher education programs must tighten their link with schools so that prospective teachers are exposed to the extensive "behind-the-scenes" thought and planning that goes into effective teaching. Prospective teachers need to be able to use the knowledge from educational research to examine the practice of teaching in new ways, and they need opportunities to discuss

their classroom experiences in the light of formal knowledge about teaching and learning.

■ *Improve teacher recruitment.*
Additional efforts should be made to recruit candidates likely to excel as science, mathematics, and technology teachers. Women, persons of color, and persons with disabilities should be aggressively recruited and supported for careers as science teachers. Interested students should be identified early and mentored by young teachers. "Bridge" programs between high school and college for prospective teachers are essential for many minority and nontraditional students, as are programs for community college students interested in teaching careers. Scholarship and career information about teaching are important, especially for students who may be the first family members to attend college.

At the same time, standards for science and mathematics teachers should be raised so that professionalism and teaching quality increase over time.

■ *Commit to long-term reform.*
Because higher education plays a crucial role in shaping future teachers, professional organizations in the sciences and education can take the lead in supporting publications, seminars, and other forms of professional development for administrators in higher education. Administrators in both higher education and K-12 education are keys to the success of any reform and should be included in professional development.

Administrators and faculty in higher education should also recognize that broad support for continued science research will come with increased public understanding and appreciation of science. Therefore, higher education will benefit by working with elementary and secondary educators to implement reform.

Serious reform requires long-term commitment. Experienced educators have seen previous reforms come and go without enduring, significant change. If they are to be recruited for reform, teachers must be persuaded that efforts will be maintained over decades, not just years. Successful reformers acknowledge the difficulty of the change process and push forward at all levels, building coalitions and developing a cadre of leaders that will continue the press for change.

REFERENCES

Abell, S. K. (1990). A case for the elementary school science specialist. *School Science and Mathematics, 90*(4), 291-301.

American Association for the Advancement of Science. (1993). *Benchmarks for science literacy.* New York: Oxford University Press.

Bonwell, C.C. & Eison, J. A. (1991). Active learning: Creating excitement in the classroom. *ASHE-ERIC Higher Education Report.* Washington, D.C.: School of Education and Human Development, George Washington University.

Gallagher, J. J., & Treagust, T. (1994). *Attempts at sense-making: Pre-service secondary science teachers' comprehension of selected science concepts.* East Lansing, MI: Michigan State University.

Giroux, H. A. (1988). *Teachers as intellectuals: Toward a critical pedagogy of learning.* Granby, MA: Bergin & Harvey.

Grossman, J. H. (1991, March). Improving the quality of college teaching. *Performance and Instruction, 30*(3), 24-27.

Holmes Group. (1990). *Tomorrow's schools: Principles for the design of professional development schools.* East Lansing, MI: Author.

Huberman, M. (1983). Recipes for busy kitchens. *Knowledge: Creation, Diffusion, Utilization, 4,* 478-510.

Kozol, J. (1991). *Savage inequalities.* New York: Crown.

Levin, H. M. (1987, March). Accelerated schools for disadvantaged students. *Educational Leadership, 44*(6), 19-21.

McDermott, L. C. (1990). A perspective on teacher preparation in physics and other sciences: The need for special science courses for teachers. *The American Journal of Physics, 58,* 734-742.

National Council of Teachers of Mathematics. (1991). *Professional standards for teaching mathematics.* Reston, VA: Author.

National Research Council. (1996). *National science education standards.* Washington, D.C.: National Academy Press.

National Science Foundation. (1995). *Teacher preparation and NSF collaboratives for excellence in teacher preparation, FY 95 awards.* Washington, D.C.: Author.

Wilson, K. G., & Daviss, B. (1994). *Redesigning education.* New York: Henry Holt.

BIBLIOGRAPHY

Abell, S. K. (1990). A case for the elementary science specialist. *School Science and Mathematics, 90*(4), 291-301.

American Association for the Advancement of Science. (1993). *Benchmarks for science literacy* . New York: Oxford University Press.

American Association for the Advancement of Science. (1990). *The liberal art of science: Agenda for action.* Washington, D.C.: Author.

American Association for the Advancement of Science. (1989). *Science for all Americans.* New York: Oxford University Press.

Anderson, L. M. (1989). Implementing instructional programs to promote meaningful, self regulated leaning. In J. Brophy (Ed.), *Advances in research on teaching*. Vol. 1 (pp. 311-343). Greenwich, CT: JAI Press, Inc.

Ben-Peretz (1990). *The teacher curriculum encounter: Freeing teachers from the tyranny of texts*. Albany, NY: State University of New York Press.

Billings-Ladson, G. (1994). *The dreamkeepers: Successful teachers of African American children*. San Francisco, CA: Jossey-Bass.

Bishop, B. A. & Anderson, C. W. (1990). Student conceptions of natural selection and its role in evolution. *Journal of Research in Science Teaching, 27*, (5), 415-427.

Comenius, J.A. (1657/1967). *The great didactic of John Amos Comenius*. New York: Russell and Russell.

Comenius, J.A. (1910). *The great didactic*, 2nd ed., (M. Keating trans.) London: A. & C. Black.

Darling-Hammond, L. (1994). *Professional development schools: Schools for developing a profession*. New York: Teachers College Press.

Feirman-Nemser, S. & Buchmann, M. (1985). Pitfalls of experience in teacher preparation. *Teachers College Record, 87* (1), 53-65.

Fullan, M.G.(1993) *Change forces*. London: The Palmer Press.

Fullan, M. G., with Stiegelbauer, S. (1991). *The new meaning of educational change* (2nd ed.). New York: Teachers College Press.

Fuller, F. P. (1969). Concerns of teachers: A developmental characterization. *American Educational Research Journal, 6*, 207-226.

Gallagher, J. J. (1991). Prospective and practicing secondary school science teachers' knowledge and beliefs about the philosophy of science. *Science Education, 10* (1), 121-133.

Giroux, H.A. (1988). *Teachers as intellectuals: Toward a critical pedagogy of leaning*. Granby, MA: Bergin & Garvey.

Glaser, R. & Silver, E. (1994). Assessment, testing, and instruction: Retrospect and prospect. In L. Darling-Hammond (Ed.), *Review of research in education*, Volume 20 (pp. 393-419). Washington, D.C.: American Educational Research Association.

Halloran, I., & Hestenes, D. (1985). Common sense concepts about motion. *American Journal of Physics, 11*, 1056-1065.

Hamburg, D. (1944). *Today's children*. New York: Times Books.

Holmes Group (1990). *Tomorrow's schools: Principles for the design of professional development schools*. East Lansing, MI: Author.

Huberman, M. (1990). Linkage between researchers and practitioners: A qualitative study. *American Educational Research Journal, 10*, 363-391.

Huberman, M. (1983). Recipes for busy kitchens. *Knowledge: Creation, Diffusion, Utilization, 4*, 478-510.

Huberman, M. & Miles, M. B. (1984). *Innovation up close*. New York: Plenum.

Joyce, B. & Showers, B. (1988). *Student achievement through staff development* . New York: Longman.

Lanier, J. E., with Little, J. W. (1986). Research on teacher education. In M. Wittrock (Ed.), *Handbook of Research on Teaching* (3rd ed., pp. 527-569). New York: Macmillan.

Little, J. W. (1990). Conditions of professional development in secondary schools. In M.W. McLaughlin, and J. E Talbert. (Eds.) *The contexts of teaching in secondary schools: Teachers' realities*, (pp. 187-223). New York: Teachers College Press,

Little, J. W., Gerritz, W. H., Stern, D. S., Guthrie, J. W., Kirst, M. W., & Marsh, D. D. (1987). *Staff development in California: Public and personal investment, program patterns, and policy choices.* San Francisco, CA: Far West Laboratory for Educational Research and Development.

Lortie, D. C. (1975). *Schoolteacher: A sociological study.* Chicago, IL: University of Chicago Press.

Marsh, D. & Odden, A. R. (1991). Implementation of the California mathematics and science curriculum frameworks. In A. R. Odden (Ed.), *Education policy implementation.* Albany, NY: State University of New York Press.

McDermott, G. W. (1994). *Realizing new learning for all students. A framework for the professional development of Kentucky teachers.* East Lansing, MI: National Center for Research on Teacher Leaning, Michigan State University.

McDermott, L.C. (1990). A perspective on teacher preparation in physics and other sciences: The need for special science courses for teachers. *American Journal of Physics, 73.*

McDiarmid, G. W. (1993). Teacher education a vital part of equity issue. *State Education Leader, 12*(1), 11.

McDiarmid, G. W. (1992). What to do about differences? A study of multicultural education for teacher trainees in the Los Angeles Unified School District. *Journal of Teacher Education, 43*(2), 83-93.

McDiarmid, G. W. (1991). What do prospective teachers need to know about culturally different children? In M. M. Kennedy (Ed.), *Teaching academic subjects to diverse learners.* New York: Teachers College Press.

McDiarmid, G. W. & Price, L. (1993). Preparing teachers for diversity: A study of student-teachers in a multicultural program. In S. O'Dell and M. O'Hair (Eds.), *Diversity and teaching: Teacher education yearbook I* (pp. 31 - 59). Fort Worth, TX: Harcourt Brace Jovanovich.

McLaughlin, M. W. & Miller, B. (Eds.), (1992). *Staff development for education in the 90's*, (pp. 61-82). New York: Teachers College Press.

Miller, B., Lord, B., & Dorney, J. (1994). *Staff development for teachers: A study of configurations and costs in four districts.* Newton, MA: Education Development Center.

National Research Council, Committee on High School Biology Education. (1990). *Fulfilling the promise: Biology education in the nation's schools.* Washington, D.C.: National Academy Press.

Odden, A. (1994). *The financial implications of Project 2061 for teachers' professional development and compensation.* Madison, WI: Wisconsin Center for Education Research, University of Wisconsin.

Raizen, S. A. & Michelsohn, A. M. (Eds.) (1994). *The future of science in elementary schools: Educating prospective teachers.* San Francisco, CA: Jossey-Bass.

Resnick, L. B. (1987). *Education and learning to think.* Washington, D.C.: National Academy Press.

Rowe, M. B. (1983). Getting chemistry off the killer course list. *Journal of Chemical Education, 6*, 54-56

Sarason, S. B. (1993). *The case for change.* San Francisco, CA: Jossey-Bass.

Sarason, S. B. (1990). *The predictable failure of education before it is too late?* San Francisco, CA: Jossey-Bass.

Sarason, S. B. (1971, 1982). *The culture of the school.* (1st and 2nd eds). Boston, MA: Allyn and Bacon.

Sato, M. (1992). Japan. In H.B. Leavitt (Ed.), *Issues and teacher education: An international handbook.* New York: Greenwood Press.

Schifter, D. & Fosnt, C. T. (1993). *Reconstructing mathematics education: Stories of teachers meeting the challenge of reform.* New York: Teachers College Press.

Shavelson, R.J., Baxter, G. P., & Pine, J. Performance assessments in science. *Applied Measurement in Education, 494*, 347-362

Treagust, D. F. (Ed.). (1996). *Improving teaching and learning in science and mathematics.* New York: Teachers College Press.

Tyson, H. (1994). *Who will teach the children: Progress and resistance in teacher education.* San Francisco, CA: Jossey-Bass.

Tyler, R.W. (1949). *Basic principles of curriculum and instruction.* Chicago, IL: University of Chicago Press.

Wilson, K.G. (1994). Wisdom-centered learning: Striking a new paradigm for education. *The School Administrator, 51*(5), 26-33.

Wilson, K.G., & Daviss, B. (1994). *Redesigning education.* New York: Henry Holt.

Wilson, S., & Shulman, L. (1987). 150 different ways of knowing: Representations of knowledge in teaching. In J. Calderhead (Ed.), *Exploring teachers' thinking* (pp. 104-124). New York: Holt, Rinehart & Winston.

Veenman, S. (1984). Perceived problems of beginning teachers. *Review of Educational Research, 54*(2), 143-178.

Zeichner, K. (1993, February). *Educating teachers for cultural diversity.* (Special Report). East Lansing, MI: Michigan State University, National Center for Research on Teacher Learning.

10

Higher Education

THE PROGRESS of K-12 science and mathematics education reform has been steady, sometimes accelerating since the publication of *A Nation at Risk* (National Commission on Excellence in Education, 1983). To maintain this progress, future science and mathematics teachers will need deep and interconnected knowledge of their subjects and of cultural and social issues with implications for teaching the subjects. Higher education has recently acknowledged its need for significant reform (Boyer, 1994), and colleges and universities have undertaken substantial efforts to change the ways they organize teaching and learning. These efforts are especially noticeable in the science, mathematics, and technology-related disciplines and bode well for the support and institutionalization of K-12 science education reform. Nonetheless, these reforms are only a beginning. It is clear that higher education must become a more active and visible participant if the reform process is to succeed in schools, colleges, and universities.

Higher education has a significant role to play in K-12 education reform. For example, if, as reformers envision, the entire K-12 science curriculum is restructured, higher education will have to rethink the way it admits, counsels, and places students; the way it organizes its curricula and teaches undergraduate science, mathematics, and technology; and the way it goes about preparing the next generation of school, college, and university faculty. Higher education can support K-12 reform by continuing to explore ways to improve science and mathematics education for undergraduate and graduate students alike.

After examining the current status of higher education, this chapter explores 1) needed changes in admissions and placement; 2) needed changes in the undergraduate curriculum; and 3) needed changes in teacher education. It then describes ways for higher education to collaborate with K-12 reformers and build on their work. Finally, it proposes some specific recommendations for changing higher education.

THE CURRENT STATUS

Science for All Americans (American Association for the Advancement of Science, 1989) asserts that in order to achieve science literacy for all, it is just as important to consider how subjects are taught as what subjects are taught. Goroff (1995) agrees, taking the argument a step further by saying that for the purposes of teacher education especially, how university faculty teach *is* what they teach. However, at most colleges and universities, "just be clear" is the standard for teaching. The attitude prevails that everyone, including professors, should focus on the material rather than the process of learning—on what to teach rather than how. Many professors may not realize that factors such as their personal expectations of students can powerfully influence student perceptions and performance. Many faculty members might find it disconcerting to know that future teachers in their courses will emulate their teaching style. Nevertheless, what students retain often has less to do with the subject matter than with what they learn about how to attack a new problem, or what to do when they get stuck or frustrated. The "just be clear" philosophy ignores the influence of teaching style and focuses on spoon-feeding students boiled-down facts.

Teacher education simply does not happen for those who teach in higher education.

Most science and mathematics faculty have heard that they should teach better, to the point of feeling harangued and harassed about it. K-12 reformers must recognize that most college and university faculty are neither lazy nor averse to teaching well, but that they might not know how to do it. Teacher education simply does not happen for those who teach in higher education. Although many campuses are implementing strategies to address this problem, much more needs to be done, especially in science and mathematics.

A great deal of teaching effort in the sciences and mathematics is for non-science majors. Higher education ascribes different purposes to science education for majors versus nonmajors. Not surprisingly then, individual faculty differ in their views of how to adjust to a cohort of incoming students better prepared through K-12 reforms than today's students. Nonetheless, this chapter asserts that the majority of college and university faculty see in reform an opportunity to reinvigorate science education for both majors and nonmajors in ways that will broaden and enrich our students' preparation for life in the next century.

BARRIERS TO CHANGE

The different ways in which the disciplines interpret the very nature of science may inhibit universities from implementing the integrated, interdisciplinary science instruction advocated by Project 2061. For scientists to become partners in a shared, common science curriculum for all students, they will need considerable convincing that their own disciplines are represented fairly and adequately. This disciplinary constraint is likely to loosen gradually during the coming years as the roles of teaching and research for university faculty reach a new balance.

College or university culture erects another set of barriers to change. In many large science departments, an instructional "pecking order" is observed: the most senior researchers teach graduate students; younger, active research faculty and older, formerly active researchers teach undergraduate majors; and those whose research careers have faltered handle the large introductory courses for nonmajors. In some research-oriented universities, departmental courses for nonmajors are viewed by both students and faculty as less attractive and less rigorous. This self-fulfilling prophecy may lead professors to devote less effort to teaching those classes and students to avoid or perform poorly in them. In addition, the recognition and reward system in much of higher education favors research over innovative teaching. This is especially prevalent in science and engineering, where the added incentive of outside funding shifts the reward balance even further toward research.

The American tradition of physically and intellectually segregating the science education of teachers from the education of science professionals has severely limited opportunities for teachers—especially elementary teachers—to learn the content and practice of science. This segregation has also limited scientists' exposure to the K-12 curriculum and their understanding of the science knowledge—and misunderstandings—that college freshmen bring into their classes. There is also a nearly complete lack of contact between those who teach science in our K-12 schools and their counterparts in colleges and universities, which renders significantly more difficult the task of changing higher education to connect with and help build a reformed K-12 science program.

NEEDED CHANGES IN ADMISSIONS AND PLACEMENT

The prospect of future students coming to higher education with a broader and more uniform knowledge of science raises several important admissions and placement issues described below.

ADMISSIONS

For higher education to join forces with the K-12 reform movement, it will have to address seriously such questions as:

■ What is science and who needs to learn it? Currently, "real" science—that is, science done in laboratories and universities—is understood and practiced only by a select few, all of whom engage in scientific work only after negotiating parlous rites of passage. On the other hand, many scientists and educators believe that every individual has the ability and should have the opportunity to understand the process of science and even to do some real science.

■ Who sets admissions standards? High schools construct their curricula in part to meet the demands of standardized assessments and in part to be acceptable to higher education. If graduates of a high school science program do not gain admission to the college of their choice, that curriculum is in danger. Science educators at all grade levels must work to ensure that reforming the K-12 curriculum does not make the transition from high school to college more difficult.

■ Will reform expand the pool of science majors? Because K-12 reform focuses on producing a more science literate populace rather than on producing more and better scientists, it could allow some universities, whose reputations rest on the latter, to ignore the reform as irrelevant to their students and faculty.

■ What is the role of community colleges? Are they more likely than four-year colleges and universities to build on K-12 reforms? Science education reformers should pay special attention to the transitions from high school to community college to university.

■ Will traditional assessment help or hinder reform? *Science for All Americans* stresses that students should perceive connections across disciplines, sometimes work collaboratively, and pursue answers through scientific inquiry. These skills are not measured by traditional assessments like the Scholastic Achievement Test (SAT) and American College Testing program (ACT). A more fruitful approach for college admissions may lie in competency measures such as the Wisconsin

Competency-Based Admission Model (University of Wisconsin Board of Regents, 1996), which asks students to work, often collaboratively, to acquire learning that is deemed important by the teacher, the receiving college, the student, and the business community.

If higher education faculty really want an enlarged pool of undergraduates to enter some of the most elite laboratories and classrooms in our nation's colleges and universities, they must work toward admitting students prepared to be science literate. This is true even if these students differ from traditional high-school honors students. More importantly, faculty who have been concerned only with the traditional "good science student" will need to work with science majors who have increasingly diverse aspirations, including teaching, and be willing to help them achieve their goals.

PLACEMENT

The prospect of future students coming to higher education with a broader and more uniform knowledge of science raises several important placement issues. With successful K-12 reform, a single set of general education courses in science would meet the needs of all incoming students. (AP [Advanced Placement] courses would have to adjust to these interdisciplinary general education courses as they become the higher education introductory norm.) When most students are taking similar general education versus content-driven courses, the point at which students make the transition from "shopping" to committing to a major may be delayed. Most science departments should welcome that change if it leads to increased numbers of able students choosing to major in their disciplines.

Meanwhile, four-year colleges and universities are becoming

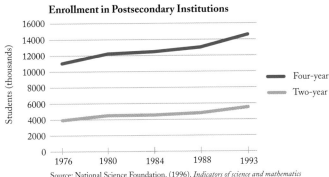

Enrollment in Postsecondary Institutions

Students (thousands) — Four-year / Two-year

Source: National Science Foundation. (1996). *Indicators of science and mathematics education 1995.* Arlington, VA: Author.

increasingly competitive for the growing number of students—older students; those with greater financial needs; culturally and racially diverse students; and more first-generation, college-going students— who launch their higher education careers in community colleges. Four-year institutions should examine their transfer policies and practices to accomodate these non-traditional students. Higher education leaders can design ways to promote and sustain more regular communication between two- and four-year colleges and between colleges and K-12 schools.

NEEDED CHANGES IN THE UNDERGRADUATE CURRICULUM

The traditional departmental organization of the disciplines in higher education is likely to remain intact, with the scientific principles and methods central to each discipline retaining their integrity and distinctiveness. However, changes in content emphasis will be necessary and desirable if higher education is committed to the goals of science education reform. Some critical elements in a new agenda for changing science content in higher education are:

■ concentrating on the central ideas of each discipline—even at the expense of less content coverage—and providing *all* students with an understanding of the interconnectedness of human knowledge, including links among the fields of science;

■ building on the scientific knowledge and habits of mind with which better prepared students will come to higher education;

■ providing a more student-centered learning environment, supporting a wider variety of learning styles, and using more varied organizational strategies and teaching materials;

■ prolonging opportunities for students to enter disciplinary majors by closing the gap between the content in major and nonmajor introductory science courses; and

■ providing majors with more explicit instruction in the history and methodology of their disciplines, enabling them to better appreciate and be able to identify features that are common to all sciences and those unique to each discipline.

The following discussion examines several of these elements and points out some necessary changes that should take place in universities and colleges in order to accommodate the goals of science education reform.

CENTRAL IDEAS AND CONNECTIONS IN SCIENCE

Material that only a decade ago was taught in graduate courses has moved into undergraduate curricula, adding to the specialized nature of science programs for majors. Inevitably, a commitment to fostering scientific habits of mind, focusing on essential principles in science, and exploring links among the sciences leaves less time and space for content-laden courses in any undergraduate programs.

If, in their first two years, undergraduate science and engineering majors study a common core of physical and life sciences laced with interconnections and links to the social sciences and humanities, they will be better equipped to choose and succeed in a science discipline. They will also be better prepared to function as professionals in the world of work, which is not neatly divided into disciplines. For departments that insist on maintaining topical coverage in their current upper division courses, "bridge" courses might be used to fill the perceived gaps created by omitting specific topics from reformed science courses.

If universities support experimentation with innovative teaching methods they will necessarily stimulate more conversation among the disciplines.

New, multidisciplinary programs will continue to emerge—just as biochemistry did within the last generation and environmental and energy studies did within the last decade. Science educators should view the practitioners of these fields as models of cross-disciplinary scientific practice and instruction. If universities support experimentation with innovative teaching methods—multidisciplinary programs; team teaching; collaborative learning; simulation; multimedia and computer-supported instruction; and exploration of the interaction of science, technology, and human values—they will necessarily stimulate more conversation among the disciplines and engender still more interdisciplinary collaboration in teaching and scholarship.

TEACHING APPROACHES

To expand the pool of potentially successful recruits to the scientific/technical professions, college curricula and instruction need to reflect the variety of learning styles present among students. Although the recommendations on teaching and learning in *Science for All Americans* are geared to K-12 education some of the suggestions have value for higher education. For example, college faculty would agree that all students need genuine experiences grappling with scientific questions, collecting data, constructing models, guessing, estimating, making mistakes, recognizing the unanswerable, and engaging in other activities that go beyond calculating solutions to routine sets of problems. Thus, undergraduates in general, and future teachers in particular, should have a wide range of learning experiences and should also come to appreciate how each teacher selects and adapts teaching approaches.

SCIENCE FOR MAJORS AND NONMAJORS

To change science education for majors and nonmajors alike, science curricula at the college level should stress the important central concepts of science, their observational basis, and the history of their development. This will require adding topics that reach outside the traditional domains of individual science disciplines.

Most campuses entertained vigorous discussions of general or liberal education in the 1980s. Project 30, which brought colleges of science, education, and liberal arts together to explore general education (see *Blueprints'* Resources for a description), and a report by the American Association for the Advancement of Science (1990) that addressed the issue of liberal arts courses in the context of the education of future teachers were notable contributions to this debate. *Science for All Americans* provides a framework that can invigorate and inform a renewed discussion of what a science and technology component in liberal education might look like. The available resources in colleges and universities provide ample opportunities to imbue students with historic and societal perspectives that will prepare them for a lifelong pursuit of science literacy. A convincing case can be made that a defined but varied selection of liberal education science courses can satisfy science requirements for science and non-science majors.

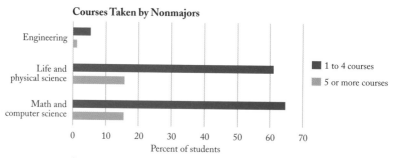

Courses Taken by Nonmajors

Engineering

Life and physical science

Math and computer science

■ 1 to 4 courses
▨ 5 or more courses

0   10   20   30   40   50   60   70
Percent of students

Source: National Science Foundation. (1996). *Indicators of science and mathematics education 1995.* Arlington, VA: Author.

Attending to the needs of prospective science teachers, science majors, and others in this way makes sense for several reasons. First, if college faculty do their jobs right, people who were planning to be teachers may decide to become scientists, and vice versa. Second, people who are neither professional educators nor scientists will have a chance to become science literate. We should insist that whatever we call good science for all Americans is good for future teachers—and that good science for future teachers is good for all Americans.

NEEDED CHANGES IN THE EDUCATION OF COLLEGE FACULTY

Transforming the pedagogy in the average college classroom to promote the kind of learning called for by Project 2061 requires attention to teacher education for higher education faculty. Many of the ideas outlined for K-12 teachers in *Science for All Americans* and *Benchmarks for Science Literacy* (American Association for the Advancement of Science, 1993) can be adapted for higher education faculty.

In helping college faculty learn to teach, colleges and universities should pay particular attention to three key principles: 1) it is important to create an emotional climate that rewards creativity, avoids dogmatism, builds on students' knowledge, supports the roles of women and minorities, and expects success; 2) teaching should engage students actively and be informed by feedback; and 3) teaching is a powerful way to learn. These ideas are discussed in the following sections.

LEARNING TO BUILD SUCCESS FOR ALL

Given that the nation's K-12 school population has a majority of students of color and females—a proportion that will grow to at least two-thirds in the next few decades—successful reform hinges on our ability to address equity issues and eliminate barriers to science for women, minorities, and students of low socioeconomic status. In addition to improving science literacy, reform of higher education must draw into the science pipeline groups who have been seriously underrepresented in scientific endeavors in the past.

Colleges with limited resources that undertake reform may fall behind the efforts of well-funded universities. At schools with fewer resources, reform may actually exacerbate resource inequities, improving opportunities for a small number of students, but not for others. State university branch campuses, community and technical colleges,

Minority Enrollment in K-12 Schools

Source: National Science Foundation. (1996). *Indicators of science and mathematics education 1995.*
Arlington, VA: Author.

and historically Black colleges and universities have led efforts to diversify the student body and encourage nontraditional students to pursue scientific careers. They have been the vanguard in designing special programs with a strong record for producing minority scientists, and they have committed admission and tuition support to students who show promise of succeeding in scientific fields. Unfortunately, these programs

Colleges and Universities Awarding the
Most Bachelor's Degrees in Engineering to Minorities

Blacks:
1. North Carolina A&T
   State University
2. Tuskegee University
3. Prairie View A&M University
4. Georgia Institute of Technology
5. Howard University
6. Southern University and A&M
   College at Baton Rouge
7. North Carolina State University
   at Raleigh
8. CUNY City College
9. Pratt Institute
10. Massachusetts Institute of
    Technology

Hispanics:
1. University of
   Puerto Rico Mayaguez
2. University Politechica de
   Puerto Rico
3. Florida International University
4. Texas A&M University
5. University of Texas at El Paso
6. California Polytechnic
   State University
7. University of Texas at Austin
8. Massachusetts Institute
   of Technology
9. New Mexico State University
10. University of Miami

Source: National Science Foundation. (1996). *Indicators of science and mathematics education 1995.* Arlington, VA: Author.

have served a limited number of students because of scarce resources. It is essential that we respond with higher priority to the needs of schools with high concentrations of minority and lower socioeconomic status students if we are to achieve a level playing field.

LEARNING TO ENGAGE STUDENTS ACTIVELY AND USE FEEDBACK

If science literacy is to become a reality, students must significantly increase their knowledge of science each year. As professors calibrate expectations, set emotional climates, select appropriate activities, and give constructive feedback to students, it is absolutely vital that they pay careful attention to students' developmental readiness to advance their knowledge and skills. How can this be accomplished?

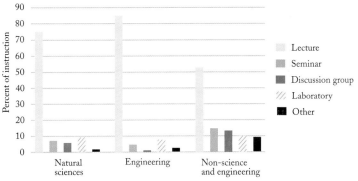

Types of Instruction at Research Universities

Source: National Science Foundation. (1996). *Indicators of science and mathematics education 1995*. Arlington, VA: Author.

Learning experiences should balance activity, reflection, and practice. If science professors reflect on the way they work and learn, they can better serve their students. In their day-to-day work, scientists ask themselves questions, devise explanations, perform experiments, and assimilate information from interactions with others. Students also need to engage in these strategies as they develop their knowledge.

On the other hand, through years of training, scientists and science faculty have internalized many active learning strategies: for example, working scientists rarely set out to memorize a formula. But students sometimes need to memorize because they may not yet be able to derive a formula based on their knowledge. Whereas many undergraduates are, at best, just beginning to acquire this level of sophistication, many faculty cannot imagine ever having been without it.

Rather than keeping students at their initial level of understanding or expecting them to suddenly jump to a higher one, faculty should instead think of "ramping students upwards."

Rather than keeping students at their initial level of understanding or expecting them to suddenly jump to a higher one, faculty should instead think of "ramping students upwards." This can be accomplished by building on students' science knowledge, helping them to learn more complex concepts, and explicitly telling them that they will be expected to climb increasingly on their own as the course progresses.

How far upward should prospective science teachers climb this ramp? The answer depends partly on what level of understanding is necessary to enable them as teachers to continually expand their scientific knowledge. Prospective science teachers should gain an appreciation for the sweep of science and have some authentic, in-depth, and positive experiences with important concepts of science.

LEARNING TO TEACH

To encourage all students to act as teachers, professors sometimes set up peer study groups, identify and train undergraduate teaching assistants or mentors, or incorporate student presentations of course material. Some colleges have developed "sidecar courses" parallel to usual science courses, in which students meet with the professor to discuss how the course is being taught. In some universities, graduate courses in teaching and learning have grown into new degree programs for people interested in science education.

However interested in encouraging their students to teach, however, college faculty sometimes neglect to reflect on their own teaching. Professors should be more involved with training graduate students and junior faculty as they begin to teach. Asking faculty to help others is not only flattering but it also makes them more articulate and reflective about education. It exposes seasoned faculty to fresh pedagogical ideas that younger colleagues bring, including those of initiatives like Project 2061. Teaching graduate students and junior faculty to teach rather than teaching them to learn would encourage professors to think of themselves as teachers and to become more aware of their own instructional techniques.

COLLABORATING ON AND SUSTAINING REFORM

By making K-12 science instruction more broadly appealing and effective, reform expands the pool of students who will study science in college. Taking a similarly broad and inclusive approach to science instruction at the collegiate level expands the pool of future scientists and science teachers. Scientists and engineers in higher education should—as acts of professional self-interest—support K-12 science education reform and re-examine their own methods of science teaching in light of it.

By collaborating with K-12 schools and aligning science education in higher education with standards-based goals, colleges and universities can reclaim public confidence. School/college alliances, such as K-16 councils and the like, are a means to aid coordinated reform of our schools and colleges (Atkin & Atkin, 1989). These councils can explore issues such as technology access for rural and urban schools, mentoring programs in science and mathematics, and access to resources for teaching science. If these alliances and collaboratives are expanded, replicated, and supported, they can bring more colleges and universities directly into an active role in K-12 educational reform.

Arguably, K-12 reform will help produce students who are more science literate and eager to achieve in science. The desire to attract these students will be powerful motivation for higher education to change, especially for under-enrolled science departments. Rethinking the admissions process might then represent the first step on the part of colleges to "buy in" to reform, and may encourage curriculum discussions between the K-12 and higher education communities.

BUILDING ON K-12 REFORMS

If colleges and universities eventually respond to K-12 reform, several organizations and strategies can ensure that the effective teaching and learning techniques that produce science literate high school graduates are sustained through college. Groups whose support is key to successful reform include: 1) professional and licensing associations, which set the standards for disciplinary content in their fields; 2) the business community, which requires a broadly trained and science literate work force; and 3) the research community, which validates the success of undergraduate students who acquire new science competencies and move to the next educational level.

To overcome the tendency to "teach as we have been taught," and to develop new teaching models, higher education should look to centers for teaching and learning such as those at Harvard University (Graduate School of Arts and Sciences, 1993) and the collaborative project at the University of Wisconsin (Wisconsin Center for Educational Research, 1996). Both of these programs illustrate how research universities have engaged their faculty in reexamining their teaching strategies and experimenting with new techniques.

Colleges and universities can advocate innovative, research-based instructional techniques and materials by developing models and by sponsoring regional workshops for school and university faculty. Because college and university faculty have nearly complete freedom to choose both their content and instructional techniques, they can be leaders in innovative instruction. Collaboration between K-12 and college science instructors should be a central component in these efforts. Working with colleagues in both K-12 and higher education, college faculty can experiment with a full range of pedagogical research and instructional technology, and can model the teacher-as-researcher role for their K-12 colleagues.

Professional societies and their umbrella organizations can educate their members about science education reform and enlist their support, nationally and locally, to reform science education at all levels. Because many higher education faculty have primary allegiance to their discipline rather than to their home institution, science educators must enlist the support of disciplinary professional societies to engage scientists and engineers from higher education faculty, as well as from industrial and government research laboratories, in reform efforts.

RECOMMENDATIONS

Change does not come easily, especially to higher education. If science education reform is to succeed with higher education, not only must university faculty interact with K-12 colleagues on an ongoing basis, but a larger number of committed faculty and administrators have to become involved.

■ Presidential leadership is critical. More than rhetoric is needed from university presidents. Resources, funds, and time commitments on the part of some of the most visible and busy individuals on campus are necessary. Presidents and provosts can bring together deans and department chairs of science, mathematics, and engineering to (a) develop models of multidisciplinary course sequences introducing science, mathematics, and technology; (b) provide incentives for excellent teaching in science and mathematics; and (c) encourage faculty involvement with K-12 science and mathematics education. They can promote *Science for All Americans* as a basis for liberal education discussions held on college campuses and at other higher education forums.

■ Equity issues are critical to the success of reform. Although K-12 science education reformers are clearly committed to an equity agenda (Kreinberg, 1995), too many students, particularly low-income and minority students, fall through the cracks in the transition from high school to higher education. Policy aimed at increasing minority participation in the sciences has had disappointing results thus far.

It is worth considering whether to extend more support to those higher education institutions with a history of contributing to the equity agenda. As reform requires ample resources, it is essential to place the needs of schools with high concentrations of minority and low income students, particularly schools in rural or urban areas, first.

■ Agents of change in higher education must be identified. Because higher education often sees the needs of the K-12 sector as peripheral to itself, it will be important for science faculty to work closely with professional and disciplinary societies. Exposure to reform materials and ideas through these interactions will provide support for college faculty as they develop courses and instruction methods.

■ Parents and college applicants should be privy to specific information about the teaching and learning culture at institutions of higher education. It is important for prospective students to consider how their future college's science and mathematics teaching and learning strategies will bear on their success. This information should be made available, especially for students who may not have traditional access to information about colleges.

■ The admissions process is critical. Across the nation, higher education has begun to adapt admissions procedures in response to the standards movement and the growth of portfolio and performance assessment programs. Flexibility in admissions should be explored further and communications between K-12 schools and higher education institutions enhanced.

■ High quality professional development for K-12 faculty and administrators is essential to science education reform. Higher education can help in this regard. To provide the appropriate content for science and mathematics teachers and school administrators, university faculty in the sciences and in education departments must be more aware of day-to-day learning in K-12 schools.

For higher education to participate fully in science reform, university faculty must change their outlook on teaching. When faculty show respect for students interested in teaching careers, encourage some of their best and brightest to think about careers in K-12 teaching, take seriously their role in developing science and mathematics teachers, and become involved in important new research that can help science teachers, they will be full participants in the education reform agenda.

REFERENCES

American Association for the Advancement of Science. (1993). *Benchmarks for science literacy.* New York: Oxford University Press.

American Association for the Advancement of Science. (1990). *Liberal education in the sciences.* Washington, D.C.: Author.

American Association for the Advancement of Science. (1989). *Science for all Americans.* New York: Oxford University Press.

Atkin, J. M., & Atkin, A. (1989). *Improving science education through local alliances.* New York: Carnegie Corporation of New York.

Boyer, E. L. (1994, March 9). Creating the new American college. *The Chronicle of Higher Education,* A48.

Commission on Faculty Recognition and Rewards. (1994). *Report to the Joint Policy Board for Mathematics.* Washington, D.C.: Author.

Goroff, D. (1995). *College teaching and the education of teachers.* Commissioned paper. Washington, D.C.: American Association for the Advancement of Science.

Graduate School of Arts and Sciences. (1993). *Teaching fellows handbook.* Cambridge, MA: Harvard University, Derek Bok Center for Teaching and Learning.

Kreinberg, N. (1995). *Equity and systemic reform.* Washington, D.C.: American Association for the Advancement of Science.

National Commission on Excellence in Education. (1983). *A nation at risk: The imperative for educational reform.* Washington, D.C.: U.S. Government Printing Office.

University of Wisconsin Board of Regents. (1996). *Study of the UW system in the 21st century.* Madison, WI: Author.

Wingspread Group. (1993). *An American imperative: Higher expectations for higher education.* Report of the Wingspread Group on Higher Education. Racine, WI: Johnson Foundation, Inc.

Wisconsin Center for Educational Research. (1996). Faculty collaboration improves undergraduate teaching. *WCER Highlights, 8*(2), 1-2.

BIBLIOGRAPHY

American Association for the Advancement of Science. (1990). *The liberal art of science: Agenda for action.* Washington, D.C.: Author.

American Association of Higher Education. (1990/1991). *Improving student achievement through partnerships.* First and Second National Conferences on School/College Collaboration. Washington, D.C.: Author.

American Federation of Teachers and National Center for Improving Science Education. (1994). *What college-bound students abroad are expected to know about biology: Exams from England and Wales, France, Germany and Japan.* Washington, D.C.: Author.

American Mathematical Society. (1994). *Recognition and rewards in the mathematical sciences.* Report of the Joint Policy Board for Mathematics, Committee on Professional Recognition and Rewards. Washington, D.C.: Author.

Bernstein, A. & Cock, J. (1994, June 15). A troubling picture of gender equity. *The Chronicle of Higher Education,* Pull-Out Section 2.

Boyer, E. L. (1994, March 9). Creating the new American college. *The Chronicle of Higher Education,* p.A48.

Brubacher, J. S. & Rudy, W. (1997). *Higher education in transition.* New York: Harper & Row.

Committee on Education and Human Resources of the Federal Coordinating Council for Science, Engineering and Technology. (1993). *Pathways to excellence: A federal strategy for science, mathematics, engineering, and technology education.* Washington, D.C.: Office of Human Resources and Education.

Derek Bok Center. (1992, May). On teaching and learning. *Journal of the Derek Bok Center.* Cambridge, MA: Harvard University.

Edgerton, R. (1993, July/August). The re-examination of faculty priorities. *Change,* 10-25.

Frazier, C. M. (1993). *A shared vision: Policy recommendations for linking teacher education to school reform.* Denver, CO: Education Commission of the States.

Graduate School of Arts and Sciences and the Derek Bok Center for Teaching and Learning. (1993). *Teaching fellows handbook.* Cambridge, MA: Harvard University.

Johnston, J. S., Jr. (1989). *Those who can: Undergraduate programs to prepare arts and sciences majors for teaching.* Washington, D.C.: Association of American Colleges,.

Laws, P. (1991, July/August). Workshop physics: Learning introductory physics by doing it. *Change.*

Lederman, L. M. (1994, November 16). A science project to change our schools. *The Washington Post,* p.A25.

Lortie, D. C. (1975). *School-teacher: A sociological study.* Chicago, IL: The University of Chicago Press.

Mathematicians and Education Reform Forum Newsletter. (1993, Fall). University of Illinois at Chicago, Department of Mathematics, Statistics, and Computer Science. Volume 7, Number 1.

Narum, J. L. (ed.). (1993). *What works: Building natural science communities.* Washington, D.C.: Project Kaleidoscope, The Independent Colleges Office.

National Education Commission on Time and Learning. (1994). *Prisoners of Time: Schools and programs making time work for students and teachers.* Washington, D.C.. Author.

National Science Foundation. (1993, February). *Beyond national standards and goals: Excellence in mathematics and science education K-16.* Washington, D.C.: Author.

Recruiting New Teachers, Inc. (1993). *State policies to improve the teacher workforce: Shaping the profession that shapes America's future.* Belmont, MA: Author.

Sato, N. & McLaughlin, M. W. (1992, January). Context matters: Teaching in Japan and in the United States. *Phi Delta Kappan,* 359-66.

Sockett, H. (1994, October 19). "School-based'" master's degrees. *Education Week,* p.35.

Steen, L.A. (1991, July/August). Reaching for science literacy. *Change.*

Stigler, J. W. & Stevenson, H. W. (1991, Spring). How Asian teachers polish each lesson to perfection. *American Educator,* 12-20, 43-47.

Stoel, C., Togneri, W. & Brown, P. (1992). *What works: School/college partnerships to improve poor and minority student achievement.* Washington, D.C.: American Association of Higher Education.

Sussman, A. (Ed.). (1993). *Science education partnerships: Manual for scientists and K-12 teachers.* San Francisco, CA: University of California.

Tobias, S. (1990). *They're not dumb, they're different: Stalking the second tier.* Tucson, AZ: Research Corporation.

U.S. Department of Education. (1993). *America's teachers: Profile of a profession.* Washington, D.C.: National Center for Educational Statistics. NCES 93-025.

U.S. Department of Education. (1993). *New teachers in the job market, 1991 update.* Washington, D.C.: National Center for Education Statistics. NCES 93-392.

Wagener, U.E. (1991, July/August). Changing the culture of teaching: Mathematics at Indiana, Chicago, and Harvard. *Change.*

Wurtz, E. & Malcolm, S. (1993). *Promises to keep: Creating high standards for American students.* Report on the Review of Education Standards to the National Education Goals Panel. Washington, D.C.: National Education Goals Panel.

11

Family and Community

FAMILIES[1] AND THE COMMUNITY have a great influence on children's learning. Families are valuable resources in educational reform, and children benefit when schools recognize and encourage parents' roles in reform efforts. Research has shown that a robust, highly interactive network of parents, community members, peers, and educators stimulates a child's learning and development (Bronfenbrenner, 1989).

The task of creating a network to support children's science learning and development is becoming more difficult. However, changes in social structures and increased economic pressures have reduced the time and energy some families can devote to school involvement: single parents are often working more than one job, and in many two-parent households both parents are working. Also, many households are changing configuration, as when extended families raise children.

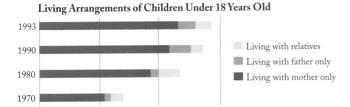

Living Arrangements of Children Under 18 Years Old

Living with relatives
Living with father only
Living with mother only

Percent of children

Source: Published on the U.S. Bureau of Census World Wide Web site at http://www.census.gov

Schools have always faced difficulties teaching students who are not prepared to learn, whether because of financial or other hardships. These challenges are especially formidable as the nation works toward

---

[1]More and more, grandparents, aunts, uncles, step-parents, and guardians may carry the primary responsibility for a child's education, development, and well-being. In this chapter, all references to "parents" and "parent involvement" include all adults who play a major role in a child's family life.

higher educational standards. This chapter discusses the role of family involvement in science education and in science education reform, and offers some strategies for addressing those issues. Some necessary changes—and specific suggestions for implementing them—are identified that can help all parents participate in their children's science education. Every family can have a role by engaging in educational activities with children at home, by being meaningfully involved with schools, or simply by supporting improved science education. Throughout the chapter, we point to specific examples of programs, projects, and resources that exemplify successful approaches to involving families and communities in science education. An annotated list of selected programs is included in *Blueprints'* Resources. These and other strategies can be used to realize the goal of involving parents in improving science literacy for all.

Some information in this chapter was collected through an extensive review of literature on parent involvement in education and through a series of twelve focus groups, each consisting of five to eight parents and other community members, in the rural, suburban, and urban areas in and around New York City, Atlanta, Chicago, and Los Angeles. Local PTA presidents and school principals in each region selected the focus group participants. Because of their involvement with the PTA, these parents may be especially active in schools and knowledgeable about the education process. Other parents may have alternative points of view.

CURRENT ISSUES

The following major concerns about science, mathematics, and technology education emerged from the focus groups:

■ the quality of teachers, their preparation, and their impact on student learning;

■ the type of instruction in schools;

■ communications between schools and families, including parents' reluctance to become involved with schools and student learning; relationships between school personnel and parents; parents' knowledge of school issues, particularly their knowledge of science curriculum and instruction; and

■ external factors, such as social and economic considerations, that may keep parents from becoming involved with schools and student learning.

These themes, as developed by parents in the focus groups, are discussed in the following sections.

QUALITY OF TEACHERS AND TEACHER TRAINING

One of the most prevalent concerns of parents in the focus groups was the quality of teachers, including the quality of preservice and inservice training that teachers receive in science and mathematics. These parents recognized that their children's motivation and interest in science and mathematics is often teacher-specific. When students perceive that their teachers are competent and confident in science or mathematics, they are more apt to become interested in these subjects. Parents of elementary school children were particularly concerned about teacher preparation because teachers at that level seemed to spend more time on subjects in which they feel comfortable—such as reading and writing—than they did on science and mathematics.

When students perceive that their teachers are competent and confident in science or mathematics, they are more apt to become interested in these subjects.

Parents in the focus groups proposed ideas for improving instruction, including better teacher education, science specialists in elementary grades, and frequent and relevant teacher development. Despite their high level of awareness and desire for their children to achieve at higher levels, these parents reported that they generally take a passive role in their child's schooling, hoping their child will be assigned to a good teacher rather than demanding that teaching improve or change.

CLASSROOM INSTRUCTION

Focus group discussions of classroom instruction identified four major needs:

- more hands-on activities and real-life applications,
- a strong foundation in the basics,
- students working and learning together, and
- increased use of technology.

Suburban and rural parents emphasized critical thinking skills. Urban parents called for curricula pertinent to the real life experiences of their children and approaches that help students apply what they learn.

Parents defined the basics as more than just reading, writing, and arithmetic. For example, they mentioned the ability to read a clock, count change, and do basic measurements. Parents recognized that science learning should extend far beyond the textbook and the classroom.

All of the focus groups indicated that hands-on activities related to real-life experiences and future career options are important in improving science education. However, they also stressed the need to include critical thinking and opportunities to apply skills to provide context and to engage students' minds.

Parents were frustrated with their limited knowledge of school reform issues. They indicated that they often hesitate to support initiatives that promote nontraditional methods of learning science because they are unfamiliar with them and uncertain about how they would work in the classroom. For example, most of the parents thought that an integrated curriculum sounded like a good idea, but were not sure exactly it would mean. Some suburban parents believed that collaborative learning would cause advanced children to suffer academically and might have a negative effect on their children's attitudes and motivations toward science.

Parents also mentioned the need to incorporate technology into student learning. Discussions focused on equipping classrooms with computers, but also recognized cost constraints and the need for training and technical support. Parents in urban areas found it hard to contemplate computer acquisition when their classrooms lacked books and basic supplies. In some urban and rural schools, the need for equity in technology use is especially critical.

COMMUNICATION BETWEEN SCHOOLS AND FAMILIES

The deep concern that parents expressed about reform clearly indicates that they understand the need to be actively engaged in the educational process. However, many parents—including those who understand that need—are not involved. Parents reported that poor communication creates large gaps in their knowledge of school issues, contributes to suspicion of reform, and results in their accepting current conditions and resisting change.

Communication with parents is especially important as schools

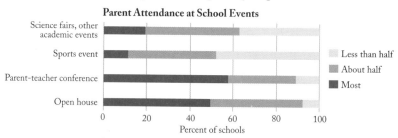

Parent Attendance at School Events

Source: National Center for Education Statistics. (1996, October). *Statistics in brief*. Washington, D.C.: Author. (NCES 96-913).

continue to integrate technology into their teaching because parents admit to a limited understanding of the potential uses of technology in classrooms. Schools often do not include parents in discussing technology acquisitions and may not inform parents of the technological options available or the rationale for decisions that they ultimately make.

Although many parents think schools are not preparing students sufficiently, they may not feel responsible for changing these conditions.

Communication also affects families' involvement in student learning. Parents who are involved in their children's schools reported that they participate mainly in activities peripheral to the learning process, such as chaperoning field trips or planning special events. For better or worse, communities trust in schools to "do the right thing." The reasons for minimal involvement include limited knowledge and uncertainty about curriculum and reform initiatives, a sometimes distant relationship between schools and families, and social and economic factors. For some parents, language differences are also a factor. Not surprisingly, these factors are interrelated. The bottom line is that, although parents may be concerned, they hesitate to discuss these concerns with school staff and remain outside the process of improving science instruction.

Although many parents think schools are not preparing students sufficiently, they may not feel responsible for changing these conditions. Many parents in the focus groups who reported that they feel responsible for ensuring that schools prepare their children to reach standards said they felt powerless to change the current system. They felt that their ability to influence the process depends on how receptive teachers and school administrators are to their input. For example, although parents in the groups have some input into decisions such as selecting textbooks, they reported having little opportunity to make a significant impact on those decisions.

Parents were especially uncomfortable with change in science, a subject in which most of them admit having little proficiency. Research indicates that even well-educated parents may be fearful of science and have low levels of science literacy (Kober, 1993). This admitted lack of scientific knowledge leads many parents to view science only in terms of mastering discrete skills, without recognizing that understanding concepts and processes is necessary for intellectual growth and further learning.

These findings have two implications. First, to motivate parents to participate in their children's education, schools need to stress the link between proposed changes and the results that parents desire. Second, schools should design strategies to engage parents in working to reach those results. Because access to and influence on school systems may be limited for rural, low-income, non-English-speaking, and minority parents, schools in their communities need to make concerted efforts to improve outreach efforts.

SOCIETAL AND ECONOMIC FACTORS

Not surprisingly, the most striking differences among urban, suburban, and rural parents in the focus groups were in how social and economic factors influence their involvement in schools. These factors can influence participation in many ways. Differences in educational levels, cultural background, language, and availability of time, money, and other resources all affect the family's ability and desire to participate fully in their children's education. School personnel can further inhibit family involvement when they act out of sociocultural assumptions that devalue the contributions of poorer, less-educated families; when they use educational jargon that deepens the communication divide; and when they ignore or disparage important economic, cultural, and language differences.

School personnel can further inhibit family involvement when they ... use educational jargon that deepens the communication divide and when they ignore or disparage important economic, cultural, and language differences.

Parents may have low aspirations for their children's school achievement in general, or in science or mathematics in particular, because of their own low achievement in these areas. Some parents attribute success in science and mathematics to innate ability, rather than to effort and perseverance.

In communities where literacy and educational levels tend to be lower, family members who wish to be involved in their children's education may lack the confidence and skill to approach school personnel or to express their interests and opinions. Parents who have had little schooling or negative school experiences may be reluctant to work with educators.

Immigrant and minority families have additional language and cultural hurdles to

"Risk Factors" Among Eighth-Graders

• Single parent
• Parents not high school graduates
• Limited English
• Income less than $15,000
• Sibling dropped out of school
• Home alone more than 3 hours daily

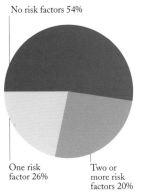

No risk factors 54%

One risk factor 26%

Two or more risk factors 20%

Source: Nelson, B.H., Weiss, I.R., and Conaway, L.E. (1992). *Science and mathematics briefing book, Vol III.* Chapel Hill, NC: Horizon Research.

overcome in order to be involved. In areas where immigrant families are concentrated, language differences may pose a substantial barrier to family involvement. These barriers challenge schools to become more flexible, more aware, and more creative in their communications with students and families and in their outreach efforts.

Families from lower income communities often find that survival issues exhaust their personal resources. Many low-income parents work two or three jobs to provide for their families. Crowded living conditions, substandard housing, inadequate nutrition, and minimal health care may have a negative impact not only on children's education but also on the amount of time and energy their parents can commit to educational reform issues. The need for child care for younger children, fear for personal safety, and lack of transportation may be deterrents, as well, that schools should consider in their outreach efforts.

Nevertheless, parents in all segments of society are keenly aware of the importance of education to the future well-being of their children. When schools learn to communicate their vision for students in ways that parents can understand and to accommodate the realities of everyday family life in all kinds of settings, they can create powerful allies in their communities.

As daunting as these obstacles may seem, they can be overcome by using well-designed, research-based programs, such as the Comer School Development Program, ASPIRA's Mathematics and Science Academies, the American Association for the Advancement of Science's (AAAS) Faith Communities Project, and Teachers Involve Parents in Schoolwork, which are described in *Blueprints'* Resources, to foster meaningful parent and family engagement in science learning. These and similar kinds of community-based projects have proven successful in reaching parents, regardless of income level, education, or ethnicity.

STRATEGIES FOR CHANGE

Families and communities can effect changes in science education by being educators in the home, by becoming actively involved with the school, and by advocating for improvements in science education.

FAMILY STRATEGIES

The first place for parents to participate in their child's education is at home. Studies show that when parents are involved in learning activities at home in a particular subject, such as mathematics, their children show higher achievement in that subject (Epstein, 1988). Parents do not need degrees in microbiology or engineering to help their children with science and math. They can start by turning off the TV and making sure homework is done. When parents monitor homework, students complete more assignments, have higher test scores, and improve their grades (Kober, 1993). There is a high correlation between students' mathematics achievement and limited television viewing (Mullis, Dossey, Owen, & Phillips, 1991). Many schools and communities sponsor homework hot lines, tutoring, parent workshops, and programs to help parents assist their children in science and mathematics homework. Some of these programs, which include Family Science, Family Math, Teachers Involve Parents in Schoolwork, and Project EXCEL-MAS, are described in *Blueprints'* Resources.

Next, families simply need to encourage children's natural curiosity and watch and learn along with them. Parents can model the pursuit of lifelong learning, inquiry, and curiosity by reading, asking questions, discussing science-related articles, and visiting museums and science centers. Comer (1986) reported that many low-income parents participating in a parent involvement program became role models for their children simply by continuing their own education.

Relationship Between Homework and Mathematics Proficiency of 17-Year-Old Students in 1992

Frequency of Doing Homework	Percentage of Students	Average Math Proficiency
Often	76	310
Sometimes	19	295
Never	5	285

Source: National Science Foundation. (1996). *Indicators of science and mathematics, 1995.* Arlington, VA: Author.

Exciting mathematics and science materials—such as *MegaSkills, Revised and Updated* (Rich, 1992) and *Helping Your Child Learn Science* (Paulu, 1991)—reinforce the value of study while building thinking and problem-solving skills.

Parents can use the radio, TV, activity books, and the Internet to engage in home-based science projects with their children. The AAAS Kinetic City Super Crew radio program engages children in science activities. KidsNet, a project of the National Geographic Society, networks parents, students, teachers, and scientists in exploring vital, real-life, science-related issues. Print materials such as *Manual for Teachers: Teachers Involve Parents in Schoolwork* (TIPS): *Language Arts and Science/ Health Interactive Homework in the Middle Grades* (Epstein, Jackson, & Salinas, 1992), *Learning Science and Math in Your Community* (National Urban League, Inc., 1994), and the series *Family Connections* (Appalachia Educational Laboratory) also provide suggestions for home science activities.

Finally, parents can promote high achievement, no matter where they live or what their income is, by letting their children know they have high expectations, especially in science and mathematics. Parents can convey the importance of high achievement and increase their child's self-esteem by setting short-term goals and providing rewards when their child reaches those goals.

SCHOOL STRATEGIES

Outreach and involvement of families and the community naturally extends the boundaries of school. By widening its sphere of influence to include parents, scientists, and other community members, the school can create a supportive dialogue for improving science education.

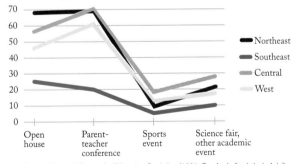

Percentage of Schools Where Most or All Parents Attend Events

Source: National Center for Education Statistics. (1996, October). *Statistics in brief.* Washington, D.C.: Author. (NCES 96-913).

Families and schools must agree on the goals set for the child, and both parties must recognize that each plays a role in the child's educational success. Walberg, Bole, and Waxman (1980) examined a school-wide K-6 program in which parents signed a contract pledging to set high expectations, provide an appropriate study environment, encourage learning by discussing work daily, and cooperate with teachers in matters related to discipline. Walberg observed significant gains in student performance. These results match similar findings by Levin (1987), who has had success in clearly specifying expectations for educators, students, and parents in the form of a contract in his Accelerated Schools.

Schools can increase family involvement by establishing parent advisory councils and involving parents in setting standards and expectations for students. It is especially important for educators to reach out to and involve minority, non-English speaking, and low-income families in developing these partnerships.

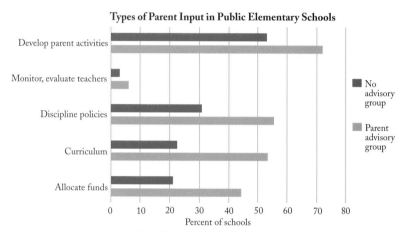

Types of Parent Input in Public Elementary Schools

Source: National Center for Education Statistics. (1996, October). *Statistics in brief*. Washington, D.C.: Author. (NCES 96-913).

Schools can also involve families directly as both learners and teachers. All parents—not just those few who are professional scientists—can teach by reading a book about science, gathering materials for an activity, mentoring or tutoring children in science and mathematics activities, or helping with a project. Teachers can develop homework assignments that involve family members and enable students to share knowledge of science and its applications.

COMMUNITY STRATEGIES

Community resources can supplement science learning in classrooms and meet the challenge of improving science education for all children in several ways. Churches, advocacy groups, and youth service agencies (e.g., health clinics, Boys and Girls Clubs, and the YMCA or YWCA) are valuable components of the reform effort, especially as science educators strive to reach an increasing number of low-income and minority students.

The National Urban League, the AAAS Faith Communities Project, and individual efforts such as Luis Moll's work with Mexican-American communities in New York have successfully engaged minority students and their parents in meaningful science learning. Some of these and similar programs are described in *Blueprints'* Resources.

Schools can use community resources such as museums, nature centers, businesses, and hospitals as sites for out-of-school learning for students and families. These informal arenas can provide an additional context for students to learn and understand firsthand the science concepts they are taught in class. Such venues—from zoos to botanical gardens—exist in both urban and rural settings. National and state parks, NASA Teacher Resource Centers, and Department of Energy Laboratories can also serve as sources of information and materials for families and teachers. Local plumbers, electricians, and mechanics apply science principles in their daily work, which they can demonstrate to students. Utilities, such as telephone switching stations and water treatment facilities, also offer possibilities for scientific inquiry. Businesses can serve as a valuable science education resource by providing science experts to work with teachers on designing instructional programs, offering applied settings for scientific inquiry, or supporting mentoring relationships between employees and students. High-profile support from business can also lead to wider political and community support for educational reform programs.

Some of the most exciting science opportunities happen when scientists become involved with students and teachers in science projects.

Although they are not available in all areas, colleges and universities can also be rich sources of scientific knowledge, expertise, and tools. Some of the most exciting science opportunities happen when scientists become involved with students and teachers in science projects. These collaborations provide role models for children and support for teachers. They also build mutual understanding and respect between K-12 schools and higher education. Community groups can play several possible roles to encourage or participate in these partnerships. For example, sponsoring a "university-school" mathematics and science night can provide the catalyst for planning long-term activities.

RECOMMENDATIONS

Together families, community leaders, and educators can develop effective strategies and programs—beyond fund-raising and occasional attendance at school events—that generate the public's enthusiasm for science learning and that use community resources to enrich science education. Following are some specific measures that all participants in science education reform can take to nurture these relationships.

■ *Promote the development of shared goals in science education and joint problem solving among educators, families, and members of the community.* Policies should be framed so that parents, community members, and schools are encouraged to communicate clearly to each other their goals for children's science literacy. Schools that are committed to change can help communities and parents connect their expectations to the specific science learning goals of the reform efforts.

■ *Convince educators that all parents have the desire and the ability to support their children's education.* Schools can bridge the gap that often exists between parents and school staff by treating all parents and other community members, regardless of ethnic or socioeconomic background, as willing and able participants in reform. While some changes—such as greater emphasis on hands-on learning—are likely to be accepted by most parents, science educators should acknowledge parents' concerns and remain forthright in their commitment when addressing more controversial issues such as the increased use of group instruction. Parents should understand that higher levels of science literacy are critical to their children's future success.

■ *Disseminate information to increase parent and community involvement in science education.* Organizations such as the National Science Foundation through its State, Rural, and Urban Systemic Initiatives Programs; professional societies; business; and the media should replicate and disseminate successful models for increasing parent and community involvement in science education.

■ *Inform families and the community about science education and involve them in meaningful decision making about education reform.* Schools can distribute existing guidelines to parents such as *What to Look for in Science Classrooms* and *What to Look for in Mathematics Classrooms*, published by the AAAS and The College Board. Professional societies can develop additional guidelines and checklists that will inform parents of science education issues and help them become involved in the decision making process.

■ *Engage parents and the community as learners and teachers.* Schools should engage all families and adult members of the community in thinking and learning, particularly in the critical area of science. Science educators at all levels of the educational system should implement models of schools that are science education resources for all community members. Parents should see schools as places to expand their own knowledge of science, mathematics, and technology. Schools could also engage parents and community members as resources to enrich school science learning.

This set of recommendations requires collaboration among schools, families, and other organizations. Implementing these recommendations independently of other changes in the nation's educational system could be beneficial. However, the radical reform of science education needed to promote science literacy among all students will occur only if players from all parts of the educational system work together toward shared science literacy goals. The full and active participation of families, community members, and community-based organizations is crucial in effecting systemic change and ensuring science literacy for all students.

REFERENCES

Bronfenbrenner, U. (1979). *The ecology of human development: Experiments by nature and design.* Cambridge, MA: Harvard University Press.

Comer, J. (1980). *School power: Implications of an intervention project.* New York: Free Press.

Comer, J. (1986, February). Parent participation in schools. *Phi Delta Kappan,* 226-442.

Epstein, J. (1988). How do we improve programs for parent involvement? *Educational Horizons, 66,* 58-59.

Epstein, J., Jackson, V., & Salinas, K.C. (1992). *Manual for teachers: Teachers involve parents in schoolwork (TIPS): Language arts and science/health interactive homework in the middle grades.* Boston, MA: Johns Hopkins University Center on Families, Communities, Schools, and Children's Learning.

Kober, N. (1993). *EDTALK: What we know about science teaching and learning.* Washington, D.C.: Council for Educational Development & Research.

Levin, H. M. (1987, March). Accelerated schools for disadvantaged students. *Educational Leadership, 44*(6), 19-21.

Mullis, I. V., Dossey, J. A., Owen, E. H., & Phillips, G. W. (1991, June). *The state of mathematics achievement: NAEP's assessment of the nation and the trial assessment of the states.* Washington, D.C.: U. S. Department of Education, National Center for Educational Statistics.

National Urban League, Inc. (1994). *Learning science and math in your community.* New York: Author.

Paulu, N. (1991). *Helping your child learn science.* Washington, D.C.: Office of Educational Research and Improvement, U.S. Department of Education.

Rich, D. (1992). *MegaSkills, revised and updated.* Boston, MA: Houghton Mifflin Company.

Walberg, H., Bole, R., & Waxman, H. (1980). School-based family socialization and reading achievement in the inner city. *In Psychology in the Schools.* Santa Monica, CA: Rand Corporation.

BIBLIOGRAPHY

American Association for the Advancement of Science. (1993). *Benchmarks for science literacy.* New York: Oxford University Press.

American Association for the Advancement of Science. (1989). *Science for all Americans.* New York: Oxford University Press.

Armor, D. (1976). *Analysis of the school preferred reading program in selected Los Angeles minority schools.* Santa Monica, CA: RAND.

Ascher, C. (1987). *Improving the school-home connection for poor and minority urban students.* (Trends and Issues Series, No. 8). New York: Institute for Urban and Minority Education, Teachers College, Columbia University. p. 5, 8, 10. (ERIC/CUE Document Reproduction Service No. ED300-484)

Baker, D., & Entwisle, D. (1987). The influence of mothers on the academic expectations of young children: A longitudinal study of how gender differences arise. *Social Forces, 65,* 670-694.

Baker, D., & Stevenson, D. (1986). Mothers' strategies for children's school achievement: Managing the transition to high school. *Sociology of Education, 59,* 156-166.

Becker, H., & Epstein, J. (1982). Parent involvement: A survey of teacher practices. *The Elementary School Journal, 83,* 85-102.

Bee, H., Barnard, K., Eyres, S., Gray, C., Hammond, M., Spietz, A., Snyder, C., & Clark, B. (1982). Prediction of IQ and language skills from prenatal status, child performance, family characteristics, and mother-infant interaction. *Child Development, 53,* 44-75.

Bempechat, J. (1990). *The role of parent involvement in children's academic achievement: A review of the literature.* (Trends and Issues No. 14). New York: ERIC Clearinghouse on Urban Education. p. 2, 4-11. (ERIC/CUE Document Reproduction Service No. ED 322 285)

Bempechat, J. Mordkowitz, E., Wu, J., Morison, M., & Ginsburg, H. (1989, April). *Achievement motivation in Cambodian refugee children: A comparative study.* Paper presented at the Biennial conference of the Society for Research in Child Development, Kansas City, MO.

Berliner, D., & Casanova, U. (1985, October 20). Is parent involvement worth the effort? *Instructor*, 20-21.

Bloom, B.S. (1986). *The home environment and school learning.* One of 46 papers commissioned by the Study Group on the National Assessment of Student Achievement and cited in Appendix B to their final report, "The Nation's Report Card" (TM 870 044).

Boardman, S., Harrington, C., & Horowitz, S. (1987). Successful women: A psychological investigation of family, class and education. In B. Gutek & L. Larwood (Eds.), *Women's career development.* Beverly Hills, CA: Sage.

Bronfenbrenner, U. (1979). *The ecology of human development: Experiments by nature and design.* Cambridge, MA: Harvard University Press.

Brown, L. (1980). *Problems in implementing statutory requirements for Title I ESEA parent advisory councils.* Boston, MA: Institute for Responsive Education. (ERIC Document Reproduction Service No. ED 204 434).

Burns-Crawford, R. (1993). *Parents and schools: From visitors to partners.* Washington, D.C.: National Education Association.

Bush, C. S. (1981). *Language, remediation, and expansion: Workshops for parents and teachers.* Tucson, AZ: Communication Skill Builders.

Center on Organization and Restructuring of Schools. (1993, Fall). Social capital and the rebuilding of communities. In *Issues in restructuring schools.* Madison, WI: University of Wisconsin-Madison.

Chavkin, N. F., & Williams, D.L. (1984). *Executive summary: Guidelines and strategies for training teachers about parent involvement.* Austin, TX: Southwest Educational Development Laboratory.

Chavkin, N., & Williams, D. (1988). Critical issues in teacher training for parent involvement. *Educational Horizons*, 66, 87-89.

Child Development Project (1994). *At home in our schools: A guide to school wide activities that build community.* Oakland, CA: Development Studies Center.

Clark, R. (1983). Family life and school achievement: *Why poor black children succeed and fail.* Chicago, IL: The University of Chicago Press.

Clark, R.M. (1988). Parents as providers of linguistic and social capital. *Educational Horizons*, 66.

Clark-Stewart, A. (1983). Exploring the assumptions of parent education. In R. Haskins & D. Adams (Eds.), *Parent education and public policy.* Norwood, NJ: Ablex.

Cochran, M., & Henderson, C.R. (1986). *Family matters: Evaluation of the Parental Empowerment Program.* Ithaca, NY: Cornell University.

Coleman, J., Campbell, E. Hobson, C., McPartland, J., Mood, A., Weinfeld, F., & York, R. (1966). *Equality of educational opportunity*. Washington, D.C.: U.S. Government Printing Office.

Coleman, J. (1988). Social capital in the creation of human capital. *The American Journal of Sociology, 94* (Supplement), S95-S120.

Coleman, J. (1991). *Policy perspectives: Parental involvement in education*. (065-000-00459-3). Washington, D.C.: U.S. Government Printing Office.

Comer, J. (1980). *School power: Implications of an intervention project*. New York: The Free Press.

Comer, J. (1986, February). Parent participation in the schools. *Phi Delta Kappan, 67*(6), 226-442.

Comer, J. (1988, November). Educating poor minority children. *Scientific American, 259*(5), 42-48.

Comer, J., & Haynes, N.M. (1991). Parent involvement in schools: An ecological approach. *The Elementary School Journal, 91*(3), 271-277.

Csikszentmihalyi, M., & McCormack, J. (1986, February). The influence of teachers. *Phi Delta Kappan, 67*(6), 415-419.

Devaney, K. (1987). Family math: Making the home an environment for problem solving. In M. Druger (Ed.), *Science for the fun of it: A guide to informal science education*, Washington, D.C.: National Science Teachers Association.

Dokecki, P., Hargrove, E., & Sandler, M. (1983). An overview of the parent child development center social experiment. In R. Haskins & D. Adams (Eds.), *Parent education and public policy*. Norwood, NJ: Ablex.

Duncan, L. W. (1969). *Parent-counselor conferences make a difference*. St. Petersburg, FL: St. Petersburg Junior College. (ERIC Document Reproduction Service No. ED 031 743).

Dunton, K., McDevitt, T., & Hess, R. (1988). Origins of mothers' attributions about their daughters' and sons' performance in mathematics in sixth grade. *Merrill-Palmer Quarterly, 34*, 47-70.

Eccles, J. (1983). Expectancies, values, and academic behaviors. In J. Spence (Ed.), *Achievement and achievement motives: Psychological and social approaches*. New York: Freeman.

Epstein, J. L. (1984). School policy and parent involvement - Research results. *Educational Horizons, 62*.

Epstein, J.L. (1987, February). Parent involvement: What research says to administrators. *Education and Urban Society, 19*(2).

Epstein, J. (1987). Toward a theory of family-school connections: Teacher practices and parent involvement. In K. Kurrelmann, F. Kaufmann, & F. Lasel (Eds.), *Social intervention: Potential and constraints*. New York: De Gruyter.

Epstein, J. (1988). How do we improve programs for parent involvement? *Educational Horizons, 66*, 58-59.

Epstein, J. (1989). Family structures and student motivation: A developmental perspective. In C. Ames & R. Ames (Eds.), *Research on motivation in education, v.3: Goals and cognitions*. New York: Academic Press.

Epstein, J. (1992). School and family partnerships. In M. Atkin (Ed.), *Encyclopedia of educational research*, (6th edition). New York: MacMillan.

Epstein, J. & Becker, H. (1982). Teachers' reported practices of parent involvement: Problems and possibilities. *The Elementary School Journal, 83*, 103-113.

Epstein, J., Jackson, V., & Salinas, K.C. (1992). *Manual for teachers: Teachers
involve parents in schoolwork (TIPS) language arts and science/health interactive
homework in the middle grades.* Baltimore, MD: Johns Hopkins University,
Center on Families, Communities, Schools and Children's Learning.

Farkas, S. (1993). *Divided within, besieged without: The politics of education in four
typical American school districts.* New York: The Public Agenda Foundation.

Flaxman, E., & Inger, M. (1991, September). Parents and schooling in the 1990s.
ERIC Review, 1(3), p. 4.

Flood, J. (1993, March). *The relationship between parent involvement and student
achievement: A review of the literature.* Springfield, IL: Illinois State Board of
Education, Department of Planning, Research, and Evaluation.

General Accounting Office (GAO). (1994, January). *Rural children: Increasing
poverty rates pose educational challenges* (Report No. GAO/HEHS-94-75BR).
Washington, D.C.: U.S. Government Printing Office.

Goodman, J. (1992, September). The school community mathematics project.
Thrust for Educational Leadership.

Gotts, E.E., & Purnell, R.F. (1985). *Improving home-school communications.* (PDK
Fastback Series No. 230). Bloomington, IN: Phi Delta Kappa Educational
Foundation.

Harris James, B. (1993). *Organizing communities for educational improvement: The
Brownsville site interim report.* Charlestown, WV: Appalachia Educational
Laboratory.

Henderson, A. (1987). *The evidence continues to grow: Parent involvement improves
student achievement.* Columbia, MD: National Committee for Citizens in
Education.

Henderson, A. (1981). Home environment and intellectual performance. In R.
Henderson (Ed.), *Parent-child interaction: Theory, research and prospects.* New
York: Academic Press.

Henderson, A. (1981). *Parent participation and student achievement: The evidence
grows.* National Committee for Citizens in Education Occasional Paper.
Columbia, MD: National Committee for Citizens in Education.

Henderson, A., Marburger, C., & Ooms, T. (1985). *Beyond the bake sale: An educator's
guide to working with parents.* Columbia, MD: National Committee for
Citizens in Education.

Hispanic Research Center. (1990). *A prospectus on project PRIME: A project to
improve minority education.* Tempe, AZ: Arizona State University-Tempe.

Hobbs, D. (1992). The rural context for education: Adjusting the images. In M.
W. Galbraith (Ed.), *Education in the rural American community: A lifelong process.*
Melbourne, FL: Krieger Publishers.

Hofmeister, A.M. (1977). *The parent is a teacher.* Paper presented at the 56th
Annual Faculty Honor Lecture in the Humanities, Logan, UT. (ERIC
Document Reproduction Service No. ED 161 541).

Holloway, S., & Hess, R. (1985). Mothers' and teachers' attributions about children's mathematics performance. In I. Sigel (Ed.), *Parent belief systems.*
Hillsdale, JN: Erlbaum.

Howard, J., & Hammond, R. (1985, September 9). Rumors of inferiority. *The New Republic.*

Iverson, B.K., & Walberg, H.J. (1982). Home environment and school learning: A quantitative synthesis. *Journal of Experimental Education, 50*(3), 144-151.

Jones, B.F., & Fennimore, T.F. (1990). The new definition of learning: The first step to school reform. A guidebook for the teleseries *Restructuring to promote learning in America's schools.* Oak Brook, IL: North Central Regional Educational Laboratory.

Kepler, L. (1986, September). We Love Science Day. *Science and Children, 24*(1), 30, 43.

Kober, N. (1993). *EDTALK: What we know about science teaching and learning.* Washington, D.C.: Council for Education Development & Research.

Kunesh, L.G., & Farley, J. (1993). Integrating community services for young children and their families (Report 3). *Policy Briefs.* Oak Brook, IL: North Central Regional Educational Laboratory.

Lareau, A. (1987). Social class differences in family-school relationships: The importance of cultural capital. *Sociology of Education, 60,* 73-85.

Ledell, M. & Arnsparger, A. (1993). *How to deal with community criticism of school change.* Denver, CO: Education Commission of the States.

Leler, H. (1983). Parent education and involvement in relation to the schools and to parents of school-aged children. In R. Haskins & D. Adamson (Eds.), *Parent education and public policy* (p. 173). Norwood, NJ: Ablex.

Levin, H.M. (1987, March). Accelerated schools for disadvantaged students. *Educational Leadership, 44*(6), 19-21.

McKinney, J.A. (1975). *The development and implementation of a tutorial program for parents to improve the reading and mathematics achievement of their children.* Fort Lauderdale, FL: Nova University. (ERIC Document Reproduction Service No. ED 113 703).

Melaragno, R.J., Keesling, J.W., Lyons, M.F., Robbins, A.E., & Smith, A.G. (1981). *Parents and federal education programs. Volume I: The nature, causes, and consequences of parental involvement.* Santa Monica, CA: System Development Corporation. (ERIC Document Reproduction Service No. ED 218 783).

Mize, G.K. (1977). *The influence of increased parental involvement in the educational process of their children.* Technical Report No. 418. Madison, WI: University of Wisconsin Research and Development Center for Cognitive Learning. (ERIC Document Reproduction Service No. ED 151 661). p. 76.

Moles, O. Wallat, C., Carroll, T., & Collins, C. (1980). *1980-1984 research area plans for families as educators.* Washington, D.C.: National Institute of Education.

Moles, O. (1982, November). Synthesis of recent research on parent participation in children's education. *Educational Leadership,* 44-47.

Moses, R., Kamii, M., Swap, S., & Howard, J. (1989). The Algebra Project: Organizing in the spirit of Ella. *Harvard Educational Review, 59*(4), 423-443.

Mullis, I.V.S., Dossey, J.A., Owen, E.H., & Phillips, G.W. (1991, June). *The state of mathematics achievement: NAEP's 1990 assessment of the nation and the trial assessment of the states.* Washington, D.C.: National Center for Education Statistics, U.S. Department of Education.

The National PTA. (1992). *A leader's guide to parent and family involvement.* Chicago, IL: Author.

National Urban League, Inc. (1994). *Learning science and math in your community.* New York: Author.

Newmann, F.M. (1991). Linking restructuring to authentic student achievement. *Phi Delta Kappan, 72*(6), 458-463.

O'Connell, S. R. (1992, September). Math pairs: Parents as partners. *Arithmetic Teacher 40*(1), 10-12.

Ogbu, J. (1989). *Academic socialization of black children: An inoculation against future failure.* Paper presented at the Biennial Conference of the Society for research in Child Development, Kansas City, MO.

Olmstead, P., & Rubin, R. (1983). Parent involvement: Perspectives from the follow-through experience. In R. Haskins & D. Adams (Eds.), *Parent education and public policy,* Norwood, NJ: Ablex.

Parsons, J. Adler, T., & Kaczala, C. (1982). Socialization of achievement attitudes and beliefs: Parental influences. *Child Development, 53,* 310-321.

Rogoff, B., & Gardner, W. (1984). Adult guidance of everyday cognition. In B. Rogoff & J. Lave (Eds.), *Everyday cognition: Its development in social context.* Cambridge, MA: Harvard University Press.

Rosen, B., & D'Andrade, R. (1959). The psychosocial origins of achievement motivation. *Sociometry, 22,* 185-218.

Sattes, Beth D. (1985). *Parent involvement: A review of the literature.* (AEL Occasional Paper 021). Charleston, WV: Appalachia Educational Laboratory.

Schorr, L. B., with Schorr, D. (1988). *Within our reach: Breaking the cycle of disadvantage.* New York: Anchor Press/Doubleday.

Schwartz, W. (1987). Teaching science and mathematics to at risk students. *ERIC Digest.* New York: ERIC Clearinghouse on Urban Education. (ERIC Document Reproduction Service No. ED 289 948)

Scott-Jones, D. (1988). Families as educators: The transition from informal to formal school learning. *Educational Horizons, 66.*

Seeley, D. (1982, November). Education through partnership. *Educational Leadership, 39,* 42-43.

Sevener, D. (1990, March). Parents and teachers: Co-navigators for successful schooling. *Synthesis, 1*(2), 1-3.

Shuck, A., Ulsh, F., and Platt, J.S. (1983). Parents encourage pupils (PEP): An inner city parent involvement reading project. *Reading Teacher, 36,* 524-528.

Sigel, I. (1982). The relationship between parental distancing strategies and the child's cognitive behavior. In L. Laosa & I. Sigel (Eds.), *Families as learning environments for children.* New York: Plenum Press.

Smith, M.B., & Brahce, C.I. (1963). When school and home focus on achievement. *Educational Leadership, 20,* 314-318.

Steller, A., & Knox, D. (1981). How to develop positive teacher-parent relationships. *Journal of Educational Communication, 5*(2), 28-31.

Stevenson, H. (1987, October). America's math problems. *Educational Leadership, 45*(2), 4-10.

Swap, S.M. (1990). *Parent involvement and success for all children: What we know now.* Boston, MA: Institute for Responsive Education.

Tinzmann, M. B., Friedman, L., Jewell-Kelly, S., Mootry, P., Nachtigal, P., & Fine, C. (1990). Schools as learning communities. *A guidebook for the teleseries* [*Restructuring to promote learning in America's schools*]. Oak Brook, IL: North Central Regional Ed. Lab.

Tinzmann, M.B., Jones, B.F., Fennimore, T.F., Bakker, J., Fine, C., & Pierce, J. (1990). The collaborative classroom: Reconnecting teachers and learners. *A guidebook for the teleseries* [*Restructuring to promote learning in America's schools*]. Oak Brook, IL: North Central Regional Educational Laboratory.

Toby, J. (1957). Orientation to education as factor in the school maladjustment of lower class children. *Social Forces, 35,* 259-266.

Walberg, H., Bole, R., & Waxman, H. (1980). School-based family socialization and reading achievement in the inner city. In *Psychology in the schools.* Santa Monica, CA: RAND Corporation.

Wilson, W.J. (1990). *The truly disadvantaged: The inner city, the underclass, and public policy.* Chicago, IL: University of Chicago Press.

Wolf, J.S. (1982). Parents as partners in exceptional education. *Theory Into Practice 21(2),* 77-81.

12

Business and Industry

THIS CHAPTER DEFINES WAYS for the business community to help implement reform in science, mathematics, and technology education. It discusses business' current involvement in K-12 reform, and examines ways for business to become involved in the reforms and to help foster an environment in which reforms can succeed. It identifies barriers to successful business involvement in education in general and science reform in particular, and suggests ways for science education reformers to address those barriers and develop and maintain useful relationships with business.

Business involvement in pre-college education in America dates to the mid-19th century, when many members of the Whig Party saw economic success and desirable socialization skills, such as punctuality and good work habits, as key goals of education. Business involvement in education reform began early in the 20th century, when the National Association of Manufacturers led a lobbying campaign that resulted in the 1917 passage of the Smith-Hughes Act— legislation that called for standardized testing, guidance counseling, and tracking in the nation's schools. More recently, business reacted to the Soviet launch of Sputnik and to the Cold War by demanding more engineers and scientists. In the 1980s, reports like *A Nation at Risk* (National Commission on Excellence in Education, 1983) justified for many business people the idea that education was both a root cause of many economic and social problems and the best hope to remedy these problems.

Although one could argue that business' historical involvement in education has been only marginally effective, there are signs that today's participation could lead to more significant results. Corporations have developed an interest in disadvantaged youth, early childhood education, and a variety of programs ranging from adopt-a-school efforts and collaborative partnerships to systemic change initiatives. Business involvement in education can reinforce science education reform's emphasis on teamwork (which many modern workplaces stress) and on professional development (which most business have long offered for their employees).

Companies involved with education for a decade or more come to understand how difficult science education reform is and how business must commit support for the long term. This understanding is key to the success of business-school partnerships, many of which have waxed and waned in past decades (Shakeshaft & Trachtman, 1986). If business becomes frustrated by the pace of education reform and begins to support more radical approaches, or goes outside the education system to solve its problems, it may be working at cross purposes with other reformers. Science education reformers should continue to encourage business leaders to take the long-term view when getting involved in education reform, and educators and business people should remain at the reform table together.

THE CURRENT STATUS

Although there is little research on the extent of business involvement in K-12 education, anecdotal evidence suggests that big business is usually more involved than smaller organizations. Though every community cannot have access to a Xerox production facility or an AT&T laboratory, every community does have businesses that can contribute to science education. Power companies, telephone companies, engineering firms, environmental businesses, and veterinarians all have the potential to help. For instance, David Coen of Vermont's State Systemic Initiative formed a partnership with a backhoe operator who visited elementary school classrooms to explain why it is not possible to operate a backhoe without a solid knowledge of math (Coen, 1993).

The key point for education reformers to recognize about business involvement in K-12 education is that businesses most likely to become involved in reform are those who feel most affected by today's competitive environment.

THE NATURE OF BUSINESS INVOLVEMENT

Recently, there have been important changes in business' priorities for education reform. For example, business is now urging a more inclusive approach, as evidenced by the Business Roundtable's 1990 education reform credo that "every student can learn at significantly higher levels." Demographic projections indicate an increasingly important role in tomorrow's work force for traditionally underrepresented groups—women, minorities and immigrants—and businesses have testified before Congress for increased Head Start funding to ensure that today's schools better serve these populations.

Second, business has changed its traditional approach of reserving most of its education investment for higher education. Recognizing the need to improve learning earlier in students' lives, business increased its giving to elementary and preschool programs considerably during the late 1980s and early 1990s and has recently increased its support of pre-K education. Financial support for K-12 education grew as a percentage of overall educational contributions during that period, peaking in 1992 (Sommerfield, 1993; Tillman, 1994).

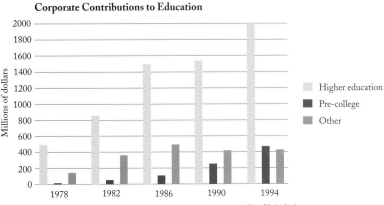

Corporate Contributions to Education

Source: AAFRC Trust for Philanthropy. (1996). *Giving USA, 1996*. New York: Author.

And third, business involvement in partnerships, alliances, and other collaborative education efforts is growing. About 50% of America's school districts are engaged in some kind of partnership with business (National Association of Partners in Education, 1991). The trend toward widespread and more systemic partnerships offers hope that business-school relationships are becoming a key part of science education reform. Although information on the types of business likely to get involved in education is as sketchy as data on the extent of their involvement, a handful of studies and surveys suggests that banks, utilities, insurance companies, financial services companies, and electronics and high-tech firms are most likely to collaborate on school reform (Shakeshaft & Trachtman, 1986). Other frequent collaborators include paper companies, manufacturers, and aerospace and automotive companies.

Most states have reform groups in which business plays a major role.

As educational policy makers at the state and national level continue to pursue systemic change, businesses are increasingly engaged in the reform effort. Most states have reform groups in which business plays a major role, and it is not uncommon for a 1990s CEO to visit the White House or the Department of Education to discuss school reform. The Business Roundtable, which includes more than 200 CEOs from America's leading companies, is committed to a ten-year, 50-state reform initiative. This initiative focuses on public policy issues, including standards, performance and assessment, school accountability, school autonomy, professional development, parent involvement, learning readiness, technology, and safety and discipline. As an important actor in the business community and therefore in the policy community, the Business Roundtable initiative is already having an impact on education.

Businesses are also increasingly encouraging well-defined content standards like Project 2061's *Benchmarks for Science Literacy* (1993) and academic content frameworks at the state level. The 1996 Governors' Education Summit—well attended by prominent CEOs—added momentum to this drive. Associations and collaborative groups are expanding their roles in education reform. The National Alliance of Business (NAB) focuses on education reform as it relates to work-force issues. Eleven business organizations belong to the Business Coalition for Education Reform, an NAB-led umbrella group that addresses legislative matters relating to education. The Council for Aid to Education exists to stimulate private support—especially business support—of education. Trade associations such as the Edison Electric Institute, Chemical Manufacturers Association, and American Petroleum Institute have well-established education programs and they also encourage members to work in concert with educators, communities, and other businesses in restructuring K-12 education. Local Chambers of Commerce have contributed significantly to resources produced by the U.S. Chamber of Commerce's Center for Workforce Preparation and Quality Education.

Not surprisingly, many of the large companies that are involved in K-12 education concentrate their efforts on science, mathematics, and technology, as these subjects naturally help to meet future work-force needs and promote U.S. competitiveness. In supporting science and mathematics, businesses emphasize curricula, motivation, achievement, school-business contacts, and technology-based instruction (Lund & Wild, 1993). Increasingly, science educators are recognizing that business can—and probably should—play an active role in effecting change. The Corporate Council for Mathematics and Science Education, the National Science Resources Center, the Triangle Coalition for Science and Technology Education, The National Science Teachers Association, and the American Association for the Advancement of Science work closely with business to solicit input about science education reform issues and to include representatives from the scientific and business communities on their advisory boards.

Finally, there is a growing interest in school-to-work transition (STW), which aims to close the gap between what happens in school and what is needed on the job by using each to reinforce the other. Many business leaders see STW as a way to improve education generally, while many educators are beginning to see possibilities for STW to go far beyond the traditional school vocational program. The goal of STW is to acknowledge, from a pedagogical and curricular perspective, that although the majority of students put their future economic life near the top of their list of educational objectives, they also think of vocational education as a dead-end track intended for someone else (Timpane & McNeill, 1991).

THE MOTIVATION FOR BUSINESS INVOLVEMENT
The desire for a highly skilled work force is a major factor motivating business involvement in science and math education reform. Many businesses contend that today's schools do not provide the highly skilled workers needed for today's work. Such thinking reflects the popular wisdom, but critics ask whether a skills shortage really exists and question the link between curriculum content and workplace needs. Still others suggest that America's lack of competitiveness in the 1970s and 1980s resulted from poor management, not poor workforce training on the part of public schools. Only now is the reality of a high-tech workplace catching up with the rhetoric. Manufacturers will increasingly demand the services of highly skilled workers as jobs become more complex. That appears to be the case with the Big Three auto makers, which in hiring production line workers reportedly check on applicants' "reading and math abilities, manual dexterity and understanding of spatial relations." These checks take the form of a three-hour group exercise in which applicants are evaluated on their contribution to a task, such as improving a production-line process (Meredith, 1996).

Many chemical, pharmaceutical, biotechnology, and other companies that depend on a highly trained work force also see a science literate public as crucial to their future success. Said one chemical company CEO, "It is important to educate all children to be literate, informed citizens and consumers—the same citizens and consumers who buy our products go to the polling booth and vote on issues which affect the success of our industry." Public relations, community relations, employee relations, economic development, and corporate social responsibility continue to motivate business involvement.

Business involvement in education always sparks debate about whether schools exist to educate students for life or for work. The answer should be both—that a school's customers are students, parents, and society. While much of the dialogue about business' relations with schools revolves around preparing students for the workplace, surveys consistently reveal that businesses do not expect schools to provide job training for future workers. Business wants workers who have mastered basic skills and who have good work habits and attitudes (Mann, 1987). "You teach 'em, we'll train 'em" remains an appropriate call for today's businesses.

A difficult issue arises when corporations promote products, ideas, or values in public schools. Many people criticize business harshly for using schools to promote ideas of free enterprise and to distribute materials reflecting the corporate view on issues such as environmental protection, labor, and energy. Some businesses recognize this fact and have structured their involvement to address broader goals such as the development of critical thinking skills.

THE NEEDED CHANGES

The ideal and useful relationship between business and science education reformers would be a truly collaborative one in which each partner understood the other's perspective and was comfortable with constructive criticism. Business would advocate reform in public policy debates and funding requests, keeping the issue high on society's agenda. Business would participate in science education reform and assist local schools—offering expertise in strategic planning and finance, encouraging employees and parents to participate in school-improvement efforts, and collaborating with schools on programs that make schooling more relevant to students' lives. Schools and business would work together to maximize schools' use of volunteers, funding, and in-kind contributions from business.

AFFECTING EDUCATION POLICY

Business would also signal to students that science literacy is important to future success and would actively participate in school-to-work programs. Business would help to develop effective science curriculum materials and provide internships and summer employment to assist minority, female, and disadvantaged students in pursuing successful careers in science.

As one of the country's most powerful political lobbies, business can help to create safe policy space for science education reform to flourish, especially in the areas of finance and implementation. Now that many business leaders have been involved for more than a decade, they are an especially powerful voice for science education reform. Having one or several respected business leaders support science benchmarks and standards can make an extraordinary difference in passing legislation that will support the type of teaching and learning promoted by science educators. But business will not always want to lobby directly on behalf of controversial reforms. In these instances, such lobbying can be done through trade associations or the many business alliances that were described earlier.

Continuing efforts to upgrade the quality of education in South Carolina illustrate how business can lead a long-term advocacy effort. Businesses there played an active role in developing reforms and pushing policymakers to provide the necessary funding in 1983-84. They also helped to implement the reforms and to sustain the momentum that so often fades from reform efforts. On several occasions they beat back efforts to gut the original legislation.

Many people believe that business' most crucial role in education reform is to be an advocate for reform efforts.

Many people believe that business' most crucial role in education reform is to be an advocate for reform efforts, convincing parents, the public, and policymakers to focus on meaningful change—just as they did in South Carolina.

In addition to being an advocate, business can place constant pressure on many levels of the system to change. As major contributors to universities, business can encourage schools of education or departments of chemistry, for instance, to reform the way they teach. Business is often the only institution with enough power and credibility to bring together key constituencies—educators, policymakers, parents, and business representatives—to support education reform.

Demanding "improvement" in education is easy; defining "improvement" is often difficult, but critical if businesses expect schools to produce an improved workforce for the next century. In support of higher standards and expectations, business can make grades and attendance important factors in hiring considerations. It can also clearly define its workplace needs and inform schools of future skills—in alignment with science standards—that will be needed on the job.

Finally, business can play a critical role in improving education by adopting workplace practices that allow parents to be with their children at key moments and to become involved in their children's education. Providing parents with paid time off to visit a child's teacher or developing a formal education policy that legitimizes employee/parent volunteerism in schools, for instance, can be an invaluable incentive for getting parents into the classroom.

DIRECT CONTRIBUTIONS TO REFORM

Although corporate grants to public schools will never rival public support, business funds can still be helpful—especially if they are available for professional enrichment activities or pilot projects. Businesses with experience in leadership, quality, and managing change can make significant contributions to the increased staff development called for in science education reform. Many companies today focus their contributions to achieve greater program leverage and results. In order to support specific changes in curriculum, professional development, materials, or assessment, businesses often combine financial assistance such as scholarships or incentives for students and teachers with employee involvement and expertise.

Breaking down walls between schools and the community directly affects business, and the day should come when the involvement of parents, business people, and others in schools will no longer be news. As students learn more meaningful science, schools will surely need more and better facilities and equipment—materials that business is in a unique position to provide. Business contributions can fill gaps in needed resources by funding supplemental booklets, films, and other needed materials.

In addition to providing facilities and materials to schools, businesses are providing schools with technology and expertise on using it. Local cable and telephone companies are wiring some schools for Internet access. The relationship between Thomas Jefferson High School in Virginia and Westinghouse—described in detail in *Blueprints'*

Chapter 6: Curriculum Connections—exemplifies how business can both provide schools with the latest technology and help students understand and use that technology.

A successful example of business providing support for classroom science and mathematics teachers is the Industry Initiatives for Science and Math Education (IISME) program in the San Francisco area. A consortium of companies and government laboratories, working with the Lawrence Hall of Science, provides summer internships for K-12 teachers.

Although we usually think of business volunteers or programs inside the classroom, volunteers often make their greatest contributions elsewhere. Industry scientists and engineers across the country design school-to-work transition programs that are showcased at school career days; participate in professional development programs for science teachers; keep teachers current on new technologies and their applications; provide technical input in developing inquiry-based curriculum

---

Industry Initiatives for Science and Math Education (IISME)

When school lets out for the summer, San Francisco area science and mathematic teachers take on careers as summer fellows. For eight weeks, teachers embark on fellowship programs that provide them with paid, mentored jobs in businesses and industries.

Teachers are given challenging work assignments to recharge their interest and motivation. Companies receive enthusiastic workers and an opportunity to show teachers the skills that students need to be productive members of the workforce. Students benefit from the ten percent of their fellowship time that teachers devote to developing an action plan to translate their summer experience into enriched instruction.

The IISME experience does not end when school resumes. More than 85 percent of mentors either make classroom visits or host student visits to their work site during the school year. Since the program started in 1985, sponsors have devoted more than 30,000 volunteer hours to improving math and science education.

IISME's reach extends far beyond the Bay Area. As one of the oldest programs of its kind, IISME has helped launch similar programs throughout the United States and abroad. More than 90 scientific work sites for teachers now exist in the United States.

Source: Industry Initiatives for Science and Math Education. (1996). *A decade of discovery.* Santa Clara, CA: Author

materials; and serve as role models and mentors for students, especially for minorities and women. Teachers find it much easier to relate classroom work to the real world if companies provide tours of facilities, workshops for students and teachers, and apprenticeships for students outside the classroom.

In one attempt to foster a school/industry partnership, Eastman Chemical Company in Kingsport, Tennessee, alternates contracts with two local school systems to have middle school science teachers spend two years with Eastman as "educators-on-loan." During that time, the teachers serve as liaisons with partnering schools and help the company evaluate school requests for help. Eastman had previously sent only professionals and managers into schools; today any employee may be found volunteering time in the classroom. The schools and the com-

---

The Jefferson Davis High School Educational Collaborative

Thanks to the work of Tenneco, Inc., and its partners in the Jefferson Davis High School Educational Collaborative, the college enrollment rates for this inner-city Houston high school jumped from 10 percent in 1989 to about 60 percent in 1994.

Tenneco formed the collaborative with the University of Houston, a coalition of churches, Communities in Schools (an organization funded by private and public sectors), and the Houston School District. The goal was to reduce the dropout rate and increase the rate of college acceptance. After 5 years, the dropout rate fell to 15 percent and the students passing the Texas Assessment of Academic Skills test rose from 37 to 86 percent.

The primary role for Tenneco is supporting the Presidential Scholarship Program which provides four-year tuition assistance to graduating seniors with grade-point averages of 2.5 or above. In addition, the company provides part-time employment for Jefferson juniors and seniors, sponsors dropout prevention programs, and supports academic achievement and attendance incentives.

Tenneco's involvement began at Jefferson Davis in 1981, when employees began volunteering as tutors. Two years later, the company funded a leadership training program for students, and in 1988 an academic bridge program was started to help students make the transition from middle school to high school.

Source: Council for Aid to Education. (1994). *Leaders for Change*. New York: Author.

pany have a written agreement that clearly identifies guidelines and expectations, and the company actively maintains contact with—and therefore the trust of—local school officials, the district superintendent, local principals and teachers, and the school board.

Various kinds of science alliances around the country help to coordinate area scientists, offer enrichment programs, and function as clearinghouses of resource materials for schools and businesses that are interested in collaborating on improving education in local areas. In Houston, Texas, the Jefferson Davis High School Collaborative, formed with the help of Tenneco, has raised the percentage of students passing the state assessment from 37 to 86%.

This type of third-party structure often provides business people with the encouragement they need to participate and shifts the burdens of collaboration—locating suitable business representatives, instructing them on effective classroom activities, and ensuring that they will show up—away from individual teachers.

Individual employees who are parents and taxpayers will carry out most of the work that "business" undertakes to implement science education reform.

Ultimately, business isn't monolithic. Individual employees who are parents and taxpayers will carry out most of the work that "business" undertakes to implement science education reform. Business as a whole cannot be expected to march in lockstep with all reform goals or to make a major financial contribution—beyond the taxes it already pays—to improve public schools generally. Finally, business can make an important contribution by letting educators know what skills the workers of tomorrow will need, while recognizing that educational decisions ultimately must be made by educators, parents, and students—not by business people.

BARRIERS TO SUCCESSFUL INVOLVEMENT

The business-education collaboration described above faces several barriers. Business is often disdainful of what it labels as education's "inefficiency," while educators have long doubted the ability of profit-making business to understand the uniqueness of school systems. This mutual mistrust is difficult to overcome. Hopefully, the kind of collaboration envisioned here and described in The Conference Board's report, *Business and Education Reform: The Fourth Wave* (Waddock, 1994), will reduce historical suspicions and enable participants to move beyond symptoms and stereotypes to underlying needs and problems. This collaboration can lead to true two-way involvement in which business and education help one another meet their needs.

Despite all that has been written about problems in American education today, and despite the involvement of corporate America in reform efforts, the majority of business people remain uninvolved in public schools. Large corporations that are not involved in education indicate that their employees lack the time to volunteer, or believe business and schools should remain separate entities (Shakeshaft & Trachtman, 1986). Recently, however, some major corporations have made commitments to providing time for their employees to do volunteer work in schools or attend school events.

Business Involvement in Education: Four Waves

First Wave: Business-Supported School Programs

Second Wave: Applying Sound Management Principles

Third Wave: Public Policy Initiatives

Fourth Wave: Collaboration for Systemic Reform

Source: Waddock, S. (1994). *Business and education reform: The fourth wave.* New York: The Conference Board.

School reform has always been and will continue to be a politically charged issue. Whether significant numbers of businesses are willing to speak out during debates on issues such as national standards remains to be seen. Although groups such as the Business Roundtable have brought some cohesion to recent business activities advocating school reform, the United States largely lacks groups that are able to speak for business as a whole on the ongoing issue of science education reform.

As long as businesses perceive reform efforts to be disjointed, relations between business and reformers will suffer.

Because a business' involvement in education is very often the result of a CEO's decision, turnover in management can have a deleterious effect on business-school partnerships. The impact of such turnover can be minimized if business adopts strategic plans to guide its grant making and program involvement.

Many corporate scientists have little knowledge of science education reform, and their nonscience counterparts have little knowledge of school reform generally. Involved business leaders often know little about the substance of school reform—curriculum frameworks, embedded assessment, and so on. Modern theories of learning and notions that problems may have no "right" answer could be troubling to those who believe that things do have one right answer or who were served well by a more traditional approach to schooling. The most consistent and emphatic plea from business is for more coherence among the plethora of science reform organizations and efforts. As long as businesses perceive reform efforts to be disjointed, relations between business and reformers will suffer.

RECOMMENDATIONS

Local efforts to build relationships between the business community and science education reformers should start with a small group of business people chosen for their prior experience with science education in public schools. This small, high-powered group could not only serve as advisers but could help forge links with other groups. Getting business people involved in the development of curriculum blocks or other "hands-on" engagement has been shown to greatly increase business interest in and support for school reform efforts.

Business is not interested in supporting multiple groups striving for what it sees as the same results. Science education reformers should either work to define the way they are unique or collaborate with others—such as Project 2061 or the National Research Council—that are seeking a national support structure for implementing reform. Business and schools can take the following steps to bring about the type of reform envisioned by Project 2061 and other reform organizations:

■ Key business leaders and science educators should agree on their roles and communicate them to the community through success stories, increasing exposure in the business community and preempting opposition to reforms.

■ To develop crucial state and local alliances science education leaders should contact key business associations that have a demonstrated interest in school reform.

■ Science educators should utilize materials—many of which already exist—that offer guidelines for local educators to work effectively with business. The Education Commission of the States, for example, publishes *Statewide Restructuring of Education: A Handbook for Business*, which presents different perspectives on subjects from assessment to teacher preparation.

■ Business can sponsor professional development and summer internships for science teachers and students and work with schools of education to support changes in science teacher training.

■ Business can encourage deeper employee/parent involvement in schools by providing flexibility for employees to attend school events or volunteer in classrooms.

■ Business produces numerous materials for America's classrooms and should be encouraged to make those materials consistent with *Benchmarks* and *National Science Education Standards* (National Research Council, 1996).

■ Business can be an especially effective advocate for reform by enhancing public understanding of the connection between well-educated students and American economic success.

■ Connections between science education and the world of work can be strengthened and encouraged through business internships and school-to-work programs.

The most significant impact is achieved when both business and schools emphasize systemic and long-term science education reform. Alliances that offer tangible benefits to both business and the schools and that build a local base of political support that includes teachers, scientists, parents, and local business and industry have the best chance for lasting change and improvement.

REFERENCES

American Association for the Advancement of Science. (1993). *Benchmarks for science literacy*. New York: Oxford University Press.

American Association for the Advancement of Science (1989). *Science for all Americans*. New York: Oxford University Press.

Coen, D. (1993, July). Personal interview by Christopher Perry.

Lund, L., & Wild, C. (1993). *Ten years after "A nation at risk."* New York: The Conference Board.

Mann, D. (1987, October/November). Business involvement and public school improvement, Parts 1 and 2. *Phi Delta Kappan, 69,* 123-128; 228-232.

Meredith, R. (1996, April 21). New blood for the Big Three's plants. *The New York Times.*

National Association of Partners in Education. (1991). *National school district partnership survey.* Alexandria, VA: Author.

National Commission on Excellence in Education. (1983). *A nation at risk: The imperative for educational reform.* Washington, D.C.: U.S. Government Printing Office.

National Research Council. (1996). *National Science education standards.* Washington, D.C.: National Academy Press.

Shakeshaft, C., & Trachtman, R. (1986, April). *Business as usual: Exploring private sector participation in American public schools.* Paper presented at the Annual Meeting of the American Educational Research Association, ED268361.

Siegel, P., & Byrne, S. (1994). *Using quality to redesign school systems: The cutting edge of common sense.* Washington, D.C.: National Alliance of Business.

Sommerfield, M. (1993, September 29). Corporate gifts to K-12 education up 13% in 1992. *Education Week.*

Tillman, A. (1994). *Corporate contribution, 1994.* New York: The Conference Board.

Timpane, M., & McNeill, L. M. (1991). *Business impact on education and child development reform: A study prepared for the Committee for Economic Development.* New York: Columbia University Teachers College.

Waddock, S. (1994). *Business and education reform: The fourth wave.* New York: The Conference Board.

BIBLIOGRAPHY

Aldridge, B. G., Crow, L. W., & Aiuto, R. (1993). *Energy sources and natural fuels.* Washington, D.C.: National Science Teachers Association and American Petroleum Institute.

Aring, M.K. (1993, January). What the "V" word is costing America's economy. *Phi Delta Kappan, 74,* 393-404.

ASCD Task Force on Business Involvement in the Schools. (1989-90, December/January). Guidelines for business involvement in the schools. *Educational Leadership, 47,* 84-86.

Baas, A. (1990). *The role of business in education.* Eugene, OR: ERIC Clearinghouse on Educational Management.

Blair, H.B., Brounstein, P. J., Hatry, H. P., & Morley, E. (1990). *Guidelines for school-business partnerships in science and mathematics.* Lanham, MD: University Press of America.

Bowsher, J. E. (1989). *Educating America: Lessons learned in the nation's corporations.* New York: John Wiley & Sons, Inc.

Business/Public Education Council (Delaware). (1992). *School & work: Closing the gap in Delaware.* Dover, DE: Author.

The Business Roundtable. (1992). *The essential components of a successful education system: Putting policy into practice.* Washington, D.C.: Author.

Celis, W., 3d. (1991, May 22) Despite touted gifts, business tax breaks cost schools money. *The New York Times, Education.*

Center for Workforce Preparation and Quality Education. (1992). *Bridging the literacy gap: An employer's guide.* Washington, D.C.: Author.

Center for Workforce Preparation and Quality Education. (1992). *Education blueprints: A 1990's guide for rebuilding education and workforce quality.* Washington, D.C.: Author.

Center for Workforce Preparation & Quality Education. (1991). *Public education: Meeting the needs of small business.* Survey by the Roper Organization. Washington, D.C.: Author.

Church, R. L., & Sedlak, M. W. (1976). *Education in the United States.* New York: The Free Press.

Council of Chief State School Officers. (1993). *State indicators of science and mathematics education—1993.* Washington, D.C.: Author.

Council for Aid to Education (CFAE). (1989). *Business and the schools: A guide to effective programs.* New York: Author.

Daggett, W. R. (1990, November/December). Future workplace is shocking. *North Carolina Education*, pp. 2-9.

Digilio, A. (1985, April 21). Bringing out the best: Helping students excel—high schools on the academic fast track. *The Washington Post Education Review.*

Doherty, D. C. (1989-90, December/January). Using corporate-sponsored materials to teach history and social science skills. *Educational Leadership, 47,* 81-83.

Edison Electric Institute (EEI). (1993). 1993-94 *Directory of Educational Services.* New York: Author.

Elisha, W. Y. (1991, April). *Executive comment on education reform.* Washington, D.C.: The Business Roundtable. (p. 11).

Fabrikant, G. (1993, August 1). Whittle to substantially scale back for-profit schools plan. *The New York Times News Service.*

Farrell, A. M. (1992, March). What teachers can learn from industry internships. *Educational Leadership, 49,* 38-39.

Flanigan, J. (1983, September 18). Business is learning it pays to help educate our youth. *Los Angeles Times.*

Fosler, R. S. (1990). *The business role in state education reform.* Washington, D.C.: The Business Roundtable.

Francis, E. (1993, July 4). Middle school girls learn technology at Randolph camp. *Rutland Herald and Times-Argus.*

Gold, G. G. (1987, January). A reform strategy for education: Employer-sponsored teacher internships. *Phi Delta Kappan, 68*(5), 384-387.

Gordon, J. (1990, August 20). Can business save the schools? *Training,* pp. 19-27.

Harty, S. (1979). *Hucksters in the classroom: a review of industry propaganda in schools.* Washington, D.C.: Center for Study of Responsive Law.

Hewlett-Packard Company. (1992). *Changing America's future today: A new perspective for K-12 education.* Palo Alto, CA: Author.

Hoyt, K. B. (1991). Education reform and relationships between the private sector and education: A call for integration. *Phi Delta Kappan, 72,* 450-453.

Illinois Mathematics and Science Alliance. (1990). *1990: The challenges are clear; The choices are before us; It is time to act.* Illinois Mathematics and Science Alliance leadership conference. Aurora, IL: Author.

Institute for Educational Leadership, Inc. (1988). *Next steps in the relationship between business and public schools.* Occasional Paper #1. Washington, D.C.: Author.

Jibrell, S. B. (1990). Business/education partnerships: Pathways to success for Black students in science and mathematics. *Journal of Negro Education, 59*(3), 491-506.

Justiz, M. J. & Kameen, M. C. (1987, January). Business offers a hand to education. *Phi Delta Kappan, 68*(5), 379-383.

Kober, N. (1993). *EDTALK: What we know about science teaching and learning.* Washington, D.C.: Council for Educational Development and Research and Triangle Coalition for Science and Technology Education.

Kupfer, A. (1990). Turning students on to science. *Fortune/Education.*

Lepkowski, A. (1987). Precollege science, math education enhanced by volunteers. *Chemical & Engineering News, 65*(38).

Levine, M. & Trachtman, R. (1988.) *American business & the public school: Case studies of corporate involvement in public education.* Washington, D.C.: Committee on Education Development.

Lewis, A. C. (1991, February). Business as a real partner. *Phi Delta Kappan, 72,* 420-421.

Link, H. C. (1923). *Education & Industry.* New York: Macmillan.

Lund, L. & Wild, C. (1993). *Ten years after "A Nation At Risk."* New York: The Conference Board.

Mann, D. (1987, October/November). Business involvement and public school improvement, Parts 1 and 2. *Phi Delta Kappan, 68,* 123-128 and 228-232.

Marquand, R. (1986, August 5). A "good deal" lures top math and science major into teaching. *Christian Science Monitor,* pp. B4-5.

Mathematical Sciences Education Board. (1991). *Strategic plan.* Washington, D.C.: National Academy Press.

McClelland, A. (1992, March/April). Lessons from the Constitution and the stage. *Drexel University TIES.*

McNett, I. (1982). *Let's not reinvent the wheel: Profiles of school/business collaboration.* Washington, D.C.: Institute for Educational Leadership.

Miller, J. A. (1993). From classroom to workplace: What do Delaware students need in science? Speech, May 11, 1993.

Molnar, A. (1990, February 9). No business: Beware of corporations bearing gifts for schools. *Wall Street Journal.*

National Academy of Sciences. (1984). *High schools and the changing workplace: The employer's view.* Washington, D.C.: National Academy Press.

National Alliance of Business (1992). *Workplace readiness: a survey of small business.* Washington, D.C.: Author.

National Alliance of Business. (1989). *A blueprint for business on restructuring education.* Washington, D.C.: Author.

National Association of Manufacturers. (1993). *Tap your workers' potential: the NAM is here to help.* Washington, D.C.: Author.

National Association of Manufacturers. (1992, June). *Workforce readiness: A manufacturing perspective.* Washington, D.C.: Author.

National Association of Manufacturers. (1992, December). *Workforce readiness: How to meet our greatest competitive challenges.* Washington, D.C.: Author.

National Association of Partners in Education. (1991). *National school district partnership survey.* Washington, D.C.: Author.

National Association of Manufacturers. (1991). *High performance work force: Corporate human resource success stories.* Washington, D.C.: Author.

National Association of Manufacturers. (1991/November). *Today's dilemma: Tomorrow's competitive edge—learning from the NAM/Towers Perrin skills gap survey.* Washington, D.C.: Author.

National Center for Education Statistics. (1993). *120 years of American education: A statistical portrait.* Washington, D.C.: Author.

National Science Foundation. (1993). *Beyond national standards and goals: Excellence in mathematics and science education K-16.* (conference report) Washington, D.C.: Author.

National Science Resources Center. (1992). *1992 Annual Report*. Washington, D.C.: Author.

National Science Teachers Association. (1992). *Scope, sequence, and coordination of secondary science: Volume I: The Content Core—A Guide for Curriculum Reformers*. Washington, D.C.: Author.

Partnerships strive to improve precollege science education. (1989). *Chemical & Engineering News, 67*, 49-50.

Perry, N. (1991, October 21). Where we go from here. *Fortune: Education*/Special Report, pp. 114-125.

Ramsey, N. (1992, November 16). How business can help the schools. *Fortune: Education*/Special Report, pp. 147-174.

Richardson, J. (1993, August 4). Reform partnership makes bridging gaps its business. *Education Week*.

Seltzer, R. (1990, June 25). Science education: Group aims to coordinate reforms. *Chemical & Engineering News, 68*(26), 4-5.

Sharp, A.G. & Sharp, E.O. (1992). *The business-education partnership*. Morrisville, PA: International Information Association, Inc.

Szabo, J. C. (1991, October). Schools that work. *Nation's Business*, pp. 20-28.

Teltsch, K. (1991, Oct. 2). Science and math get most support. *The New York Times*.

Triangle Coalition for Science and Technology Education. (1991). *A guide for building an alliance for science, mathematics and technology education*. College Park, MD: Author.

Triangle Coalition for Science and Technology Education. (1990). *Providing for the future: The state of science education reform in the nation*. College Park, MD: Author.

Unseem, E. L. (1986). *Low tech education in a high tech world: Corporations and classrooms in the new information society*. New York: The Free Press.

U.S. Department of Labor. (1992). *Learning a living: A blueprint for high performance*. SCANS Report for American 2000. Washington, D.C.: Author

Walsh, M. (1993, August). And now, a word from our sponsor. *Teachers Magazine*.

Walsh, M. (1993, May 12). Some educators casting a wary eye on corporate curriculum materials. *Education Week*.

Waltner, J. C. (1992, March). *Educational Leadership, 49*, 48-52.

Weisman, J. (1993, January). Skills in the schools: Now it's business' turn. *Phi Delta Kappan, 74*, 367-369.

Wentworth, E. (1993). *Agents of change: Exemplary corporate policies and practices to improve education*. Washington, D.C.: The Business Roundtable.

Resources and Contacts

ONE OF THE TENETS underlying the recommendations in *Blueprints* is that good ideas should be replicated. Rather than reinventing programs in thousands of places, systemic reform seeks to bring efficiency into the educational system, building on quality work where it exists. As the Project 2061 staff prepared the *Blueprints* chapters, they could see that many exemplary programs and projects related to reform were already underway.

To assist *Blueprints* readers in their own efforts to improve mathematics, science, and technology education, we have included in this Resources section a selected list of programs and projects mentioned in the chapters, as well as others that are especially relevant and/or noteworthy. Most of these programs are national in scope and outreach, making it possible for individual schools or districts to adapt their materials or strategies.

The *Blueprints* chapters represent the variety of disciplines and organizations that are involved in reform. As reform in science, mathematics, and technology education has progressed over the past decade, scores of groups and organizations have become prominent. The Contacts section provides information on selected national organizations, agencies, and programs that are key players in science, mathematics and technology education, or in education reform.

Although it was beyond the scope of this work to identify all projects and groups that are dedicated to reform, the Resources and Contacts are a starting point for those seeking more information. As with the *Blueprints* chapters themselves, these lists are a work in progress, and Project 2061 welcomes your additions and updates.

Resources

Accelerated Schools Project

The *Accelerated Schools Project* was designed to improve schooling for children in at-risk situations. Each school uses three principles—unity of purpose, empowerment coupled with responsibility, and building on the strengths of all members of the school community—to develop and work toward its own specific goals. Instead of placing at-risk students into remedial classes, accelerated school communities—staff, parents, administrators, students, and local community members—provide them with the types of challenging activities that are generally reserved for gifted students. Members of the school community encourage students and teachers to think creatively, explore their interests, and achieve at high levels. Accelerated schools seek out, acknowledge, and build on every child's natural curiosity, encouraging students to build knowledge and develop complex reasoning and problem-solving skills through exploration and discovery and by making connections between school and home activities. More than 700 schools in 38 states are affiliated with the *Accelerated Schools Project.*

National Center for the Accelerated
Schools Project
Stanford University
CERAS 109
Stanford, CA 94309-3084
415/725-1676
E-mail: hf.cys@forsythe.stanford.edu
http://www-leland.stanford.edu/
group/ASP

Access Science

Access Science is a project of the National Easter Seal Society (NESS). Funded by the National Science Foundation, *Access Science* was developed in collaboration with the American Association for the Advancement of Science. Children with disabilities and their families gather in monthly workshops to conduct hands-on science activities and to test and suggest adapted equipment for each activity so that every child can participate. *Access Science* introduces children to

role models with disabilities who are professionals in science, math, and technology fields and who describe the career opportunities that are available to them.

Marilyn Hamper
Access Science Project Manager
National Easter Seal Society
230 West Monroe
Suite 1800
Chicago, IL 60606
312/726-6200

Alliance for Technology Access

Making technology a regular part of the lives of people with disabilities is the goal of the *Alliance for Technology Access. The Alliance* works to increase the awareness, understanding, and implementation of assistive technologies. More than 40 community-based technology resource centers and 70 technical designers and developers comprise the *Alliance for Technology Access.* Based on a spirit of collaboration and partnership, the *Alliance* is run by children and adults with disabilities, their families and friends, teachers, service providers and employers. The *Alliance* joins with industry, such as IBM and Mattel Foundation, to expand the possibilities of integrating students with disabilities into educational settings where they can use computers and other technology to learn.

Russ Holland, Executive Director
Alliance for Technology Access
2173 East Francisco Boulevard
Suite L
San Rafael, CA 94901
415/455-4575

ASPIRA Mathematics and Science Academy

Working primarily with Puerto Rican and other Latino middle-school students, the *ASPIRA Mathematics and Science Academy (MAS)* strives to increase the interest and skills of underrepresented students in mathematics and science. In Spanish, mas means plus or more; ASPIRA believes that all children should have more access to the adequate academic environment and social support they deserve, especially in science and mathematics. *MAS* offers a computer learning lab for students, after-school tutoring and homework monitoring, seminars about the importance of parental involvement in mathematics and science, field trips to various facilities that employ scientists and mathematicians, and summertime activities and seminars for students. ASPIRA has established *MAS* academies in Chicago, Illinois and Bridgeport, Connecticut.

Hilda Crespo,
Interim National Executive
1112 16th Street, NW
Suite 340
Washington, DC 20036
202/835-3600
FAX: 202/223-1253
E-mail: aspira1@aol.com

Blue Ribbon Schools Program

The *Blue Ribbon Schools Program* identifies and nationally recognizes a diverse group of public and private elementary and secondary schools that are unusually effective in meeting local, state, and national education goals and in educating all of their students. The program aims to improve schools through the self-evaluation that is required of participating schools and to encourage the pursuit of excellence by providing national recognition. A review panel composed of school educators, college and university faculty, state and local government officials, school board members, and community members selects Blue Ribbon schools. Their criteria include the candidate schools' leadership; teaching environment; curriculum and instruction; student environment; parent and community support; organizational vitality; student performance on measures of achievement; daily student and teacher attendance rates; students' postgraduate pursuits; and student, staff, and school awards.

U.S. Department of Education
Recognition Division
Washington, DC 20208-5645
202/219-2149

The Business Round Table Education Initiative

In 1989, the Business Round Table (BRT) undertook a 10-year effort to promote the nationwide systemic reform of public schools. The BRT and its member companies work with governors, chief state school officers, and business and educational organizations to create comprehensive reform strategies in all 50 states. The *Essential Components of a Successful Education System* is a nine-point agenda for educational reform that is based on the belief that all children can and must learn at increasingly higher levels.

The Business Round Table
1615 L Street, NW
Washington, DC 20036
202/872-1260

Closing the Gap

Exploring the use of microcomputers as personal and educational tools for people with disabilities, especially students in K-12, *Closing the Gap* is a cutting-edge newsletter that comes out six times a year. This publication includes practical computer application, software reviews, and related news and information with and emphasis on special education. *Closing the Gap* sponsors an annual conference featuring a wide range of workshops and seminars on microcomputers and their applications.

Closing the Gap
P.O. Box 68
Henderson, MN 56044
612/248-3294

The Coalition of Essential Schools

The *Coalition of Essential Schools* is a school-university partnership that redesigns American high schools to improve student learning and achievement. The *Coalition of Essential Schools* offers no specific model or program for schools to adopt; however, each school uses the project's nine common principles to redesign its structure and practices and to develop programs that best serve its own students, faculty, and community. The *Coalition of Essential Schools* provides professional development activities and programs for faculty members and develops seminars

and workshops to promote and support change. The project includes more than 230 member schools in more than 30 states, with an additional 250 schools in the planning stages and 530 schools in the exploratory stage.
Carrie Holden, Schools Coordinator
Coalition of Essential Schools
Box 1969
Brown University
Providence, RI 02912
401/863-3384
http://home.aisr.brown.edu/ces/

Comer School Development Program
In keeping with the African proverb that it takes a whole village to raise a child, the Yale Child Study Center Team in New Haven, Connecticut, developed a program in 1967 that brings together educators, parents, and community members as a school-based team and helps build meaningful parental involvement into the culture of the school. Under the School Development Program a management team of parents and teachers sets objectives and strategies regarding school climate, academics, and staff development. Parents develop workshops for parents, become actively involved in tutoring, help teachers plan and implement the school's social calendar, and serve as classroom assistants. The *School Development Program* has been adopted by more than 600 schools in 21 states and the District of Columbia.
Cynthia Savo
School Development Program
53 College Street
New Haven, CT 06510
203/737-1020
E-mail: cynthia.savo@yale.edu
http://pandora.med.yale.edu/comer/welcome.html

Council of the Great City Schools
The *Council of the Great City Schools* is a coalition of more than 50 of the nation's largest urban public school systems that works to promote urban education through legislation, research, media relations, management, technology, and special projects.

The *Council* serves as the national voice for urban educators and provides a vehicle for them to share information about promising practices and address common concerns.

Urban Education Service Corps
The *Urban Education Service Corps* seeks to enhance the educational achievement of inner-city students and improve teacher recruitment and professional development. The *Corps* builds on existing partnerships between public school systems, colleges of education, and community groups in Philadelphia, Long Beach, Omaha, Denver, and Toledo. Each local partnership addresses school issues by broadening the range of school services to increase educational achievement for students in urban schools who lack basic academic skills; expanding and diversifying the pool of teachers for urban schools; and enhancing the skills of AmeriCorps members in community service, civic responsibility, and teaching.
Shirley Schwartz
Renee Carr
Council of the Great City Schools
1301 Pennsylvania Avenue, NW, Suite 702
Washington, DC 20004
202/393-2427
FAX: 202/393-2400
http://www.cgcs.org

Urban Education Technology Forum
The *Urban Education Technology Forum* (The *Forum*) is a partnership between the *Council of Great City Schools* and selected businesses and institutions. The *Forum* addresses outreach assistance, information exchange, cooperative program design and development, and discussions of critical issues and concerns related to applying technology to urban education. *The Forum's* activities are designed to reduce duplication of efforts, reduce costs related to implementing technology in urban schools, exchange information, establish joint funding projects, and increase program effectiveness.
Mark A. Root, Manager of Technology and Information Services
Council of the Great City Schools

1301 Pennsylvania Avenue, NW,
Suite 702
Washington, DC 20004
202/393-2427
FAX: 202/393-2400
http://www.cgcs.org

DO-IT (Disabilities, Opportunities, Internetworking, Technology)
The *DO-IT* Program, funded by the National Science Foundation and located at the University of Washington College of Engineering, introduces high school students with disabilities to college and careers in engineering and science. Students spend two weeks on campus participating in labs in different disciplines and learning how to access information via the Internet. Following the summer program, students communicate with one another and an international network of volunteer mentors using electronic mail. A larger discussion group, "do-itsem," shares information on assistive technology, adapted hardware and software of special value to students with disabilities in precollege and postsecondary settings.
Sheryl Burgstahler
College of Engineering/FH-10
University of Washington
Seattle, WA 98195
206/543-0622

Dwight D. Eisenhower Mathematics and Science Education Program
The *Eisenhower Program* is designed to improve the skills of teachers and quality of mathematics and science instruction in the nation's elementary and secondary schools. The *Eisenhower State Grant Program* funds opportunities for teacher professional development. The *Eisenhower National Program* supports innovative projects that are designed to improve the quality of teaching in mathematics and to provide quality instruction to all students.
Eisenhower National Program
U.S. Department of Education
55 New Jersey Avenue, NW
Washington, DC 20208
202/219-2126
http://www.enc.org

EQUITY 2000
This project, currently underway in six major school districts nationally, is designed to close the gap in college-going and success rates between non-minority and minority students and advantaged and disadvantaged students. The project seeks to eliminate tracking, set high standards for all students and provide the support to enable all students to reach those standards, and increase students' aspirations to attend college. *EQUITY 2000* combines counseling and classroom instructional strategies with teacher preparation to prove that all students can master algebra and succeed in college.
Vinetta Jones, National Director,
EQUITY 2000
The College Board
45 Columbus Avenue
New York, NY 10023
212/713-8268
http://www.collegeboard.org

Faith Communities Project
The AAAS *Faith Communities Project* helps churches across the country incorporate hands-on science, mathematics, and technology activities into their non-religious educational programs. The *Faith Communities Project* seeks to engage parents and children in hands-on science activities in communities where the church is a central institution. The AAAS assists churches with program planning and implementation, trains church volunteers to conduct hands-on science and mathematics activities, and provides activity manuals and materials to churches.
Sandra Parker or Brenda Files
AAAS
Education and Human Resources
1200 New York Avenue, NW
Washington, DC 20005
202/326-6783 or 202/326-6682
E-mail: sparker@aaas.org or bfiles@aaas.org

FAMILY MATH
The EQUALS staff at the University of California's Lawrence Hall of Science developed *FAMILY MATH* in 1982 to help parents learn the mathematical skills they needed to help their children with their homework. *FAMILY MATH*'s primary aims

are to prevent parents from passing negative attitudes about mathematics on to children, help parents familiarize children with the broad scope of mathematics through routine family activities, and teach parents and children to approach mathematics as problem solvers. Through the program's activities, parents learn to stimulate their children's mathematical and scientific thinking in the home just as they foster their children's literacy by reading to them. Communication between teachers and parents in the *FAMILY MATH* program increases parental interest in improving the mathematics curriculum to prepare all students for high school mathematics.

Jose Franco, Director
EQUALS
Lawrence Hall of Science
University of California
Berkeley, CA 94720
510/642-1823
FAX: 510/643-5757
E-mail: equals@uclink.berkeley.edu
http://equals.lhs.berkeley.edu

FAMILY SCIENCE

This national outreach program combines teacher inservice education with a family learning program. *FAMILY SCIENCE* provides opportunities for families to have enjoyable science experiences, relate learning science to future studies and work, and involve parents in their child's science education. The program uses hands-on learning activities to increase the study of science by K-8 students, particularly among female and minority students. *FAMILY SCIENCE* includes an inservice program that is designed to provide educators and community members with science and career activities, organizational information, and program philosophies.

Peggy Noon, Director
Northwest EQUALS
Portland State University
P.O. Box 751
Portland, OR 97207
800/547-8887 ext. 3045
FAX: 503/725-4838
E-mail: equals@pdx.edu

Full Option Science System

The *Full Option Science System (FOSS)* is an elementary school science program that was designed to provide meaningful science education for all students in diverse American classrooms and preparing them for life in the 21st century. Its modular design allows *FOSS* to be used in a variety of ways in many school settings and to be adapted to almost every science framework, guide, and program. *FOSS* incorporates hands-on inquiry, interdisciplinary projects, collaborative learning groups, and multisensory observation.

Linda DeLucchi
Lawrence Hall of Science
Center for Multisensory Learning
University of California
Berkeley, CA 94720
510/642-8941

High School/High Tech Programs

As an enrichment program for students with disabilities interested in science, math, education, and technology, the *High School/ High Tech* programs offers mentor programs, professional shadowing, workshops in science and math, and work opportunities. This program, available in several states, identifies and motivates talented high school students with disabilities to pursue science and technology careers.

Richard Sheppard
President's Committee for the Employment of People with Disabilities
1331 F Street, NW
Suite 400
Washington, DC 20004
202/376-6200
202/376-6205(TDD)

Mathematicians Education Reform Forum

The *Mathematicians Education Reform Forum* is a National Science Foundation project that brings together college and university mathematicians across the nation to promote educational reform efforts within the mathematics community. The *Mathematicians Education Reform Forum* conducts national workshops that focus on mathematicians' participation in education reform,

publishes materials that address mathematics and education reform issues, provides professional programs for mathematicians, and develops educational initiatives in the mathematics community.
Naomi Fisher, MER Co-Director
Department of Mathematics, Statistics, and Computer Science (M/C 249)
University of Illinois at Chicago
851 S. Morgan Street
Chicago, IL 60607
312/413-3749
E-mail: NDFisher@uic.edu
http://www.math.uic.edu/MER/

National Alliance of Business
The *National Alliance of Business* (The *Alliance*) is a business-led nonprofit organization that provides business leadership to reform education and enhance job training by shaping public policy; building partnerships among business, education, and community leaders; and increasing public awareness of the need to improve education and job training. The *Alliance* works to achieve excellence in education by sponsoring programs that ease the transition from school to work and by providing publications that contain information about and models of business involvement in education reform locally and nationally.
1201 New York Avenue, NW, Suite 700
Washington, DC 20005
202/289-2888

National Assessment of Educational Progress
Under the mandate of Congress and the direction of the U. S. Department of Education's National Center for Education Statistics, the *National Assessment of Educational Progress* (NAEP) monitors the educational progress of nationally representative samples of 4th, 8th, and 12th graders and reports group trends over time. *NAEP* assesses student achievement in reading and mathematics every two years, science and writing every four years, and history and geography at least once every six years; examines in detail the performance of a cross section of students that are assessed in each subject, highlighting home and school factors related to achievement; and reports

teachers' descriptions of their backgrounds, teaching experience, and instructional approaches. *NAEP's* assessments are designed to expand our knowledge of students' problem solving abilities and offer challenging performance tasks for students.
Archie Lapointe, Executive Director
P.O. Box 6710
Princeton, NJ 08541
800/223-0267
http://www.ed.gov/NCES/

National Center for Fair & Open Testing (FairTest)
FairTest works to ensure that the evaluation of students and workers is fair, open, accurate, accountable, and educationally sound. To achieve these goals, *FairTest* serves as a source of information about testing and alternatives for educators, parents, public officials, journalists, and other policy makers; provides information, training, and strategic advice to parents, educators, and civil rights and womens' organizations; and coordinates and catalyzes educators, citizen groups, and parents to effect testing reforms.
Bob Schaeffer, Public Education Director
342 Broadway
Cambridge, MA 02139-1802
617/864-4810
FAX: 617/497-2224

National Science Foundation Systemic Initiatives
NSF's Division of Educational System Reform sponsors several programs that encourage coordinated approaches to the standards-based reform of science and mathematics education to ensure a comprehensive impact on curriculum, policy, professional development, assessment, resource allocation, and student performance. Among these programs are the *Statewide Systemic Initiatives, Urban Systemic Initiatives,* and *Rural Systemic Initiatives,* which improve coordination within states, cities, rural areas, school systems, and other educational organizations to effect change.

Statewide Systemic Initiatives

The *Statewide Systemic Initiatives Program* (*SSI*) encourages improvements in science, mathematics, and engineering education through comprehensive systemic changes to the education systems of the states. The program seeks to strengthen the infrastructure for science and mathematics education by supporting the states on issues such as leadership development, strategic planning, selecting materials, equity, assessment, public awareness, and project evaluation. *SSI* encourages collaboration between educators at all levels, business and industry, parents, and community members.

Janice Earle, Senior Program Director
Carolyn Mahoney, Program Director
Julia Wan, Program Director
Statewide Systemic Initiatives Program
Office of Systemic Reform
4201 Wilson Boulevard, Suite 875
Arlington, VA 22230
703/306-1682
FAX: 703/306-0456
TDD: 703/306-0090
http://www.nsf.gov

Urban Systemic Initiatives

The *Urban Systemic Initiatives Program* (*USI*) in science, mathematics, and technology education fosters experimentation, accelerates the rate of change, and implements system-wide improvement in student learning for grades K-12 in the 25 U.S. cities with the largest number of school-aged children living in poverty. *USI's* goals are to improve the scientific and mathematical literacy of all students in urban communities; to develop the mathematics and science fundamentals that will enable students to participate fully in a technological society; and to enable a greater number of urban students to pursue careers in mathematics, science, and technology. The program seeks to change the way school systems deliver mathematics, science, and technology education to all students by providing a learning environment that includes continuous assessment, a challenging curriculum with hands-on and inquiry-based learning components, skilled educators, adequate resources, and individualized support opportunities.

Urban Systemic Initiatives Program
Directorate for Education and Human Resources
National Science Foundation
4201 Wilson Blvd., Room 875
Arlington, VA 22230
703/306-1684
TDD: 703/306-0090
http://www.nsf.gov

Rural Systemic Initiatives

The goal of the *Rural Systemic Initiatives Program* (*RSI*) is to promote systemic improvements in science, mathematics, and technology education for students in rural, economically disadvantaged regions of the United States. To significantly impact the achievement levels of disadvantaged students, *RSI* supports consortia that are formed to address curriculum reform, teacher preservice and inservice education, policy restructuring, assessment, implementation of national standards, and the social and economic well-being of the targeted regions. *RSI* seeks to sustain those improvements by encouraging community development activities in conjunction with instructional and policy reform.

Rural Systemic Initiatives Program
Directorate for Education and Human Resources
National Science Foundation
4201 Wilson Blvd., Room 875
Arlington, VA 22230
703/306-1684
TDD: 703/306-0090
http://www.nsf.gov

Operation SMART

Girls Incorporated developed *Operation SMART* in 1985 to provide girls with experiences that would encourage them to persist in science and mathematics in school and stay on the track to good jobs and satisfying lives. Girls in *Operation SMART* make their own plans and decisions about their activities and projects. The program provides a variety of activities that are designed to help girls become confident inquirers and explorers. Many *Operation SMART* programs are designed to provide girls with the types of hands-on, science-related experiences that are generally reserved for boys—building, dismantling, using tools and computers, and playing games and sports that help teach geometry and spatial relations. *Operation SMART* distributes materials to assist others in developing similar programs for girls nationwide.

Susan Ellis
Girls Incorporated
National Resource Center
441 West Michigan Avenue
Indianapolis, IN 46202
317/634-7546
FAX: 317/634-3024
E-mail: hn3580@handsnet.org

Professional Development Schools
The *Professional Development Schools* project is a long-term partnership between universities and schools nationwide to bridge the gap between research and practice in the teaching profession. Faculty of *Professional Development Schools* work with university faculty to assist educators, administrators, and counselors in creating exemplary schools in which all children achieve educational excellence. The project is committed to improving pre- and in-service educational programs for practicing and future teachers, engaging school staff in studies of teaching and learning, and using the results of those studies to improve education.

Dr. Frank Murray, President
The Holmes Partnership
101 Willard Hall, Education Building
University of Delaware
Newark, DE 19716
302/831-2557
FAX: 302/831-3013
E-mail: fmurray@udel.edu

Project 30
Project 30 is a collaborative, nationwide effort of 30 representative higher education institutions to redesign the way prospective teachers are educated in the nation's colleges and universities. *Project 30's* efforts focus on subject matter understanding; general and liberal knowledge; pedagogical content knowledge; multicultural, international, and other human perspectives; and teacher recruitment.

Dr. Frank Murray
101 Willard Hall, Education Building
University of Delaware
Newark, DE 19716
302/831-2557
FAX: 302/831-3013
E-mail: fmurray@udel.edu

Project EXCEL-MAS
Through *Project EXCEL-MAS* (Excellence in Community Educational Leadership-Math and Science), the National Council of La Raza (NCLR) aims to increase and strengthen informal math and science education opportunities for Hispanics and to help students stay in and succeed in school. Project *EXCEL-MAS* builds on two existing NCLR projects—*Academia del Pueblo* and *Project Success*—that emphasize cooperative learning to help at-risk students acquire skills in observing, measuring, collecting data and other mathematical and science skills that they can use in everyday life. Demonstration sites in ten communities work with partner schools to offer after-school enrichment programs for elementary, middle school, and junior high school students and their parents.

Antonia Lopez, Director
Center for Community Education Excellence
National Council of La Raza
1111 19th Street, NW, Suite 1000
Washington, DC 20036
202/785-1670
FAX: 202/776-1792

Project MOSAIC
In 1992, the AAAS and the Association of Science Technology Centers launched a three year project called National Resources for Equity in Science: Connecting Museums and Community Groups, also known as *Project MOSAIC* (Museums Offering Science Assistance in the Community). The project developed plans for three science museums in different regions of the country to appeal to a broader, more diverse audience and to engage the total community in the life of the museum. *Project MOSAIC* disseminates materials for all museums that are interested in broadening their audience participation.

Yolanda S. George,
Principal Investigator
Judy Kass, Project Director
Elizabeth Spring, Project Assistant
American Association for the Advancement
of Science
Directorate for Education and Human
Resources Programs
1200 New York Avenue, NW
Washington, DC 20005
202/326-6667
http://www.nextwave.org/ehr/

**Project on Science, Technology
and Disability**

The AAAS *Project on Science, Technology
and Disability* was founded in 1975 to
improve the entry and advancement of people with disabilities in science, math and
engineering. Primarily an information center, the *Project* links people with disabilities,
their families, professors, teachers and counselors with scientists, mathematicians and
engineers with disabilities who can share
their education and career coping strategies
in technical fields. The AAAS *Resource
Directory of Scientists and Engineers with
Disabilities,* 3rd ed., 1995 lists over 600
individuals who are available to serve as role
models and mentors. The *Project* works with
NSTA and other organizations to give technical assistance to classroom teachers and
disseminates videos and publications on
access to science, education, and career
choices.
Virginia Stern, Director
Project on Science, Technology
and Disability
American Association for the Advancement
of Science
1200 New York Avenue, NW
Washington, DC 20005
202/326-6672 (V/TDD)
http://www.nextwave.org/ehr/

Proyecto Futuro (Project Future)

Proyecto Futuro is designed to build excellence in K-8 science and mathematics education for Hispanic students nationwide. The
project seeks to change parent and student
attitudes about science and mathematics and
to promote a learning environment in which

children receive positive reinforcement from
teachers and parents about how to learn and
succeed in science. *Proyecto Futuro* develops
coalitions of local school councils, principals,
teachers, and parents; develops materials that
are culturally relevant for Hispanic students
and that facilitate hands-on inquiry and
problem-solving; provides parents with specific strategies for encouraging children in
mathematics and science; and provides training, technical support, and resources to
implement instructional strategies that incorporate scientific process skills and culturally-
related activities.
Edward Gonzalez
AAAS
Education and Human Resources
1200 New York Avenue, NW
Washington, DC 20005
202/326-6673
E-mail: egonzalez@aaas.org
http://www.nextwave.org/ehr/

**Quality Education for Minorities (QEM)
Network Teacher Education Action Plan**

Since 1992, the Quality Education for
Minorities (QEM) Network has sponsored
four teacher-related initiatives—which are
the foundation of the *Teacher Education
Action Plan*—that probe issues of minority
student access to challenging mathematics
and science courses and to qualified teachers.
The *Teacher Education Action Plan's* goals are
to expand the pool of well-qualified minority
teachers, especially of mathematics and
science; strengthen the teacher education
institutions that produce the most minority
teachers; provide quality professional development programs for teachers; produce a culturally and ethnically diverse cadre of teachers
that represent the community that represents
the community it serves; and coordinate
efforts and share resources across institutions.
J. Arthur Jones, Senior Associate
1818 N Street, NW
Suite 350
Washington, DC 20036
202/659-9525
FAX: 202/659-9528
E-mail: jajones@qem.org
http://qemnetwork.qem.org

Say Yes to a Youngster's Future

Say Yes to a Youngster's Future is a comprehensive, family-centered education program that motivates and trains students of color and girls, their families, and their teachers in mathematics, science, and technology to prepare them for the high technology workplace. *Say Yes* offers in-school programs, provides family learning centers and activities, and provides role models and mentoring in schools and in the community for pre-K through junior high school students and their families.

The National Urban Coalition
1875 Connecticut Avenue, NW, Suite 400
Washington, DC 20009
202/986-1460
FAX: 202/986-1468
http://www.chron.com/content/houston/k-12/sayyes/sayyes.html

School Community Mathematics Project

Faced with the need to effectively reach its diverse student population, the Pittsburgh, California, Unified School District is teaching students to become active learners in mathematics. The *School Community Mathematics Project* provides teachers and parents in the district's elementary schools with the financial resources and materials to explore nontraditional teaching methods and has made mathematics more accessible to students who traditionally don't succeed in mathematics. Schools host informal meetings between staff from the nearby Lawrence Hall of Science, parents, and students. Parents learn about hands-on mathematics activities that can be easily executed at home with common household materials and are encouraged to assist with different mathematics opportunities in the classroom. Teachers receive quality inservice, follow-up throughout the school year, and numerous opportunities for leadership.

Steve Gare, Curriculum Coordinator
Pittsburgh Unified School District
2000 Railroad Avenue
Pittsburgh, CA 94565
510/473-4289
FAX: 510/473-4265

School to Work

The *School To Work Initiative* stems from The School-to-Work Opportunities Act of 1994, which provides seed money to states and to local partnerships of business, labor, government, education, and community organizations to develop school-to-work systems. Although *School-To-Work* programs vary from state to state, each program allows students to explore different careers, provides students with structured training and work-based learning experiences that teach them work-related skills, and develops education and training standards that ensure that students receive the proper education for each career. Employers, teachers, and workers outline the skills necessary for each job and work together to help students acquire them. Employers create a structured learning program that is closely connected to the school curriculum to ensure that students learn as they work. Teachers, administrators, and counselors work with businesses to find better ways to incorporate workplace concepts and technologies into the curriculum.

The School-to-Work Learning and Information Center
400 Virginia Avenue, Room 210
Washington, DC 20024
800/251-7236
FAX: 202/401-6211
E-mail: stw-lc@ed.gov
http://www.ed.gov/Programs/stw.html

Science Access for All Students

The Center for Accessible Technology has established a model for improving instructional delivery in science for students with disabilities. The intention of this model is to prepare science educators and staff developers in California to meet the needs of students with disabilities. The Center will produce a video/workbook kit that will model the process of planning for inclusion and full participation in science.

Lisa Wahl, Executive Director
Center for Accessible Technology
2547 8th Street, 12-A
Berkeley, CA 94710-2572
510/841-3224
http://www.el.net/CAT

Science Activities for the Visually Impaired/Science Activities for Learners with Physical Handicaps (SAVI/SELPH)
The *SAVI/SELPH* program was originally developed to meet the science learning needs of students with disabilities, but has recently been successfully applied in all types of upper-elementary school classrooms. The program materials include print and video activities and optional student science kits.
Linda DeLucchi
Lawrence Hall of Science
Center for Multisensory Learning
University of California
Berkeley, CA 94720
510/642-8941

Science Association for Persons with Disabilities (SAPD)
This organization promotes and advances the teaching of science, and the development of curricular and instructional materials for students with disabilities at all levels. *SAPD* is supported by membership dues and is associated as a sub-group with the National Science Teachers Association.
Ben Van Wagner, President
Fresno-Pacific College
1717 South Chestnut Ave
Fresno, CA 93702
209/453-2278
FAX: 209/453-2007

Teachers Involve Parents in Schoolwork (TIPS)
Teachers helped design, implement, and test this program for interactive homework, called *Teachers Involve Parents in Schoolwork* (*TIPS*). With *TIPS*, any teacher can help their students' families stay informed and involved in their children's learning activities. *TIPS* programs encourage students to share what they are learning about a specific mathematical skill and obtain reactions from parents before completing regular mathematics homework. The programs also provide a format for students to conduct and discuss with their parents a hands-on lab or data collection activity related to the science topics they study in class. *TIPS*

enables all families to become involved—not just those who already know how to discuss mathematics, science, or other subjects. All activities require students to talk to someone at home about what they are learning in class, and *TIPS* asks families to comment on their children's work. Thus, homework becomes a three-way partnership involving students, families, and teachers.
Joyce Epstein, Co-Director
Center on Families, Communities, Schools, and Children's Learning
Johns Hopkins University
3505 N. Charles Street
Baltimore, MD 21218
410/516-0370

YouthALIVE!
The Association of Science-Technology Centers launched this national youth program in 1991 to generate excitement about science learning in populations that are traditionally underrepresented in science and museum programs. Children aged 13 to 17 work in one of more than 40 museums or science centers—often for more than one year—as interns and interpreters. For younger children, more than 80 *YouthALIVE!* programs at museums and science centers provide hands-on science learning through workshops, classes, clubs, research projects, and camps. Through these programs, students increase their aptitude for and interest in science by encountering scientific phenomena and ideas in personally meaningful ways.
Tanya Tucker
Association of Science-Technology Centers, Inc.
1025 Vermont Avenue, NW, Suite 500
Washington, DC 20005-3516
202/783-7211
FAX: 202/783-7207
http://www.astc.org/astc/info/youth/ya!.htm

Contacts

**NATIONAL SCIENCE, MATHE-
MATICS, AND TECHNOLOGY
EDUCATION ORGANIZATIONS:**

American Association of Physics Teachers
Bernard V. Khoury, Executive Officer
One Physics Ellipse
College Park, MD 20740-3845
301/209-3300
E-mail: bvk@aip.org
http://www.aapt.org

American Chemical Society
Sylvia A. Ware, Division Director, Education
1155 16th Street, NW
Washington, DC 20036-4800
202/872-4388; FAX: 202/872-8068
E-mail: saw97@acs.org
http://www.acs.org

**American Indian Science and
Engineering Society**
Norbert Hill, Executive Director
5661 Airport Blvd.
Boulder, CO 80301-2339
303/939-0023, FAX: 303/939-8150
http://bioc02.uthscsa.edu/aisesnet.html

**International Technology
Education Association**
Kendall Starkweather, Executive Director
1914 Association Drive
Reston, VA 22091-1502
703/860-2100, FAX: 703/860-0353
http://www.iteatwww.org

National Association of Biology Teachers
Kathleen Frame
11250 Roger Bacon Drive, No. 19
Reston, VA 22090-5202
703/471-1134, FAX: 703/435-5582
http://gene.com/ae/RC/NABT

National Association of Geology Teachers
Robert Christman, Executive Director
Department of Geology
Western Washington University
Bellingham, WA 98225
206/650-3587, FAX: 206/650-7295
E-mail: xman@henson.cc.wwu.edu
http://oldsci.eiu.edu/geology/NAGT/NAGT
.html

**National Association for Research in
Science Teaching**
Dr. Arthur L. White
Ohio State University
1929 Kenny Road, Suite 200E
Columbus, OH 43210
(614) 292-3339, FAX: (614) 292-1595
http://science.coe.uwf.edu/narst/narst.html

**National Council of Teachers
of Mathematics**
Linda Rosen, Executive Director
1906 Association Drive
Reston, VA 22091
703/620-9840, FAX: 703/476-2970
http://www.nctm.org

**National Earth Science
Teachers Association**
Frank Watt Ireton, Executive Advisor
American Geophysical Union
2000 Florida Avenue, NW
Washington, DC 20009-1277
202/462-6900 ext. 243, FAX: 202/328-
0566
E-mail: fireton@kosmos.agu.org
http:// www.agu.org

**National Science
Teachers Association**
Gerry Wheeler, Executive Director
1840 Wilson Blvd.
Arlington, VA 22201-3000
703/243-7100, FAX: 703/243-7177
http://www.nsta.org

POLICY, RESEARCH, AND REFORM ORGANIZATIONS:

American Education Research Association
William J. Russell, Executive Officer
1230 17th Street, NW
Washington, DC 20036
202/223-9485, FAX: 202/775-1824
http://tikkun.ed.asu.edu/aera/home.html

Consortium for Policy
Research in Education
Peg Goertz, Co-Director
3340 Market Street, Suite 560
Philadelphia, PA 19104-3325
215/573-0700 ext. 228, FAX: 215/573-7914
E-mail: pegg@nwfs.gse.upenn.edu
http://www.upenn.edu/gse/cpre

Council of Chief State School Officers
Gordon Ambach, Executive Director
1 Massachusetts Ave., NW, No. 700
Washington, DC 20001-1431
202/408-5505, FAX: 202/408-8072
http://www.ccsso.org

Education Commission of the States
Frank Newman, President
707 17th Street, No. 2700
Denver, CO 80202-3427
303/299-3600, FAX: 303/296-8332
http://www.ecs.org

Mathematical Sciences
Education Board
Joan Ferrini-Mundy, Executive Director
2101 Constitution Avenue, NW
Harris 476
Washington, DC 20418-0007
202/334-1273, FAX: 202/334-1453
E-mail: mseb@nas.edu
http://www.nas.edu/mseb/mseb.html

National Academy of Sciences
National Research Council Center for
Science, Mathematics, and Engineering
Education
Rodger Bybee, Executive Director
2101 Constitution Avenue, NW
Washington, DC 20418
202/334-2353, FAX: 202/334-2210
http://www.nas.edu

National Board for Professional
Teaching Standards
James A. Kelly, President
300 River Place, No. 3600
Detroit, MI 48207
810/351-4444, FAX: 810/351-4170

National Center for Improving
Science Education
Senta Raizen, Associate Director
2000 L Street, NW, Suite 603
Washington, DC 20036
202/467-0652, FAX: 202/467-0659

National Center for Research on
Evaluation, Standards, and Student
Testing (CRESST)
UCLA Graduate School of Education
405 Hilgard Avenue
145 Moore Hall
Los Angeles, CA 90024-1522
310/206-1532, FAX: 310/825-3883
http://www.cse.ucla.edu

Office of Science and Technology Policy,
National Science and Technology Council
Angela Phillips Diaz, Executive Secretary
Old Executive Office Building
17th and Pennsylvania Avenue, NW
Washington, DC 20500
202/456-6100, FAX: 202/456-6026
http://www.whitehouse.gov/WH/EOP/OS
TP/html/OSTP_Home.html

National Institutes of Child Health and
Human Development
Clarissa Wittenberg, Chief
31 Center Drive, Room 2A32
Bethesda, MD 20892-2425
301/496-5133, FAX: 301/496-7101
http://www.nih.gov/nichd

School Mathematics and Science
Achievement Center
Thomas A. Romberg, Director
University of Wisconsin
1025 West Johnson Street
Madison, WI 53706
608/263-4285, FAX: 608-263-3406
http://www.wcer.wisc.edu

NATIONAL EDUCATIONAL ORGANIZATIONS:

**American Association
for Higher Education**
Louis Albert, Vice President
One Dupont Circle, NW
Suite 360
Washington, DC 20036
202/293-6440, FAX: 202/293-0073
http://www.aahe.org

American Federation of Teachers
Alice Gill, Assistant Director
555 New Jersey Ave., NW
Washington, DC 20001
202/879-4000, FAX: 202-879-4545
http://www.aft.org

Council for Exceptional Children
Nancy Safer, Executive Director
Information Services
1920 Association Drive
Reston, VA 22091-1589
703/620-3660
http://www.cec.sped.org/home.htm

**National Council for
Measurement in Education**
Don Cameron, Executive Director
1230 17th Street, NW
Washington, DC 20036
202/223-9318, FAX: 202/775-1824
http://www.assessment.iupui.edu/
ncme/ncme.html/

National Education Association
1201 16th Street, NW
Washington, DC 20036
202/833-4000
http://www.nea.org

**National Association of
Elementary School Principals**
1615 Duke Street
Alexandria, VA 22314-3483
703/684-3345, 800/386-2377
800/396-2377
http://www.naesp.org

**National Association of
Secondary School Principals**
1904 Association Drive
Reston, VA 22091
703/860-0200, FAX: 703/476-5432
http://www.nassp.org

National PTA
National Headquarters
330 North Wabash Ave., Suite 2100
Chicago, IL 60611-3690
312/670-6782, FAX: 312/670-6783
http://www.pta.org

SCIENCE CURRICULUM MATERIALS DEVELOPERS:

**Activities Integrating Math and Science
(AIMS) Education Foundation**
1595 S. Chestnut Avenue
Fresno, CA 93702
209/255-4094, FAX: 209/255-6396
E-mail: aimsed@fresno.edu
http://www.aimsedu.org

Biological Sciences Curriculum Study
Pikes Peak Research Park
5415 Mark Dabling Blvd.
Colorado Springs, CO 80918
719/531-5550, FAX: 719/531-9104

Educational Development Center, Inc.
Judith Opert Sandler,
Managing Project Director
EDC Publishing Center
55 Chapel Street
Newton, MA 02158
617/969-7100
800/225-4276, FAX: 617/965-6325
http://www.edc.org

Lawrence Hall of Science
Ian Carmichael, Director
University of California
Centennial Drive
Berkeley, CA 94720
510/642-5132, FAX: 510/642-1055
http://ucaccess.uirt.uci.edu/rescenters/ber/la
wrence.html

Technical Education Research Centers
(TERC)
Barbara Sampson,
Chief Executive Officer
2067 Massachusetts Avenue
Cambridge, MA 02140
617/547-0430
http://www.terc.edu

INFORMATION AND SUPPORT ORGANIZATIONS:

American Association of University
Women
Carole Rogin, Interim Executive Director
1111 16th Street, NW
Washington, DC 20036
202/785-7700, FAX: 202/872-1425
http://www.aauw.org

Council for Aid to Education
342 Madison Avenue, Suite 1532
New York, NY 10173
212/661-5800, FAX: 212/661-9766
http://www.cae.org

Derek Bok Center For Teaching
and Learning
Harvard University
Science Center 318
J. Wilkinson, Director
1 Oxford Street
Cambridge, MA 02138
617/495-4869, FAX: 617/495-3739

Eisenhower National Clearinghouse for
Math and Science Education
Len Simutis, Director
1929 Kenny Road
Columbus, OH 43210-1079
614/292-7784, FAX: 614/292-2066
http:// www.enc.org/

Junior Engineering Technical Society
Dan Kunz, Executive Director
1420 King Street
Alexandria, VA 22314-2570
703/548-5387, FAX: 703/548-0769
E-mail: jets@nas.edu
http://www.asee.org/jets

NASA Central Operations of Resources
for Educators (CORE)
Tina Salyer
Lorain County Joint Vocational School
15181 Route 58 South
Oberlin, OH 44074
216/774-1051, FAX: 216/774-2144
E-mail: nasaco@leeca8.leeca.ohio.gov
http://spacelink.msfc.nasa.gov/CORE

NASA Educational Workshops for
Math and Science Teachers/NASA
Educational Workshops for
Elementary School Teachers
Wendell Mohling, Program Director
National Science Teachers Association
1840 Wilson Blvd.
Arlington, VA 22201-3000
703/312-9226, FAX: 703/243-7177
E-mail: nem-request@nsta.org

National Action Council for Minorities
in Engineering
Lea K. Williams, Executive Vice President
3 West 35th Street
New York, NY 10001-2281
212/279-2626, FAX: 212/629-5178
http://www.nacme.org

National Council for the Accreditation
of Teacher Education
Arthur Wise, President
2029 K Street, NW, Suite 500
Washington, DC 20006
202/466-7496, FAX: 202/296-6620

National Energy Information Center
Paula Altman, Energy Information Specialist
Energy Information Administration
Room 1F-048
1000 Independence Avenue, SW
Washington, DC 20585
202/586-8800, FAX: 202/586-0727
http://www.eia.doe.gov

National Science Resources Center
Douglas M. Lapp, Executive Director
Smithsonian Institution
MRC 50-2
Washington, DC 20560
202/357-2555, FAX: 202/786-2028
http://www.si.edu/nsrc

Triangle Coalition for Science and
Technology Education
John M. Fowler, Executive Director
5112 Berwyn Road
College Park, MD 20740
301/220-0870, FAX: 301/474-4381
http://www.triangle-coalition.org

U.S. Department of Education
Luna Levinson, Education Program Specialist
Office of Educational Research
and Improvement
555 New Jersey Avenue, NW
Washington, DC 20208-5572
202/219-2164, FAX: 202/219-2109
World Wide Web: http://www.ed.
gov/offices/OERI/oeribio.html

U.S. Department of Education
Office of Bilingual Education and
Minority Languages Affairs
Delia Pompa, Director
600 Independence Avenue, NW
Washington, DC 20202-6510
202/205-5463
http://www.ed.gov/offices/OBEMLA

U.S. Department of Education
National Center for Education Statistics
Emerson J. Elliot, Commissioner of
Education Statistics
555 New Jersey Avenue, NW
Washington, DC 20208
202/219-1828, FAX: 202/219-1736
http://www.ed.gov/NCES

SCHOOL-BASED PROGRAMS:

UCLA Science Project
Janet Thornber, Director
1041 Moore Hall
Box 951521
Los Angeles, CA 90095
310/825-1109

**Thomas Jefferson High School for Science
and Technology**
Geoffrey A. Jones, Principal
6560 Braddock Road
Alexandria, VA 22312
703/750-8300, FAX: 703/750-5010

Middle College High School
Cecilia Cullen, Principal
3110 Thompson Ave.
Long Island City, NY 11101
718/349-4000

ORGANIZATIONS FOR SCIENTISTS AND STUDENTS WITH DISABILITIES:

Committee on Chemists with Disabilities
American Chemical Society
1155 16th Street, NW
Washington, DC 20036
800/227-5558, 202/872-4438 (V/TDD)

Foundation for Science and Disability
E.C. Keller, Jr., President
236 Grand Street
Morgantown, WV 26505-67509
304/293-5201

*For Information on The Americans with
Disabilities Act (ADA):*

Americans with Disabilities Act
Equal Employment Opportunity
Commission
1801 L Street, NW
Washington, DC 20507
800/669-EEOC (V)
800/800-6860 (TDD)

For Information on Assistive Technologies:

Center for Special Education Technology
The Council for Exceptional Children
1920 Association Drive
Reston, VA 22091-1589
703/620-3660

*For Information on Specific Disabilities and
Advocacy Training:*

**National Center for Learning Disabilities
(NCLD)**
381 Park Avenue South
Suite 1420
New York, NY 10016
212/545-7510
202/789-1505(in Washington, DC)

National Federation of the Blind
1800 Johnson Street
Baltimore, MD 21230
410/659-9314

American Foundation for the Blind
11 Penn Plaza, Suite 300
New York, NY 10001
800/232-5463, 212/502/7600

Alexander Graham Bell Association
for the Deaf
3417 Volta Place, NW
Washington, DC 20007
202/337-5220 (V/TDD)

National Technical Institute for the Deaf
Rochester Institute of Technology
52 Lomb Memorial Drive
P.O. Box 9887
Rochester, NY 14623-0887
716/475-6200 (V/TDD)

National Spinal Cord Injury Hotline
C/o Montebello Rehabilitation Hospital
2201 Argonne Drive
Baltimore, MD 21218
800/526-3456

United Cerebral Palsy Associations
1660 L Street, NW
Suite 700
Washington, DC 20036-5602
202/776-0406

WORLD WIDE WEB SITES FOR INFORMATION AND RESOURCES:

American Association for the
Advancement of Science Home Page
http://www.aaas.org/

Educational Resources Information Center
(ERIC) Home Page
http://www.aspensys.com/eric/

Eisenhower National Clearinghouse
for Mathematics and Science Education
Home Page
http://www.enc.org/

NASA Education Home Page
http://www.hq.nasa.gov/office/codef/
education

North Central Regional
Educational Laboratory
Pathways to School Improvement—
Assessment
http://www.ncrel.org/ncrel/sdrs/areas/
as0cont.htm

Technology Education Resources
http://ed1.eng.ohio-state.edu/TechRes/pro-
forgs.html

The Regional Alliance for Mathematics
and Science Education Reform Hub
http://ra.terc.edu/HubHome/html

DIRECTORIES:

IDEAAAS Sourcebook for Science,
Mathematics, and Technology Education
Barbara Walthall, Editor
AAAS
1200 New York Avenue, NW
Washington, DC 20005
202/326-6646

To Order:
The Learning Team
Suite 256, 10 Long Pond Road
Armonk, NY 10504
800/793-TEAM, FAX: 914/273-2227

Acknowledgements

Blueprints for Reform was developed with the effort and advice of hundreds of people representing every aspect of the education system, and beyond. It is meant to suggest how systemic reform can support the vision of science literacy put forth by *Science for All Americans*. Although not everyone's idea of a "blueprint for reform" may be represented by the book, sketching how all parts of the system might work together toward science literacy should be a real and significant goal for reformers. The current version of *Blueprints* is a small step toward that goal, representing an attempt at synthesizing ideas from the many contributors, but not implying their agreement or endorsement. The institutions listed are the affiliations of contributors at the time of the contribution.

PROJECT 2061
STAFF

As with other Project 2061 publications, *Blueprints* is a collaborative effort of the staff, whose contributions are acknowledged and appreciated. Gerald Kulm directed the final phase, completing the current version of the book and on-line publication.

Andrew Ahlgren
Associate Director

Kelvin Bennett
Computer Specialist

Lucia Buie
Administrative Support Specialist

Mary Ann Brearton
Field Services Coordinator

Sherelle Derrico
Financial Analyst

Ann Cwiklinski
Writer

Barbara Goldstein
Administrative Support Specialist

Sofia Kesidou
Research Associate

Mary Koppal
Communications Director

Gerald Kulm
Program Director

Lester Matlock
Project Administrator

Francis Molina
Electronic Resources Manager

George Nelson
Deputy Director

Natalie Nielsen
Writer

Keran Noel
Administrative Support Specialist

John Owens
Webmaster

Lawrence Rogers
Consultant

Jo Ellen Roseman
Curriculum Director

F. James Rutherford
Director

Luli Stern
Research Associate

Diane Surati
Project Coordinator

Cheryl Wilkins
Secretary

Former Project 2061 staff members who contributed to the *Blueprints* project included Andrea Hoen Beck, Kathy Comfort, Walter Gillespie, and Patricia O'Connell Ross. Editorial consultant Susan Yoder worked closely with the staff, providing invaluable support and help with final drafts.

PROJECT 2061 SCHOOL-DISTRICT CENTERS

The cooperation and assistance of Project 2061 School-District Centers was also important to the *Blueprints* work. The centers serve as sites for exemplary reform work and help to review and react to reports.

Georgia
Susan Matthews
Center Director

Wisconsin
Leroy Lee
Center Director

Philadelphia
Marlene Hilkowitz
Center Director

San Antonio
Joan Drennan-Taylor
Center Director

San Diego
Danine Ezell
Center Director

San Francisco
Bernard Farges
Center Director

COORDINATORS, CONTRIBUTORS, ADVISORS

Project 2061 commissioned experts to prepare reports on each of the twelve *Blueprints* topics. Most coordinators formed committees which developed background papers that the coordinator incorporated into a synthesized report. In some cases, advisors

were consulted by the coordinators and, for some reports, a team of authors worked to develop the report. The thoughtful work by these coordinators and their teams provided the foundation for the current *Blueprints* book.

Assessment

Wayne Welch
(Coordinator)
University of Minnesota

Leigh Burstein
University of California, Los Angeles

Senta Raizen
National Center for Improving Science Education

Richard Walker
Illinois State Department of Education

Business

Christopher Perry
Perry Associates Inc.

Curriculum Connections

Patte Barth (Coordinator)
Council for Basic Education

Ruth Mitchell
American Association for Higher Education

Graham Down
Council for Basic Education

Equity

Sharon Lynch
(Coordinator)
George Washington University

Mary Atwater
University of Georgia

Jack Cawley
SUNY, Buffalo

Jacquelynne Eccles
University of Michigan

Okhee Lee
University of Miami

Cora Marrett
(Coordinator)
National Science Foundation

Doreen Rojas-Medlin
Daugherty County Public Schools, Georgia

Walter Secada
University of Wisconsin

Gregory Stefanich
University of Northern Iowa

Abbie Willetto
Boulder, Colorado

Finance

David Monk (Coordinator)
Cornell University

Allan Odden
University of Wisconsin

William Clune
University of Wisconsin

Higher Education

Carol Stoel (Coordinator)
American Association for Higher Education

Bruce Albert
American Association for Higher Education

Ronald Archer
University of Massachusetts, Amherst

Deborah Bowles
Rutgers University, Camden

Ramona Brown
City College of New York

Peter Buck
Harvard Summer School

Prassede Calabi
TERC

Arthur Camins
New York City Urban Systemic Initiative

Brian Coppola
University of Michigan

Joseph Diescho
Fund for the University of Namibia

Eleanor Duckworth
Harvard University

Naomi Fisher
University of Illinois, Chicago

Andrew Gleason
Harvard University

Daniel Goroff
Harvard University

Kip Herreid
SUNY, Buffalo

Leslie Hornig
Allee Laboratory

James Kaput
University of Massachusetts, Dartmouth

Nancy Kaufmann
University of Wisconsin

Scott Langhorst
Virginia Community College System

Priscilla Laws
Dickinson College

J. Ivan Legg
Memphis State University

Lourdes Monteagudo
Illinois Institute of Technology

Frank Murray
University of Delaware

Jeanne Narum
Independent Colleges Office

Timothy O'Sullivan
San Francisco State University

Richard Panofsky
University of Massachusetts, Dartmouth

Bryan Pollack
American Association for Higher Education

Ruben Puentedura
Bennington College

John Russell
University of Massachusetts

Paul Sally
University of Chicago

David Sanchez
Texas A&M University

Judah Schwartz
Massachusetts Institute of Technology

John Stevenson
LaGuardia Community College

Uri Treisman
University of Texas

Tom Venables
Rutgers University, Camden

Philip Wagreich
University of Illinois, Chicago

Charles Watkins
City College of New York

James Wilkinson
Harvard University

Kea Williams
National Action Council for Minorities in Engineering

Sandra Williams
Simmons College

David Wilson
Rutgers University, Camden

Materials, Media & Technology

Alan Hofmeister
(Coordinator)
Utah State University

Douglas Carnine
University of Oregon

Richard Clark
University of Southern California

Parents and Community

Cathy Belter (Coordinator)
The National PTA

William Quinn
North Central Regional Educational Laboratory

Gilbert Valdez
*North Central Regional
Educational Laboratory*

Todd Fenimore
*North Central Regional
Educational Laboratory*

Shannon Cahill
*North Central Regional
Educational Laboratory*

Policy

Margaret Goertz
(Coordinator)
Rutgers University

Diane Massell
(Coordinator)
University of Pennsylvania

Bari Anhalt
Stanford University

Richard Elmore
Harvard University

Beverly Hetrick
Consultant

Michael Kirst
Stanford University

Robert Marine
Stanford University

Andrew Porter
University of Wisconsin

Research

Ron Good (Coordinator)
Louisiana State University

Charles Anderson
Michigan State University

Jere Confrey
Cornell University

Sherry Demastes
University of Utah

Kathleen Fisher
San Diego State University

Jack Fraenkel
San Francisco State University

Barry Fraser
Curtin University

Dorothy Gabel
Indiana University

James Kaput
*University of Massachusetts,
Dartmouth*

David Kirshner
Louisiana State University

Gloria Ladson-Billings
University of Wisconsin

Norman Lederman
Oregon State University

Marcia Linn
*University of California,
Berkeley*

Mary Jo Magee-Brown
University of Georgia

Thomas Romberg
University of Wisconsin

Robin Sharp
*San Francisco Community
College*

James Shaver
Utah State University

James Shymansky
University of Iowa

Patrick Thompson
San Diego State University

Judith Torney-Purta
University of Maryland

James Wandersee
Louisiana State University

James Whitson
University of Delaware

Larry Yore
University of Victoria

School Organization

Robert Donmoyer
(Coordinator)
Ohio State University

Larry Cuban
Stanford University

Rick Lear
Sedona High School, California

Charol Shakeshaft
Hofstra University

Theodore Sizer
Brown University

Teacher Education

James Gallagher
(Coordinator)
Michigan State University

Robert Floden
(Coordinator)
Michigan State University

Mary Kennedy
(Coordinator)
Michigan State University

Charles Anderson
Michigan State University

Alphonse Baartmans
*Michigan Technological
University*

Audrey Champagne
SUNY, Albany

Donald Dryden
Duke Univesity

Marcia Fetters
University of North Carolina, Charlotte

Timothy Goldsmith
Yale University

Barrett Hazeltine
Brown University

Glenda Lappan
Michigan State University

James Leitzel
University of Nebraska, Lincoln

Walter Massey
University of California

William McDiarmid
Michigan State University

Kathleen Ochs
Colorado School of Mines

Kathleen Roth
Michigan State University

Carol Stoel
American Association for Higher Education

Gary Sykes
Michigan State University

Kenneth Tobin
Florida State University

Sylvia Ware
American Chemical Society

Kenneth Wilson
Ohio State University

David Wong
Michigan State University

BLUEPRINTS REPORT REVIEWERS

The draft Blueprints Reports were reviewed externally by experts in each of the twelve topics. In addition, the other Blueprints coordinators reviewed the drafts and identified issues from their own areas that were related to the report. Project 2061 staff summarized the suggestions and comments from reviewers and coordinators, then forwarded them to the Blueprint coordinator to incorporate into the final Blueprints Report. The contributions by these experts were critical in producing the reports.

Assessment

Joan Baron
Connecticut State Department of Education

Paul Black
University of London

Rolf Blank
Council of Chief State School Officers

Rodney Doran
University of Buffalo

Richard Duschl
University of Pittsburgh

Drew Gitomer
Educational Testing Service

Mary Ellen Harmon
Boston College

Nan Jackson
Harcourt, Brace & Co.

Gerald Kulm
Texas A&M University

Jay McTighe
Maryland Assessment Consortium

John Rigden
American Institute of Physics

Joan Solomon
University of Oxford

Iris Weiss
Horizon Research, Inc.

Business and Industry

William Baker
AT&T Bell Telephone Laboratories (Retired)

Edward Bales
Motorola, Inc.

Chris Cross
Business Roundtable

William Linder-Scholer
Cray Research

Alan McClelland
Science Alliance of Delaware

Carlo Parravano
Merck Institute for Science Education

Edwin Przybylowicz
Eastman Kodak

Michael Timpane
Columbia University

Sylvia Ware
American Chemical Society

Curriculum Connections

Gordon Cawelti
Alliance for Curriculum Reform

Arthur Ellis
Seattle Pacific University

Paula Evans
Brown University

David Kennedy
Washington State Department of Education

Mary Hanson
National Science Foundation

Eugenia Kemble
American Federation of Teachers

Joseph Krajcik
University of Michigan

Mary Lindquist
Columbus State University

Judith Renyi
CHART

Equity

Bernice Anderson
Educational Testing Service

Diane August
National Research Council

Shirley Malcom
American Association for the Advancement of Science

Iris Weiss
Horizon Research, Inc.

Family and Community

Pamela Buckley
Appalachia Educational Lab

Joyce Epstein
Johns Hopkins University

Peggy Noone
Northwest Equals

Michael Webb
National Urban League

David Williams
Southwest Educational Development Laboratory

Finance

Jacob Adams
Vanderbilt University

Patrick Galvin
University of Utah

Stephen Jacobson
SUNY, Buffalo

David Moberly
Washington State Department of Education

Lawrence Picus
University of Southern California

Higher Education

Alfred Bortz
Duquesne University

Timothy Goldsmith
Yale University

Barrett Hazeltine
Brown University

Alice Kehoe
Marquette University

Judith Kildow
Massachusetts Institute of Technology

John Layman
University of Maryland

Leroy Lee
Wisconsin Academy of Sciences

James Leitzel
University of Nebraska–Lincoln

Duncan Luce
University of California–Irvine

John Moore
University of California, Berkeley

Kathleen Ochs
Colorado School of Mines

Kenneth Wilson
Ohio State University

Materials and Technology

Henry Becker
University of California, Berkeley

Gary Bitter
Arizona State University

Daniel Caton
Addison-Wesley Publishing

James Ellis
Biological Science Curriculum Study

Gregory Jackson
Massachusetts Institute of Technology

Marcia Linn
University of California, Berkeley

David Malouf
U.S. Department of Education

Carolee Matsumoto
*Educational Development
Center*

Joyce McLeod
Math, Science and Health

David Morrisson
Northwest Regional Lab

David Moursund
University of Oregon

Cary Sneider
Lawrence Hall of Science

Herbert Thier
Lawrence Hall of Science

Policy

Cherry Jacobus
Goodwill Industries

Floretta McKenzie
The McKenzie Group

Thomas Shannon
*National School Boards
Association*

Michael Usdan
*Institute for Educational
Leadership*

School Organization

Victoria Boyd
*Southwest Educational
Development Laboratory*

Carl Glickman
University of Georgia

Fred Newmann
*National Center for
Organization &
Restructuring of Schools*

Robert Slavin
Johns Hopkins University

David Zuckerman
NCREST

Teacher Education

Sandra Abell
Purdue University

Joan Duea
University of Northern Iowa

James Gates
*National Council of Teachers
of Mathematics*

John Layman
University of Maryland

Sharon Lynch
George Washington University

Cheryl Mason
San Diego State University

Lillian McDermott
University of Washington

Patricia McWethy
*National Association of
Biology Teachers*

Kathleen O'Sullivan
*San Francisco State
University*

Albert Shanker
*American Federation of
Teachers*

Barbara Spector
*University of Southern
Florida*

Kendall Starkweather
*International Technology
Education Association*

Carol Stuessy
Texas A&M University

CONSULTANTS

Michael Kirst, Stanford University, and Steve Schneider, Woodside Research Consortium, were commissioned to prepare summaries of the Blueprints Reports, to assist Project 2061staff in developing chapter-length syntheses of the topics. Ron Havelock and Michael Huberman, Knowledge Transfer Institute, were commissioned to prepare a paper discussing the Blueprints user audience and recommendations for connecting the work to other Project 2061 efforts. These consultants helped to focus the Blueprints efforts and synthesize important ideas from the reports.

CHAPTER REVIEWS

Project 2061 staff edited the summaries of the reports in an attempt to add consistency in format and language, producing drafts of the current *Blueprints* chapters. These drafts were sent for review to hundreds of people, representing a broad spectrum of the educational, scientific, business, and client community. Many reviewers expressed their reactions via telephone or email. Some reviews were formal and written; others were informal suggestions. All of them were valuable in sensing reactions to Blueprints ideas and in preparing revisions to the summary papers.

REVIEW
CONFERENCES

During the summer of 1996, three working meetings were held to provide input to Project 2061 staff in interpreting outside reviews, looking at cross-cutting themes, and making suggestions for future work. Each conference included coordinators or others who wrote the original Blueprints Reports, along with representatives of potential audiences in states and schools. The following participants in the working meetings helped to shape the final product.

Martin Apple
Council of Scientific Society Presidents

Patte Barth
Council for Basic Education

Michael Battista
Kent State University

Sharon Bolster
Arizona State Department of Education

Alphonse Buccino
Contemporary Communications

Juanita Clay Chambers
Detroit Public Schools

Hilda Crespo
ASPIRA

Robert Donmoyer
Ohio State University

Margaret Dutcher
Michigan Department of Education

John Eggebrecht
Illinois Mathematics and Science Academy

Joseph Exline
Science Education Consultant

John Fackler
Texas A&M University

James Gallagher
Michigan State University

Eva Gavillan
American Association for the Advancement of Science

Yolanda George
American Association for the Advancement of Science

Ron Good
Louisiana State University

David Hill
University of Texas, Austin

Alan Hofmeister
Utah State University

Tricia Kerr
Kentucky State Department of Education

Sharon Lynch
George Washington University

James Lytle
Philadelphia Public Schools

Maria Mike-Mayer
Texaco, Inc.

Alma Miller
District of Columbia Public Schools

David Monk
Cornell University

Sigrin Newell
New York State Systemic Initiative

Alicia Parra
El Paso Public Schools

Christopher Perry
Perry Associates, Inc.

Joseph Peters
University of West Florida

Carolyn Prescott
Center of Occupational Research and Development

John Russell
University of Massachusetts, Dartmouth

Linda Sand-Guest
Colorado Teacher Education Collaborative

Nehemiah Smith
Governor's Task Force, Former President, North Carolina School Boards Association

Richard Walker
Illinois State Board of Education

Patricia Watts
Northeast Louisiana University

Wanda White
University of Georgia

James Zuhn
Texas A&M University

DESIGN

Liz Clark and John Isely
Isely and/or Clark Design

PRODUCTION

Charts/Production:
Gretchen Maxwell

Cover Art Production:
Kathleen Cole

General Production:
Studio 405
Carol Hardy

ART RESEARCH

Steve Diamond, Inc.

ART CREDITS

Page X: The Comet
Page XVIII: Charles Sheeler,
The Open Door, 1932.
The Metropolitan
Museum of Art. Edith
and Milton Lowenthal
Collection. bequest of
Edith Abramson
Lowenthal, 1991
(1992:24.7)
Page 98: Paul Klee, *der*
gefundene Ausweg
(The Way Out
Discovered), 1935.
Private Collection,
Switzerland. ©1998
ARS, New York
Page 182: David Smith,
Cubi I, 1963. Detroit
Institute of Arts,
Founders Society Pur-
chase, Special Purchase
Fund. Photograph
©1996 The Detroit
Institute of Arts.

So many people have been involved with the prepara-tion of *Blueprints* that it is nearly impossible to make a comprehensive and accurate list. We apologize to those who have not been men-tioned and acknowledge their important contribu-tions to this work.

Index